OPERATION RALEIGH

Adventure Unlimited

By John Blashford-Snell

Weapons and Tactics (with Tom Wintringham)
The Expedition Organiser's Guide
Where the Trails Run Out
In the Steps of Stanley
A Taste for Adventure
In the Wake of Drake
Operation Drake
Mysteries: Encounters with the Unexplained
Operation Raleigh: The Start of an Adventure

Co-authored by Ann Tweedy and John Blashford-Snell

Operation Raleigh: Adventure Challenge

Co-authored by Ann Tweedy and John Man

Gold-Dive

Operation Raleigh gratefully acknowledges the kind support of British Gas plc and British Telecom plc in the production of this title

This book is dedicated to our Honorary Presidents

WALTER H. ANNENBERG, KBE
and
GENERAL SIR JOHN MOGG, GCB CBE DSO DL

who, together with their wives, have always
supported us to the hilt. They were never too busy
or too tired to answer the call of an
old explorer, occasionally by satellite
and often late at night. It was their
wisdom and advice that really fashioned
Operation Raleigh and their generous help
that did much to ensure its success.

CONTENTS

ILLUSTRATIONS

ACKNOWLEDGEMENTS

The success of Operation Raleigh is due to the enormous amount of work, mainly voluntary, of thousands of people all over the world. It would be marvellous if they could all be given the credit they are due, but then this would be a book of names rather than adventures.

Especially appreciated are the efforts of our solicitors, Birkbeck Montagu's, our honorary accountants, Ernst and Young, and honorary auditors, Peat Marwick McLintock.

The support of many British government ministers and their staffs has been greatly encouraging, and the Foreign and Commonwealth Office could not have been more helpful. We have also enjoyed the support of many other governments around the globe: Operation Raleigh is an international concern.

The assistance of the armed forces everywhere has been valuable – and indeed vital – to our success. As one Latin American corporal remarked: 'It does make a change from guarding the President's palace.'

In writing this book we have relied considerably on the staff of Raleigh's central headquarters, and we are particularly grateful to Sally Cox, Alison Blyth-Brook, Felicity Bowden, Nick Horne, Barbara Carlisle, Sue Holmes, Cecilia Neville, Jamie Robertson-McLeod, Louie MacPherson, Anne Pease, Bob Estridge and Peter Lee-Jones. Thanks, too, for contributions from Clive Barrow, Frank Esson, Peter Masters, Wandy Swales, Louise Fothergill, Dick Festorazzi and Richard Snailham.

Many Venturers have also sent anecdotes and diary extracts. The illustrations were contributed by a host of artists and photographers, and much credit is due to Chris Sainsbury, our chief photographer.

The book can tell only part of the tale. It is a tribute to all who have taken part, and to those who will follow on this trail to adventure.

JOHN BLASHFORD-SNELL
ANN TWEEDY
Harthill Castle
Scotland
February 1990

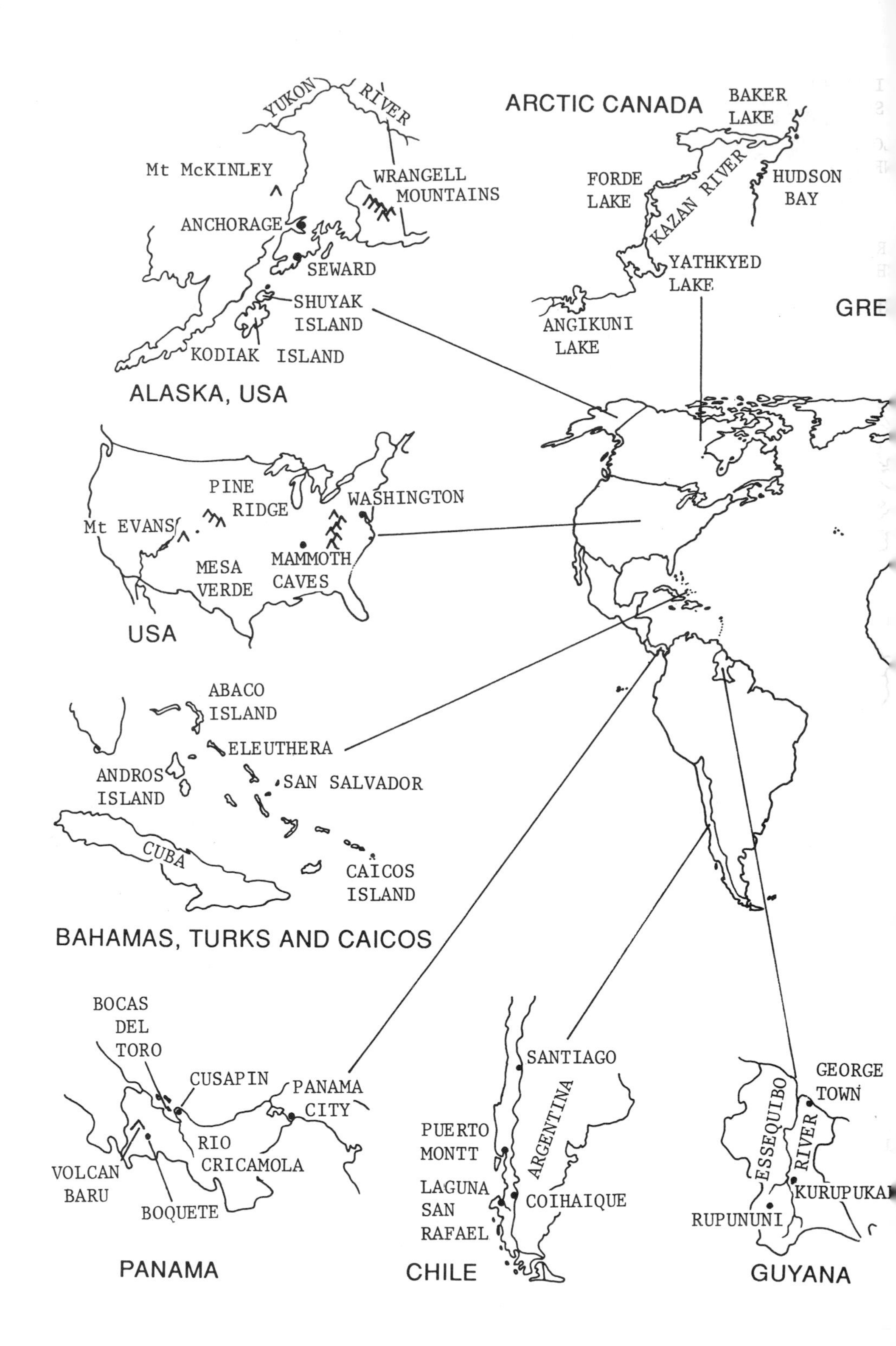
ARCTIC CANADA
BAKER LAKE
FORDE LAKE
KAZAN RIVER
HUDSON BAY
YATHKYED LAKE
ANGIKUNI LAKE
GRE
YUKON RIVER
Mt McKINLEY
WRANGELL MOUNTAINS
ANCHORAGE
SEWARD
SHUYAK ISLAND
KODIAK ISLAND
ALASKA, USA
PINE RIDGE
WASHINGTON
Mt EVANS
MESA VERDE
MAMMOTH CAVES
USA
ABACO ISLAND
ELEUTHERA
ANDROS ISLAND
SAN SALVADOR
CUBA
CAICOS ISLAND
BAHAMAS, TURKS AND CAICOS
BOCAS DEL TORO
CUSAPIN
PANAMA CITY
RIO CRICAMOLA
VOLCAN BARU
BOQUETE
PANAMA
SANTIAGO
ARGENTINA
PUERTO MONTT
LAGUNA SAN RAFAEL
COIHAIQUE
CHILE
GEORGE TOWN
ESSEQUIBO RIVER
KURUPUKAI
RUPUNUNI
GUYANA

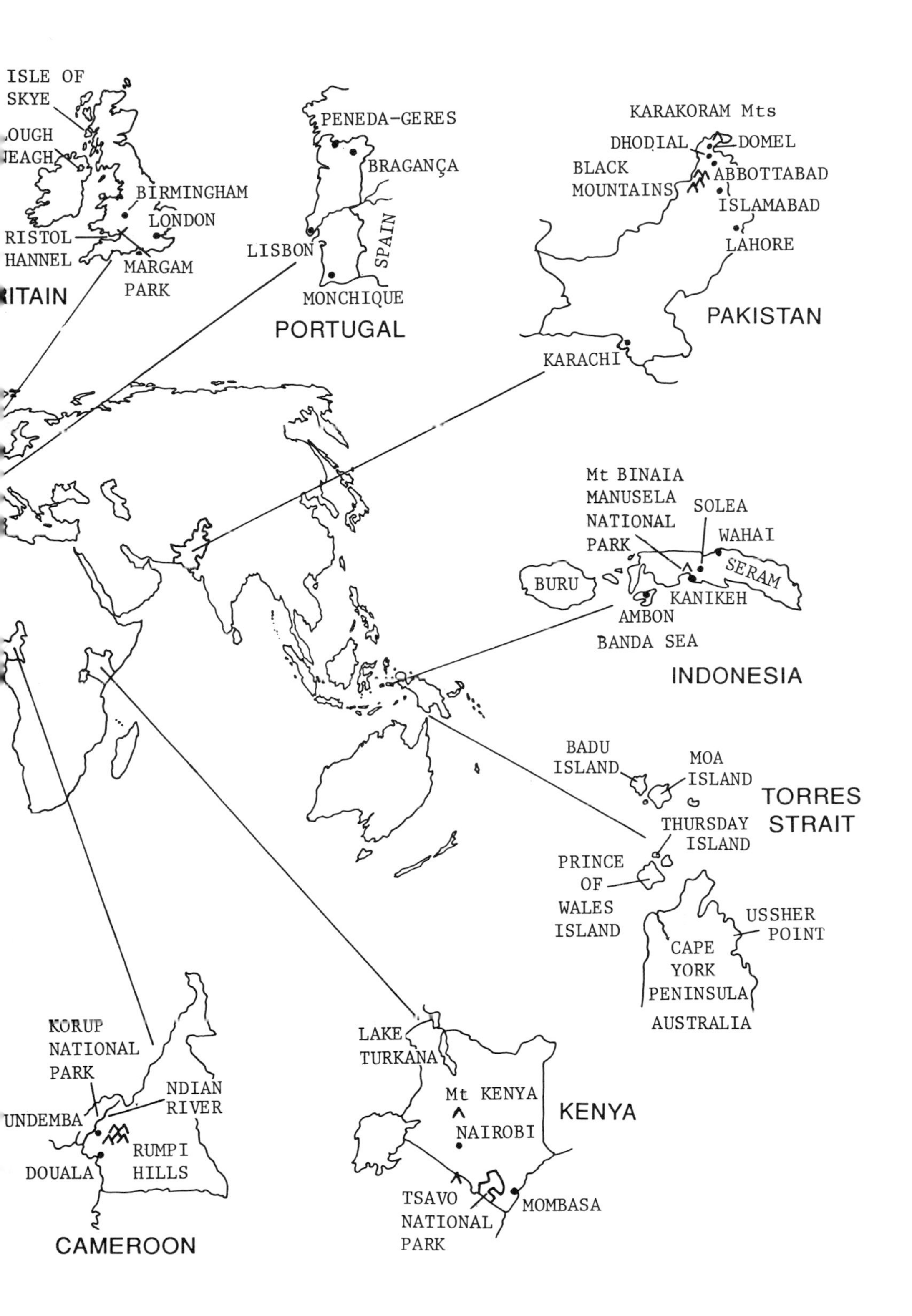
ISLE OF
SKYE
OUGH
EAGH
BIRMINGHAM
LONDON
RISTOL
HANNEL
MARGAM
PARK
ITAIN
PENEDA-GERES
BRAGANÇA
LISBON
SPAIN
MONCHIQUE
PORTUGAL
KARAKORAM Mts
DHODIAL
DOMEL
BLACK
MOUNTAINS
ABBOTTABAD
ISLAMABAD
LAHORE
PAKISTAN
KARACHI
Mt BINAIA
MANUSELA
NATIONAL
PARK
SOLEA
WAHAI
SERAM
BURU
KANIKEH
AMBON
BANDA SEA
INDONESIA
BADU
ISLAND
MOA
ISLAND
TORRES
STRAIT
THURSDAY
ISLAND
PRINCE
OF
WALES
ISLAND
USSHER
POINT
CAPE
YORK
PENINSULA
AUSTRALIA
KORUP
NATIONAL
PARK
NDIAN
RIVER
UNDEMBA
RUMPI
HILLS
DOUALA
CAMEROON
LAKE
TURKANA
Mt KENYA
KENYA
NAIROBI
TSAVO
NATIONAL
PARK
MOMBASA

PREFACE

BY WILFRED THESIGER

Operation Raleigh, the successor to Operation Drake, offers young men and women adventure in countries all round the world. Many young people wish to meet a challenge: some can do so intellectually, but most need to test themselves physically, to discover how to stand up to hardship or to confront danger. Thwarted by our urban civilization, many now resort to the kind of violence associated with football matches.

I have in recent years encountered some of the Venturers from Operation Raleigh in a remote part of northern Kenya. Some of the time they travelled on foot with camels across the desert. They endured weariness and thirst, as they laboured in intense heat across the lava fields around Lake Turkana. They spent their nights under the stars, with the camels and the tribesmen who accompanied them, alert for prowling lions. They helped to water their camels at occasional wells, where Rendile and Turkana were assembled with their cattle, camels and goats. All too briefly they took part in a way of life that had not yet changed, among people whose world is still measured by the distance they can walk. But there was always a purpose to the time they spent here in Kenya. On their journeys they collected information for scientists working in the country. At other times the Venturers worked on projects to assist the local people and by so doing got to know them. I watched them building a clinic in our isolated area. Near where they worked was a magnificent forest where they had the opportunity to see elephant, buffalo and even some leopard.

Operation Raleigh has given them the adventure which they sought, with the opportunity to test themselves; but it has given them more than this. They have experienced comradeship with others of different nationalities; they have met and worked with tribesmen and seen something of their lives. They have seen wild animals at first hand, and travelled through varied and fascinating scenery, and they have had the satisfaction of doing something to help the people among whom they lived. I am sure they will never forget the months they spent in Kenya; indeed, their time spent here will permanently affect their attitude to life.

Maralal
N. Kenya
1989

INTRODUCTION

It was dark and cool inside the shed that served as a ration store. Protected from the African sun, the waxed cardboard boxes stood in piles. Clean and dry as it was, the shed was nevertheless a haven for rats and mice and the occasional reptile that fed on them. The rations would also feed our Kenyan expedition for the next three months.

Selina Migeot, a blonde American, and Dave Horwood, whose custom of tying a bandanna around his head earned him the nickname 'Hippy', were stacking camp stores, disturbed only by the occasional rustle of a rodent. Gradually the Venturers' eyes became accustomed to the shadowy light. Snakes were commonplace at the Lake Baringo science camp, so when Selina moved a box and saw a thick, brownish tail, she wasn't unduly alarmed.

'Dave,' she called. 'Do you recognize this one?'

Her colleague peered into the darkness. 'Can't really see. Wait while I get a snake stick and we'll take it out to identify it,' he said, ducking out through the doorway. As he left the shed, Selina saw the snake come towards her, and rear up in one sinuous movement, its dreaded hood flaring wide. The girl had no time to turn from the fine spray of silver that flew from the snake's fangs. The venom lashed her eyes.

With a scream, Selina bolted for the door, her hands over her face. In her blind rush she nearly knocked over David, just returning with the stick. He knew immediately what had happened and yelled to Andy Thompson for help.

'Drench her eyes with water and keep flushing them until I'm back,' shouted Andy as he leapt into the Land Rover to fetch someone who could give expert aid.

Fortunately for the stricken girl, help was at hand. Janet Leakey and her husband Jonathan, a member of the famous Leakey family of anthropologists, live on the far side of the lake where they actually had a snake farm. Janet had been with me on Operation Drake in Kenya in 1980 and was an experienced expeditioner too. Within the hour she was back at the camp with Andy. She praised their quick action in flushing out Selina's eyes; their first aid had been exactly right and Selina's sight was saved from the spitting cobra's deadly venom.

Listening to this terrifying tale I was reminded of a snake-collecting team that I had led in Ethiopia in 1964, when I was an instructor at the Royal Military Academy, Sandhurst. Under the army's new adventure training programme we despatched hundreds of eager officer cadets to remote parts of the globe. In the words of the Commandant, General Mogg, the objective was the 'betterment of their character and, it was hoped, the least possible detriment to the Empire'.

As more civilians joined these projects, a group of my friends founded the Scientific Exploration Society, a registered charity, to handle the planning and administration of the more complex expeditions. The SES became an international body of servicemen, scientists and explorers. We have always given special emphasis to including young people in our projects: in 1978 with the considerable backing of His Royal Highness, The Prince of Wales, and the generous support of Mr Walter Annenberg, former American Ambassador to Britain, we launched Operation Drake.

This was the most ambitious and imaginative expedition for young people ever mounted. It also marked the 400th anniversary of Sir Francis Drake's circumnavigation of the globe. Aimed to combine the thrill of adventure with scientific research and community aid projects, it attracted over 50,000 young people from 27 nations, but only 414 could be taken. Nevertheless, it was a huge success, and by 1980 Prince Charles was urging us to do it all again – on a bigger scale.

Drake, Sir Walter Raleigh's cousin, had been a fiercely nationalistic and successful privateer, whereas Raleigh was more of an internationalist, trying to found a society in a New World. It was felt that the new expedition should be named after him and, by starting in 1984, it would also commemorate the 400th anniversary of the settlement of English-speaking America, in what is now North Carolina. Once again the Prince kindly agreed to be our Patron and planning for the new venture began.

Our aim was, quite simply, to develop leadership potential in young people through their experience of the expeditions. The hope was that they would return home to give service to others. Having witnessed Britain's inner city riots in 1982, it was clear to me that young leaders had a far better chance of communicating with the underprivileged than older counsellors – or the police.

Each Venturer, as the youngsters came to be called, would spend approximately three months in the field. Weather charts dictated that we should 'go west' and an invitation from Sir Jack Hayward to visit the Bahamas for our first expedition proved irresistible. One of our first ports of call would be in America, the very site where Raleigh's colonists had landed, then south to the Caribbean, Central and South America before crossing the Pacific to Australasia.

The scientists were fascinated by what Indonesia had to offer and we wanted to break new ground in Japan and Tibet. There were also interesting possibilities in

Pakistan. Africa, of course, could not be missed from the route of any worldwide expedition, and after that we planned to spend time in South America before returning to Britain five years later, via the wastes of Arctic Canada.

However, before anything could be set in motion, we needed considerable financial backing. Once again our good friend Walter Annenberg stepped into the breach and provided the necessary seed money. The next essential was a dedicated, hardworking staff, who could not expect much remuneration, and a team of experts to advise us on setting up such an international venture. Thanks to the generosity of IBM, a giant computer was installed in the London HQ to program finance, logistics and Venturer selection.

A worldwide recruiting and selection system was set up to find young people, aged seventeen to twenty-five, who were fit, compatible, spoke English (for safety reasons) and could swim well. They also needed to have leadership abilities and a willingness to place service to others before self. We planned to select 4000 Venturers.

There was a danger that Raleigh might become an expedition for the élite. To offset this, our selection procedure in Britain was consciously designed to help the underprivileged who lacked only the opportunity to reach their potential. This process included an interview and, for the finalists, a weekend in the wilderness where they were put through their paces under adverse conditions. Those selected had to raise some of the funds themselves, and a large number of companies, as varied as British Gas, the Post Office and British Telecom, sent employees.

Publicizing Operation Raleigh in Britain began with a special television programme in which Prince Charles interviewed three ex-members of Operation Drake. His Royal Highness then called for other young people to join Raleigh. Candidates were advised to apply to any branch of the Trustee Savings Bank, the only bank with branches in every part of the United Kingdom. TSB's enthusiastic support and help has been a major factor in the success of the operation.

Applications poured in and the selection process went into full swing. Eager youngsters faced giant pythons in darkened rooms, handled hairy tarantulas and were made wet, cold, hungry, frightened and furious by turns so that we could discover just how well they would get on together. Two vessels were acquired to support the enterprise. Our search for a sail training ship led us to discover the brigantine *Zebu*. She had begun life in a small, busy Swedish shipyard in 1938 and spent the next thirty-five years carrying cargoes across the Baltic. During World War II she smuggled arms for resistance movements, and carried many refugees to safety. In 1980 she competed in the Tall Ships Race, but later that year foundered in a severe storm in the Channel Islands. A young couple, Nick and Jane Broughton, bought her and *Zebu*'s new life began.

We found our support ship, MV *British Viking*, in Hull, A 1900-tonne former factory vessel, built in West Germany in 1965, she had been converted into a North Sea oil exploration vessel, equipped with submersibles. She still retained the distinctive features of a stern trawler and the massive A-frame across her after-deck, originally used to haul nets up a sloping stern ramp, could lift mini-subs. Her cavernous hold could stock expedition supplies and the former submarine base could be converted to house landing craft.

British Viking was owned by J. Marr & Sons of Hull and it was Hull City Council and the Department of the Environment who donated her to us. Her new name became *Sir Walter Raleigh*, or *SWR* for short. Many companies offered to help equip her and a refit committee was formed in Hull under the driving force of Councillor Jim Mulgrove. The people of the city soon took the ship to their hearts, no one more so than Alan Marr, the enthusiastic Chairman of J. Marr & Sons.

As the United States committee had been allocated 40 per cent of the Venturer places, I paid particular attention to their problems. The determination and persistence of Ann Smith and Mark Bensen in North Carolina held Operation Raleigh USA together, and around the globe other marvellous friends gave up their time to help. On the operational front we were desperately short of qualified staff. Encouraged by The Prince of Wales, the US Defense Secretary, Caspar Weinberger, kindly agreed to assist by allowing members of the American armed forces to take part. Australia, New Zealand, Panama and Portugal followed suit. In January 1984 the Prime Minister, The Rt. Hon. Margaret Thatcher, was our guest of honour at a luncheon organized by our commercial director, David King. Mrs Thatcher and her husband became keen supporters. Whilst David worked flat out at the fund raising I concentrated on expedition planning and logistics. The lights in our HQ at London's St Katherine's Dock were rarely out.

By September 1984 we were nearly ready. Our chairman, General Sir John Mogg, had decided to hand over to a sailor, Vice-Admiral Sir Gerard Mansfield, who took over in time for the flagship's commissioning on 4 September. It was a marvellous day. Her Royal Highness Princess Alexandra won everyone's hearts when she commissioned the ship in bright sunshine. Although we only discovered it at the last minute, our royal guest had a special interest in Raleigh; her daughter, Marina, had applied as a Venturer, passed the selection tests and would join us later in Honduras.

On 11 October 1984 *Zebu* was ready. The lovely ship sailed from Tower Pier, London, with arch sea-Goon, Sir Harry Secombe, at the helm for a few minutes. Aboard were sixteen Venturers and nine professional crew under the watchful eye of Captain Peter Masters. 'America next stop!' cried Sir Harry as her square sails filled and she left for the open sea and four years of adventure.

Meanwhile in Hull field director Charlie Daniel was working his teams round the clock to have *SWR* ready for departure on 13 November. By the dawn of that day, miracles had been achieved and The Prince of Wales gave us a wonderful send-off: to the cheers of a large crowd, *Sir Walter Raleigh* sailed for New York by way of the Channel Islands.

Our first book, *Operation Raleigh: The Start of an Adventure* (Collins, 1987), describes the events of 1984 and 1985. Supported by the ships, we carried out twenty-four exciting expeditions in the Bahamas, the Turks and Caicos Islands, Costa Rica, Belize, Honduras, Panama, Bolivia, Peru, Chile and Hawaii. On New Year's Day 1986, *Zebu* was in Australian waters and a new expedition was forming in Southern Chile, where *SWR*, having served us so well for fourteen months, was refitting.

The second book, *Operation Raleigh: Adventure Challenge* (Collins, 1988), is the story of the enterprise as it developed from January 1986 to October 1987, and covers expeditions in Chile, the Pacific crossing by *SWR*, work in the Solomons, Papua New Guinea and Malaysia. It tells of adventures in the Australian bush, the epic diving project to discover the wreck of HMS *Pandora* on the Great Barrier Reef and tasks undertaken in the scenic lakeland and mountains of New Zealand's Fiordland. There are tales of little-known areas of Japan and the home-coming of *Sir Walter Raleigh* after her successful 69,000-kilometre circum-navigation. There is also an account of a challenging expedition to Mt Xixabangma in Tibet that took me twelve years to arrange, and of a muscle-stretching endeavour in Pakistan's Karakoram.

With this, the third volume in the series, events between October 1987 and April 1989 are described. At this point it should all have ended, but Operation Raleigh had proved such a huge success that sponsors, young people around the world and conservation organizations pressed for the operation to carry on. However, the SES did not feel it could continue to run the mammoth scheme, although it would happily support those who might do so. There were several contenders for the role and the Society invited the international yachtsman Graham Walker, a prominent British businessman with a youthful spirit, to take over and establish a new charity.

Thus the Raleigh Trust was founded which is today responsible for Operation Raleigh. Expeditions continue across the world with young men and women of many nations, hell bent on adventure, travel, conservation and helping the community, whilst strengthening their leadership skills and enhancing their prospects in life.

In October 1987 we launched a major scientific expedition in Indonesia, where Sir Francis Drake's *Golden Hind* had run aground in 1580. That story begins this tale.

The spirit of Drake and Raleigh lives on.

CHAPTER ONE

Indonesia

Journey to the Centre of the Earth

(*Expedition Director*: Major Wandy Swales, TD)

(*Field Leaders*: Captain Christopher Kendall, GR
Jeremy Holloway)

Seram, Indonesia, 15 May 1987

Operation Raleigh was going to the centre of the world, the island republic of Indonesia which harbours a sacred cave believed to be the earth's navel, guarded by a demon dwarf. Stories abound in Indonesia: stories of tribes of invisible men who fly through the air, of fierce nomads who guard the forest peaks, of prehistoric Komodo dragons, of an array of spirits which, quick to anger, must be appeased by elaborate rites and ceremony. During the two expeditions mounted here by Operation Raleigh in 1987, we would learn to respect these tales, and the people who live in such close harmony with their surroundings.

It was the hard facts of science, however, and not folklore which we had come to find. Many of the country's 13,677 islands, cobbled together across the equator, have never been explored, and the region is of immense interest to scientists. Wedged between vast bodies of water – the Indian and Pacific Oceans and the seas of South China, Java and Banda – the islands of Indonesia span an area as wide as the United States. Cutting straight through the islands is the famous Wallace Line, where the Indo-Australian tectonic plate dips below that of Eurasia and forms a boundary between the Asian and Australian ecosystems.

Indonesia is a predominantly Muslim country of great beauty and contrast. It is a country of over 180 million people who speak 250 different languages but have only two seasons to cope with – the dry, from April to October, and the wet, from November to March. Thus our two expeditions were alternately parched or flooded. This hot, tropical archipelago studded with over 300 volcanoes, is the home of tigers and panthers, elephants, one-horned rhino, huge wild oxen and tiny mouse deer. Apes, monkeys, crocodiles and wild boar roam the plains and jungles while the air is fragrant with nutmeg and cloves and filled with parrots, birds of paradise and swifts, whose nests are so prized by Chinese gourmets.

Just which biogeographic region the bow-shaped island of Seram belongs to is uncertain. Scientists have long debated whether the island which was pushed above the surface of the sea five million years ago and now nudges New Guinea, belongs to the Australasian or to the Asian mainland. Indeed, one of the aims of the research undertaken by Operation Raleigh was to try to shed additional light on the question. A backbone of high, jungle-covered mountains splits the land from east to west: almost in the centre rises the highest peak in the Moluccan archipelago, Mt Binaia, or, in Indonesian, Gunung Binaia. Like the other high mountains on Seram, Kobipoto and Merkele, mist-covered Binaia is sacred, soaring 3027 metres above the lowland forest in Manusela National Park, itself one of the least explored places in the world.

We were intrigued. After discussions with many scientists from the East and the West, with the senior member of the Indonesian Institute of Sciences, Miss Moerjini and her assistant Mr Napitipulu, Seram was chosen as the site of the expedition. It would be a joint venture between Operation Raleigh in London and the talented and hardworking Indonesian committee.

Such was the island's remoteness that even before the advance party set off, Wandy Swales, an experienced traveller and ex-Royal Marine who had spent many years in the Parachute Regiment of the Territorial Army, flew from London to Jakarta, to begin organizing materials and renewing contacts. Wandy was no stranger to Indonesia: he had been deputy leader of the Operation Drake expedition to the country in 1979 and had kept in touch during his stint later at our London headquarters. Communications and transport, he knew, would be almost non-existent. There was limited sea transport, but no roads, cranes or helicopters to bring the twenty-six tonnes of stores and equipment into the remote area of central Seram. There were also no telephones or telexes; airmail letters from London took twenty-five days. The logistics, Wandy told Nick Horne, were going to be a nightmare.

With this cheerful thought in mind, Nick helped wind up one of the last Australian expeditions and flew to Ambon, the capital of the Moluccas and an island just south of Seram. There he met with Dave Hudson, an Australian who spoke the official language, Bahasa Indonesia. Dave had participated in the previous Drake adventure as a young explorer. Jumping on to an ancient wooden ferry grossly overloaded with chickens and cows, Nick and Dave spent two days on the choppy Banda Sea, the time it took the ferry to cough its way around the western end of Seram to the town of Wahai on the north coast. Their job was to confirm the suitability of base camp sites suggested for the first of the two expeditions by botanist Ian Edwards from the Royal Botanic Gardens in Edinburgh a year earlier. Solea in the northern lowlands and Kanikeh, a village nestled high in the foothills of Gunung Binaia further south, were their destinations.

After Wahai, leg and back muscles would be their only transport. But before striking out on a week's trek across the plains, rivers and tropical forests in search of the two sites, Nick and Dave were careful to observe the protocol of the country, and paid a courtesy visit to the Bapakrajah – the 'chief'. Before entering even the smallest hamlet or climbing the most remote peak, respect must be shown to the authority of the chief, for it is he who is able to intercede on the visitor's behalf, and ask for the gods' protection. There are many strict customs in Indonesia, as Wandy had briefed all members of the expedition. One must never, ever touch a person's head; never use the left hand to give or receive anything; never be rude or abrupt; and never sit with the soles of one's feet towards another person.

Nick and Dave set a fast pace through the humid lowlands and headed south to Solea. After wading through a wide river, they began to climb, first through primary rainforest, then over the Kobipoto Ridge to the mountain villages of Solumena, Manusela and finally, Kanikeh.

Nick looked up at the great mountain cloaked in a forest untouched by man. Beards of grey moss hung from the trees and steamy white mist swirled around the mountain like waves on a ship's prow. 'The mountain could be eerie,' he thought, 'if you were on your own.'

Seram, 4 July 1987

At the eastern extremity of Indonesia, Seram possesses all the ingredients required for a first-class adventure: tropical rainforests, rivers, mountains, the fascinating culture of a proud people – the Moluccans – and a wealth of unexamined scientific phenomena. Here, on this remote island where Sinbad the Sailor found his pearl divers and cannibal kings, Wandy Swales and his international team mounted two remarkable expeditions. Backed by our chief scientist Dr John Proctor, Nick Payne and Gayatri Reksodihardjo co-ordinated the efforts of an impressively well-qualified task force of scientists and Venturers. Their brief was to study a host of projects each of which could absorb a lifetime: the zoology, botany and marine life of Seram.

In what was probably the most exhaustive scientific survey ever conducted by Operation Raleigh, changes in altitude and their effects on the genetic diversity of the rainforest were studied. Manusela National Park provided the widest possible range of forest ecosystems, rising from sea level to the peak of Binaia. The work would provide a crucial link in a chain of rainforest research projects undertaken by Raleigh around the world. The results would be compared with the information on the rainforest obtained from studies undertaken by teams in Costa Rica in 1985 and on Mt Cameroon a year hence. These studies were planned years before the public took up the cry of 'Save the rainforest' and newspapers splashed green issues across their front pages. Not everyone is aware of the differences between lowland and upland rainforest, however. According to Dr Robert Payton, a member of the first Indonesian expedition who would join us again in Cameroon, 'There is a lot of talk about "rainforests" in general, but compared to the very small amount of mountain rainforest left in the tropics, there is quite a lot of lowland rainforest. It is critical to safeguard them all, but particularly the forests of the mountains: there are fewer of them, and once cut, the soil erodes on the steep slopes and the environment degrades. Who knows what resources they hold for the future.'

Indeed, the world is fast running out of trees at any altitude: one-third of the earth is arid and tropical forests are being cut at the unbelievable rate of over 1200 hectares per hour. Approximately eleven million hectares of tropical forest are lost each year, cleared for mining, farming and the sale of the wood itself. With their loss goes the habitat of insects, plants and animals, and it is estimated that one-fifth of all species on earth may disappear within twenty years: an average of 100 species every day.

To help provide the research needed to save these unique areas, the first group of Venturers and staff from all over the world flew into Jakarta on 4 July and slung their rucksacks aboard the ferry that twice a month points its bow to the east and heads off hopefully across the Java Sea for Seram.

Solea, Seram, 21 July 1987

Drenched by sudden tropical downpours and wet most of the time from rain or rivers or sweat from packing heavy loads over rough terrain in ninety degrees of humidity, Wandy knew that even the fittest members of the expedition would find it hard to adjust to the harsh climate of Indonesia. But no one expected death – and the death of a local man accustomed to the altitude and the heat. It happened on the first day of the trek south from Wahai to the science camp at Solea.

By dawn the brilliant sun already threatened the earth with its heat, and the Venturers had spent a sleepless night steaming in humid darkness, thick with mosquitoes. Based on Nick's and Dave's reports, Wandy estimated that the group marching to the lowland camp of Solea would make it in about four hours. Those heading further south, to the mountainous region of Kanikeh near Gunung Binaia, would need longer, about three days.

Strapping on their rucksacks, the two groups set off in the early morning. The heavy green leaves of the lowland vegetation crowded in around them, holding in the heat and humidity like an oven. As usual at the start of any expedition, people carried far too much in their packs; later, they would learn to live happily for weeks with little more than a change of clothes, malaria pills, foot powder, soap and a toothbrush. And some didn't bother with the soap.

Bringing up the rear, Wandy watched as the pace slowed to a crawl after the first hour. The heat was oppressive. Venturers and porters carrying scientific equipment had to stop often for rest and water, unable to carry their heavy loads as fast or as far as he had hoped. At this rate, some would need eight hours to reach Solea and over a week to walk up to Kanikeh. The gently undulating trail broke into the open, affording little protection from the sun. Ahead a punishing slope sheered off into the distance and finally, at the top of a ridge overlooking the forest, was the village of Solea. A month before, Steve Rose, an ex-Venturer, had led an energetic advance party to the site to construct the base camp. The five tarpaulin-covered long-houses were the largest structures on Seram.

That last steep hill to Solea was to take its awful toll. Walking with Mick Day, an entomologist from the British Museum, Wandy Swales discovered a dark body stretched across the path. One of the porters, Eddy, had died of a heart attack on the last push to the camp. Aided by local people, the two men carried Eddy's body back down to his village. There they attended the funeral before again setting off for Solea.

More tragedy lay ahead. This time it struck on Gunung Binaia. A few weeks after the porter's death, an expedition photographer, Paul Claxton, fell from the mountain and was killed on the rocks 200 metres below. Paul was a man with a rare combination of talents. At twenty-five, he was a physicist, an expert photographer and experienced outdoorsman. He had been a Venturer on one of Raleigh's Chile trips, cycled 12,800 kilometres across the Arctic and traversed part of the Sahara. With Paul was Venturer Ashley Hyett, a geography graduate from the London School of Economics who had joined Paul to climb the summit and photograph the sunrise.

Their night on the summit had been cool and quiet. The peak's silence was a welcome change from the rainforest below, filled with the loud noises of insects and birds and shut in on every side. The sunrise had been spectacular, a mixture of reds and yellows spilling over the sky. But the mountain's beauty held a dreadful danger. Geologically, the island is very young, and much of the rock is soft limestone. That stone was one of the main reasons we came to Seram, for there were no previous studies of limestone rainforests in the tropics. The crumbly, treacherous rock was also one of the reasons why Paul Claxton died. Looking down, Ashley could see the body of his friend lying across the rocks. There was no movement and no sound. 'I was sure Paul was dead,' said Ashley. 'No one could have survived that kind of fall.'

Twenty minutes later, struggling up the side of the ravine for help, Ashley felt the rock he held break from the face and suddenly he, too, was shrugged off the mountain's shoulder. Two or three hours passed before he regained consciousness. Ashley could still see Paul, but this time the motionless body was above him. A combination of pure instinct to survive and knowledge of first aid learned from eight years of Scout training took over.

'I checked all my injuries and realized I was wet not only from rain but equally from my blood,' wrote Ashley. 'My chest was distorted and the difficulty I had taking deep breaths led me to think I had broken ribs. I was unsure about my ankles which, although painful and prone to collapsing under me, could be walked on. My kit was strewn over the mountain and charted my descent. The larger items had travelled as far as I had, and I collected them up.

'I moved into the trees to rest and assess the situation. While I was awake, I kept calling to Paul, but in vain. There was no answer.'

Warmth, water, shelter and food were the four essentials. Leaving on his boots to support his ankles, Ashley pulled on all the clothes he could find, ate a few nuts and raisins and built a rain trap, ripping his plastic bivouac bag down one side and hanging it on a tree with spring clips to form a funnel. Beneath it he set the empty plastic first-aid box to catch the rain. Then, exhausted, he slept.

Gunung Binaia, Sunday, 16 August 1987

As soon as the pair failed to return on time, the Raleigh team went into action. On the mountain, deputy leader Chris Kendell sent out a search party led by ex-Royal Marine sergeant, Steve Oliver. Steve was no stranger to tropical forests. Trained in jungle and Arctic warfare, parachute jumping and rock climbing, he had been with Operation Raleigh in the steamy highlands of Honduras. A second search party was led by jungle expert and ex-officer in the Singaporean Army, Tay Soo Jin: both men were trained in the techniques of search and rescue.

On Ambon, Nick Horne scoured the archipelago for helicopters and managed to secure a Singaporean chopper on lease to a logging company. In Jakarta, Wandy Swales and David Stables alerted the Indonesian Army, co-ordinated the rescue efforts and kept in close touch with the rest of the expedition and with CHQ in London.

But the mountain was vast, and there were many places which could swallow a man without trace. While waiting for his rescuers, Ashley was on his own for four

William Collins Sons & Co. Ltd
London · Glasgow · Sydney · Auckland
Toronto · Johannesburg

ISBN 0 00 215855 8

First published 1990

Photoset in Itek Plantin Light by
Ace Filmsetting Ltd, Frome, Somerset
Made and printed in Great Britain by
William Collins Sons & Co. Ltd, Glasgow

Photoset in Itek Plantin Light by
Ace Filmsetting Ltd, Frome, Somerset
Made and printed in Great Britain by
Butler & Tanner Ltd, Frome, Somerset

OPERATION RALEIGH

Adventure Unlimited

John Blashford-Snell
and Ann Tweedy

COLLINS
8 Grafton Street London W1
1990

days. By the second day his ankles had swollen to the size of his thighs and he could no longer move. Perversely, the rain stopped and the air cleared, providing kaleidoscopic sunrises but putting no water in his rain trap. Finding the first-aid box dry each morning, he licked the droplets that condensed on the plastic and ate only raisins; the nuts were impossible to swallow without water. During those four days, Ashley had time to come to terms with the horror of his friend's probable death.

On the third day, he heard shouts. On the fourth he heard them grow louder until, unable to believe his eyes, he recognized the voices of the local villagers from Kanikeh. Two hours later, expedition doctor Stephen Hill reached Ashley; the prompt medical treatment saved his life. The following day, the doctor confirmed that Paul Claxton's body had been found. He had died instantly from his injuries.

Unappeased, the spirits of Binaia only grudgingly released their second victim. Bad weather made the planned helicopter lift impossible, and Ashley had to be carried off the mountain to the village – a two-day trek – then flown to Ambon, Jakarta and home.

I have seen Ashley many times since, but the last time was two years after the accident, on the Operation Raleigh expedition to Cameroon. His ankles were still a bit weak; he sometimes walked with a stick, and his infectious enthusiasm was tempered with reflection. Inspired by the rainforest project in Indonesia, however, he had always known he would join another expedition. 'It only took minutes to decide I wanted to join the Cameroon expedition,' said Ashley. 'I was fascinated to continue the study begun in Indonesia: how species – flora and fauna – vary with a change in altitude, not just with a change in weather and temperature.'

After Cameroon, he had more plans. To travel further, to the north of the country and across Chad to Niger Burkina and Mali, to Senegal and Gambia, before returning to his work at a children's home in Richmond, London.

Had he lived, I know Paul Claxton would have pursued life with equal vigour. Paul was a born adventurer, in tune with the beauty of the world around him. His photographs in this volume and elsewhere are a fitting memorial to his zest for life.

During those sad and troublesome days, the support and wisdom of the British Ambassador, Sir Alan Donald, and his wife, Janet, were an inspiration to the Venturers, as was the kindness of our Indonesian patron, Professor Emil Salim, and committee chairperson, Mrs Erna Witoeler.

The shock of the accident had affected the morale of everyone on the expedition, but the projects continued as planned and soon regained momentum. During the teams' six months on Seram almost nothing in the Manusela National Park went unexamined. For the benefit of the collections and records of scientific institutions situated all over the world, members of the two Indonesian expeditions of 1987 searched out death adders and orchids, butterflies, moths, bats, bees and birds.

Using techniques developed by John Proctor on the Costa Rican expedition, they marked off fifty-metre-square plots on the hillsides, divided each one into smaller areas and tagged every tree with a number. They made notes of the girth of the trees, their buttresses and support roots, measured the height of the canopy and compared the soils of the old alluvial flood plains with the high coastal terraces. The work was exhausting and intensive and had never been done before. Its purpose was to collect soil samples and plant specimens to be sent to botanic gardens in Leiden, Edinburgh and Ambon for identification.

Building on the work of Raleigh expeditions in Peru, the Solomon Islands, Papua New Guinea and Australia, scientists co-ordinated an extensive bio-resources project. The basic idea behind the study was to identify local medicines and plant uses. One day these might save more lives and produce needed products, thereby generating income for local people while encouraging the protection of the environment which nurtures them.

The work of many of the international scientists associated with the expeditions, such as Femi Hukom and Sven Loupati, is still being collated for publication. Other scientists such as Djoko Iskandar, British Museum scientists Mick Day and Martin Brendell, and York University's Chris Rees and Meg Huby assembled a remarkable collection of insects ranging from the tiny fruit fly, *Drosophila*, to the horned rhinoceros beetle, the antlered stag beetle that measures a full twenty-three centimetres from heel to horn, and, most startling of all, the largest bug in the world, *Bellostoma indica*. This extraordinary creature the size of a rat haunts murky river bottoms and hunts in the darkness of night. Its venomous claws make short work of prey, and, the locals claim, it has been known to attack small children.

Like the bugs of Seram, the island's bats could be cast in a science fiction film. Along with Benny Kristiansen who studies them, Venturer and radio amateur Jeremy Fish was impressed by the graceful night-flyers. So were Denis De Gruchy from Jersey, Mark Wilson and others who spent their nights nursing the home-made bamboo radio aerial – a two-element cubicle quad – and sending signals to virtually every country in the world. Frustrated by many a frequency problem of their own, the Raleigh radio 'hams' were captivated by the creatures which have a more finely tuned mechanism than any made by man.

Some evenings, waiting for a radio frequency to open, Jeremy would shake the larger bugs from his clarinet and perch on a tree stump. For a few hours the heart of the jungle would beat to the rhythms of Coltrane, Parker and Lester Young.

'We used to sit on the beach and, as the sun went down, thousands and thousands of bats flew out of the forest away from the sun directly over our heads,' recalls Jeremy. 'They were bigger than herons and you could hear their wings flap against the air. Lying on the beach with the whole sky black with bats, you thanked the Lord they had insects on their minds.'

If the earth and the air proved rich hunting grounds for study, the Banda Sea was just as exciting. In the mint-green waters surrounding the island, Operation Raleigh expedition members examined the rich variety of crustaceans, corals and molluscs – including the rare Nautilus. A beautiful 'living fossil' which evolved twenty-four million years ago, the Nautilus is housed in a segmented shell of chocolate and silver; the elegant ancestor of the naked squid.

Seram was a paradise for herpetologists too. Over a dozen new species of reptiles and amphibians were discovered during the six months, and scientists Ron Lilley and Paul Edgar – a Venturer in Costa Rica who had also been with us in Australia's Northern Territory – captured a reticulated python, one of the largest snakes in the world, swimming casually between islands.

One doesn't expect land-dwelling snakes to take to the sea, but anything is possible on Seram.

Time was running short and there was still so much to do. A savage storm at Manusela, northeast of Gunung Binaia, had reduced one of the two school huts to rubble, and the second was in a precarious state. On the expedition were three talented architecture students who soon mobilized the other Venturers and built a new school with a weatherproof roof.

My old friend and our chief photographer Chris Sainsbury, a veteran of more Drake and Raleigh expeditions than he cares to count, remembers that for many, working closely with the community was the highlight of the expedition. 'There were about the same number of Indonesians and internationals on the projects, and living in a long-house or with the villagers gave everyone a remarkable insight into the local culture and way of life,' said Chris. 'As we worked, waves of laughter would erupt at the slightest provocation, and the villagers would often talk the night away until their chatter was drowned by the dawn chorus of the village cockerels and packs of dogs.'

Following the school construction, Raleigh helped villagers build a new community centre at Solea, to the north of Manusela, and a spate of other projects soon followed in the widely scattered mountain hamlets. Along the southern coast, they repaired a mosque, and built or repaired several foot bridges.

Wandy had christened the two Indonesian phases 'The Impossible Expeditions'. For once, I was glad he was wrong. Working in a harsh climate over hazardous terrain, with almost no communications or transport, across a spray of islands spanning the distance from London to Moscow, there was every possibility that he could have been right. That he was not is a tribute to Wandy and to the support of the Indonesian and international members of the team.

As we dismantled our island camps, patched the Avon inflatables and released the pet python, thoughts were already focusing on another group of islands famous for pearl luggers and palm trees, lost and found treasures and the stories of Somerset Maugham. We were heading for the islands of the Torres Strait above the sharp pinnacle of Australia's Cape York.

Compared with Seram, it's really quite simple to find the islands of Thursday, Moa, and Prince of Wales. I flew to Cairns on the east coast of the Cape, turned my compass to due north, and kept heading in that direction.

CHAPTER TWO

The Torres Strait

Islands in the Sun

(*Expedition Leader*: Clive Barrow)

The Torres Strait, Australia, 5 October 1987

The old DC3 had only reached cruising altitude yet the twenty Venturers aboard were already beginning to enjoy the experience of flying in the workhorse of World War II. Darwin's drab desert coastline receded into the haze and beneath them the choppy, shark-infested sea was flecked with breaking waves.

'Should be in TI in three hours,' shouted the crewman above the engine's roar as they headed for the Raleigh base on Thursday Island, or TI as the Australians know it. Twenty-year-old Isobel Taylor, who worked for a children's charity in Northern Ireland, thought 'What a great way to start an expedition.' Just a few days earlier she'd been at home in Derry, now all the months of selection tests, fund raising and preparation were over and her excitement mounted as the DC3 neared its destination. Glancing out, Isobel was musing over the tasks that lay ahead when suddenly oily black smoke and flames poured out of the starboard engine. With a few splutters and coughs, its propeller stopped. The lively chatter was replaced by cold fear. The plane banked, its remaining motor straining to keep it airborne as the pilot swung back to Darwin.

Thursday Island, 5 October 1987

At the expedition base, Sergeant-Major Pat Langan of the Royal Green Jackets put down the radio microphone and drawing heavily on his cigarette, shrugged as if to say, 'Just another Op Raleigh day.' Turning to Clive Barrow, the tall, bronzed leader of Expedition 11F, he remarked, 'One of the planes has blown an engine in mid flight.'

'We'd better put the dinner back,' grunted Clive.

Meanwhile the disabled Dakota limped into Darwin where the wary passengers squeezed themselves into an unlikely assortment of small aircraft to restart their trip to TI.

The Torres Strait islands consist of seventy small islets dotted along the Barrier Reef between the Cape York Peninsula and Papua New Guinea (PNG). Ten thousand years ago this area was a dry isthmus connecting Australia to Southeast Asia and it was by this route that man first reached the southern continent.

The islands fall into two types, coral atolls and high rock outcrops. The 145-kilometre-wide Strait forms a bottleneck for the large swells from the Western Pacific. As a result, immensely strong currents make navigation dangerous through the reefs. A steady trade wind keeps the islands cooler than the mainland. Monsoonal rainfall occurs in January, February and March but the rest of the year is fairly dry. Hurricanes have been recorded during the wet season which starts at the end of November. Thus, the expedition was taking place just prior to the really dangerous weather cycle.

Originally the islanders were a mixture of Polynesian and Melanesian with a strong tribal structure separate from those of their neighbours in PNG to the north and the Aboriginal Australians to the south. Inter-island wars were common. The Spanish navigator, Torres, first passed through the Strait in 1606 mistaking mainland Australia for just another small island.

During the colonization of Australia in the early nineteenth century many boats foundered on the Torres Strait reefs, and the cannibalistic islanders often killed those who reached the shore. These fierce attacks by the powerful natives in their war canoes became the basis of the 'explorer in the cooking pot' humour of the Victorian era. The colonists were not so amused, especially when some of the most aggressive attacks were instigated by Europeans, escapees from prison camps who made incredible journeys up to the Torres Strait and befriended the natives, sometimes becoming island chiefs.

Punitive raids by colonists from the nearby Jardine Settlements of the Cape York Peninsula cowed the islanders, and eventually in 1871 missionaries settled there. Slowly cannibalism died out, but cases were still being reported early this century. Before World War II, pearling brought adventurers to the islands and the people became a diffuse mixture of Polynesian, Chinese, Melanesian and Japanese. When the advent of synthetic materials destroyed the pearl-shell industry in the 1960s, many young men became labourers on the mainland. Today there is a severe shortage of males, but the people still maintain some of their old ways.

The islanders are self-governing and elect a Council every three years. Thursday Island is the administrative centre complete with shops, a hospital, sealed roads and a number of infamous hotels and bars. Being expert fishermen and navigators the natives live from the sea. Merchant ships passing through the

Opposite: The scientific camp at Kanikeh, Seram Indonesia.

Strait often collect a pilot at Thursday Island to guide them through the maze of the Great Barrier Reef.

Seventeen islands are inhabited but fourteen of them are 'reserves' which outsiders can only visit by special permission. Very few people try. Although many islands are much nearer PNG than the mainland, in a recent boundary dispute the islanders voted to remain within the Australian administration.

As an extension of the Great Barrier Reef the Torres Strait is part of the world's largest coral system. The islands themselves vary in their ability to support life depending on the amount of fresh water available. Vegetation depends on what type of water it grows in. The mangroves and coconut palms are halophytic plants that survive on salt water. Snakes and lizards, a wide variety of bird life, wild pigs and fruit bats inhabit the lusher islands. The people hunt turtles and dugongs, the latter being the rare 'sea cows' that early sailors mistook for mermaids.

In 1987 I'd visited our earlier expedition that was involved with various projects in the area. The island community was delighted with our work and entertained us lavishly. They pressed us to return and it was in this semi-paradise that the sixty-three Venturers of the new expedition were to spend the next two and a half months.

The expedition's four project sites were based principally on two of the largest islands, Moa and Badu. At St Paul's, a 200-strong mission community on the eastern side of Moa, Venturers were to continue building two substantial houses for local families already started by the previous expedition. Construction materials were mostly local – mangrove wood, termite mounds and clay for cement and brick-making. On the south coast of the island, at the smaller community of Kubin, another group would renovate an old schoolhouse, clear thick scrub from the local school playground and cemetery, then carry out extensive bush-walking including an ascent of the highest hill in the Torres Strait, Bank's Peak.

After the opening drama involving the DC3, things progressed well until the Venturers were assigned to their sites. A ridiculously overladen passenger ferry, sailing under what could well have become the appropriate name of *Spirit of Torres*, wallowed like an inebriated monster while taking them out of TI harbour. Fortunately for all aboard it was a beautifully calm morning as they made their precarious way across the forty-eight-kilometre, reef-strewn channel to the next island. On arrival Clive Barrow disembarked in ambassadorial style to introduce his party, leaving instructions that the ferry was not to depart until he was back aboard.

All appeared to be in order until Clive saw the project leader, Val Hunt, racing down the village street towards him shouting that the *Spirit of Torres* had weighed anchor and was steaming away. Clive hailed a passing islander in an aluminium dinghy. The chase was short-lived – the young man stood his boat on its transom in hot pursuit. Once reunited with his vessel our gallant leader was loath to leave it again at the next port-of-call.

The rest of the Venturers were set down without incident and their projects commenced. The only problem appeared to be a lack of building materials at Kubin. Because of this, project leader Jim Bury asked the local people for an alternative task for the Venturers to do until the materials arrived. An initial week at Kubin was thus spent clearing scrub from the local cemetery. After a short while it became apparent that this activity was causing consternation within the superstitious local community. When asked the reason for their alarm, their simple and blindingly logical answer came back, 'Jes mek sure yous doan clear too many scrub, udderwise yous mek too much room. Den we go die too!'

Paddling amongst uninhabited islets including the now well-documented Tuin Island of *Castaway* fame, the Venturers were guided by the lean and weathered Australian, Greg Malone. The team gained remarkable first-hand insight into the unique flora and fauna of the region, including the magnificent giant turtle, the shy dugong and a vast array of other marine life. Tiger sharks, deadly poisonous stonefish and stingrays were regularly spotted.

As the weather deteriorated during the final weeks of the expedition, navigation by small craft became more and more hazardous. On the final leg of the last group's journey through the islands, the aim was to hop from the smaller island of Kulbai Kulbai to the west coast of Badu, and then to paddle on to a mangrove-swathed river mouth at the northern tip of the island. Instead, with both wind and tide pushing them inexorably northwards, the Venturers were swept on to the rocky shores of North Island, a short distance north of Badu. During this perilous journey the towering seas made it necessary for many of the canoes to be towed by Greg Malone's support craft.

Kulbai, 8 December 1987

Nick Harborne from Grimsby will not easily forget setting out in his canoe with some others and being towed by Greg across the Strait to the island of Obelish. Three-metre swells were rolling in as Greg sailed: with a heavy load aboard he could not manoeuvre easily. Worried by the size of the waves, he positioned a Venturer with an axe to slice through the tow ropes if his support craft became swamped and foundered.

A hundred metres offshore a big roller threatened them; Greg turned his craft head on and rode it, but the foaming wall of water caught the canoes sideways.

Nick Harborne's flipped over, hurling the crew into the boiling sea. Struggling beneath the upturned craft Nick swam deep to avoid the trailing ropes and equipment. 'I hope my kit was tied in properly,' was his only thought. He didn't consider the sharks. As his life jacket took him up through the water, he made out the orange blur of his canoe and surfaced beside it, gasping for air. Issy Taylor, from Ireland, came up beside him. Nick hauled himself on to the canoe bottom and putting his emergency training to good use managed to right his capsized craft.

Other Venturers who had spilled out had also climbed back aboard, but Issy was still in the water, left behind and rapidly losing strength. Despite her life jacket she couldn't keep her head out of the waves, and already her lungs were filling with water. With cool courage and swift action Samantha Ewing dived in and pulled the frightened girl to the safety of Greg's violently bucking boat. On finding a safe landing spot they all got first-aid treatment from the nurse – a hot cup of tea.

Nonetheless, the canoe project was not all mortal peril and high adventure. The weather fluctuated according to the cycles of the moon, the last quarter bringing oily calm seas and crystal blue skies. It was then that the tiny islands came close to anyone's vision of a tropical paradise; palm-fringed beaches of soft white sand caressed the soles of the feet in morning and evening and scalded them brutally as the sun grew stronger. The explorers discovered a water source known only to one native, and carried out bird-banding and mist-netting in an attempt to gain a better understanding of the migratory patterns of birds crossing the Strait. The profusion of marine life, however, provoked their greatest wonder. Venturers would return from snorkelling among the reefs wide-eyed with amazement at the sharks, stingrays, reef fish and coral formations they had seen.

Huge turtles of various species abound in the warm tropical sea. Sitting in our Thursday Island HQ one evening, as the daily Sitreps came in from project sites, Clive overheard the voice of accountant David Murray become incredulous as he manned the radio link: 'You can't be serious? Over.'

His curiosity aroused, Clive was keen to find out the reason for the disbelief in David's voice.

'Listen!' cried David. 'They came across a family of baby green turtles heading up the beach, caught one and wrote Gary's name on its shell to see where it would turn up next. They have just caught a shark and opened it up to find the very same turtle in its gut!'

A happier turtle tale occurred later in the second phase of the expedition. A team had been waiting with bated breath for their first sighting of a female turtle laying her eggs. In the dead of night they found a large lady trying desperately to dig a nest. The sand was too soft, however, and the more she struggled to dig a hole with her shovel-like flippers, the less success she had. Eventually, to the watchers' surprise, Greg Malone sauntered casually over to where the creature was becoming more and more frustrated and poured water on to the sandy patch. Finding the wet sand easier to deal with, the turtle finished digging her nest with ease, laid her eggs without further ado and trundled back to the ocean.

On Badu our team found the people suspicious of all foreigners: a bestselling novel had misrepresented the ways of the islanders, making them wary of authors and all outsiders. Nevertheless they soon took to the youngsters who worked hard under the infectious, indefatigable enthusiasm of project leader Steve Hide.

During their stay on Badu his group carved a football pitch, complete with spectators' benches, out of virgin scrub. This would permit the people to invite teams from other islands and thus improve relations. On the west side of Badu they built, in the unforgiving heat, a rock causeway through dense bush. Spanning a deep creek, it opened the way to a part of the beach hitherto inaccessible to the islanders during the wet season.

In their primitive camp the Venturers shared digs with an alarming number of extremely venomous death adders. Nurse Linda Mutti of London managed to tread on one but luckily was not bitten. Fortunately the poisonous reptiles appeared more timid than we were, although Steve seemed to possess an almost magnetic attraction for them, and indeed any other snake which happened along. He found pythons in the well, death adders at every turn, and was even caught with a small black snake in his hammock. In the final weeks a number of crocodiles, over two metres in length, were seen in the mangroves. This delighted the more adventurous Venturers, who had longed to spot some of the fabled nine-metre-long, saltwater monsters said to exist in these parts.

Greg Malone decided that the canoe group should explore the Badu River from the seaward side, using his boat and also our five-metre aluminium vessel *Dirty Dugong* which was powered by twin 40-horse Mariner outboards. The Raleigh boat was skippered by marine engineer Grant McPherson, who kept our battered old fleet afloat, to act as taxi, stores transport and ambulance. The most dramatic moment came for Grant and his crew when snaking their tortuous way up the river. Negotiating a sharp bend, Grant felt the steering arm break in his hand and the maverick boat plunged, out of control, into the bank, rearing bow-first on to two exposed mangrove roots which formed a natural ramp. The receding bow-wave swamped the small craft; she sank with all hands to the muddy bottom. In time-honoured fashion, Skipper Grant went down with his ship, a cataclysmic turn of events rectified by some furious baling by the crew. *Dirty Dugong* was soon re-floated. The engines had been a metre under, but after cleaning plugs and filters, they roared into life. Further proof, if Raleigh needed it, of the amazing reliability of Mariner outboards.

As the expedition drew to an end, the canoeists watched as dark clouds heralding the monsoon started to roll across the sky. Soon rain beat down on them with tropical force. A shrouding sea-mist billowed across the Strait; on land the dry creeks became torrents of dark brown flotsam-flecked water. It would have been madness to have attempted to navigate inflatable canoes in these conditions, so the canoes were deflated and taken by boat round to their final destination at Badu community. Their crews were put ashore at the mangroves and waded through flooded creeks and the now completely transformed landscape to the haven of the medical aid post. Their hopes of drying off were dashed when they realized that the building did not yet have a roof.

As swiftly as it had come, the rain vanished into a bright blue sky which the Venturers had learnt to bless and curse in the same breath during their sojourn amongst the islands and the lovely people of the Torres Strait. They bade farewell to the curious mixture of peoples who have unified to form the islands' population. All played their part in the trials and tribulations, the feasting and fishing, the heartache and humour - not to mention the sheer hard work - that made up a memorable experience for the members of the expedition in a place few outsiders have ever seen.

Meanwhile our plans to go to the Persian Gulf had been thwarted by the Iran–Iraq war and thus once again Operation Raleigh returned to South America.

CHAPTER THREE

In Chile's Icy Mountains

(*Expedition Leaders*: Major Tony Walton, TD RA
Major Henry Sawrey-Cookson, RA)

Lago Caro Base Camp, Southern Chile, 19 November 1987

'Down there – that's where we find them,' shouted the Chilean Army pilot as our shuddering helicopter banked above the emerald forest. Looking into the trees I realized that what I'd believed to be the ground was, in fact, just the top of an impenetrable bamboo matrix that rose five metres skyward between the larger timber.

In this thick jungle of wild forests, mountains, glaciers and fiords, it was a miracle that Captain Juan Henriquez had spotted our lost and totally exhausted patrol. Here, the rainfall can be torrential and the days often cold and stormy. Fifteen days before, the weather had been glorious when 23-year-old British aeronautical engineer Sally Armitage and ten colleagues set out to seek the rare huemule deer and chart its habitat in this remote and almost unexplored region of Southern Chile.

Back-packing ice axes, crampons, rope and dehydrated rations, their spirits were high, even if their rucksacks weighed a ton. They were an interesting mix of young people. Boat designer Neil Homeshaw carried the Plessey radio that was to be their vital link with the outside world. He was a perfectionist and had made most of his own equipment from orange Gortex. Fish farmer Paul Finnegan, from Hemel Hempstead, was used to a tough outdoor life. He wore a faithful old Barbour jacket and a pair of strong boots tied with one green lace and one red. Behind him trudged Andy Horsley, a well-travelled pop singer, who soon became great pals with Lara Norris, a cheerful blonde from Haywards Heath; James Ward, a fell runner from Derby; and engineer Alison Kempson, the patrol's leader whose hobby, fortunately, was orienteering.

The other members of the deerhunters patrol were staff member and expedition photographer Tony Painter and Alejandro Colomes, a young Chilean scientist. Shrugging off their heavy packs for a brief rest, they all wondered if they'd need the attention of bespectacled osteopath Tony Bush, who, together with conservationist John Dutton, made up the team.

In spite of a muddy track, the deerhunters made good progress on the first day and Adan, a local farmer, arrived with horses to ferry kit and equipment across the torrent at the Rio Cajou Blanco. At dusk they camped at Adan's remarkable hilltop house set above the river. Everything for the house, from ceiling boards to a home-made hydroelectric plant, had been transported by pack horse from the regional capital, Coyhaique, four days' journey away. That night the patrol formed new friendships as they sat round the homestead fire listening to Andy's Cat Stevens' tape – *Tea for the Tillerman*.

Stepping out into the night, Sally Armitage gasped as she saw the stars. 'They hit me like an explosion,' she wrote in her diary; 'someone has been scattering diamonds across the sky. I felt their force, the insignificance of my existence, the futility of the things that Western society considers so important, the power of nature.'

That power became more evident the next day. Following the river, the group hacked its way through the flaying bamboo, pulling bulging rucksacks through the narrow spaces they cut. Ominously the bamboo closed behind them. Ahead lay fifteen river crossings. Negotiating the freezing water took care, skill and the old technique of using a stout branch as a third leg, transforming a biped into a tripod. Like most good ideas, it is simple and efficient. Facing upstream against the powerful current they inched their way diagonally across the stream. Soon the river became fast and narrow, and slippery logs became an additional hazard. Lara and Sally were up their waists most of the time, but still managed to laugh as the water swirled around them.

On the fourth day the group left the river and began to climb. With relief they broke out of the forest and into clearer ground covered with small cabbage-like plants. This was huemule deer country. The wind whistled and tugged at their anoraks as they looked north to the snow-covered mountains and the great black massif of Volcán Hudson. Using ice axes for the first time they struggled on across steep gullies. The awesome sight of a soaring condor took their minds off their aching legs. The great bird circled, framed against a perfect blue sky, its characteristic wingtip feathers splayed.

In the shadow of Volcán Hudson they repacked their gear, and bade farewell to Adan whose wellies weren't made for mountaineering. Then, taking advantage of a lucky break in the gathering cloud, they scrambled up to the snowline. The scenery was fascinating; ice bridges, black from the mountain's 1971 eruption, stood out against clean walls of fresh blue ice. But there was still no sign of the huemule they had come to find.

Descending quickly, the group passed through thickets of prickly bushes, feasting on the red and white berries that grew on the alpine slopes. All too soon they were back in the claustrophobic forest. They found the Rio Desplayado in a steep gorge but couldn't get down to its waters, and it was evening before they found a campsite near a spring. Clouds blocked out the sky and the rain began.

The days passed quickly as the small expedition pushed deeper into Chile's interior. Used to river crossings though they were, the Venturers nevertheless found the fast, tumultuous waters a constant challenge. One of the most difficult crossings occurred a week after they set out. Swollen with rain, the river rushed through a deep chasm, its waters far too fast and deep to wade. Fortunately, a fallen log bridged the wide expanse; a precarious crossing, slippery and narrow, high above the water. Sally Armitage, an experienced climber, rapidly thought out the options. Helped by Tony Painter, she set up a safety system with their ropes.

'We put a rope around the log on the northern bank, ran the line along the length of the trunk and secured it on the far side,' she said. 'As I fastened my harness to it and wound the surplus rope around my neck, my heart missed a beat. Crouched on all fours I crossed the log slowly, remembered not to look down, and concentrated on the other side, respecting the danger. A back pack makes you inherently unstable, and, even with the harness around my chest, the traverse required great care.'

Once across, she turned when she heard a small voice exclaiming, 'I can't move, I can't move.' Behind her, Lara's face was rigid, her body frozen to the log with fear. 'I stretched out to reach her hand,' remembers Sally, 'trying to reassure her that she was OK, that she was safe. There had been times in the past when I had frozen too, when my legs had become uncontrollable and the shakes had set in. If you begin to imagine the danger, the battle is lost.'

This time Lara managed to win the battle. In what seemed like an eternity, she edged her way past a small stump jutting up from the log, and reached the bank. Soon the others crossed too and the group moved on.

Up and down the gullies, sliding between moss-covered trunks they pressed on, but still saw no sign of the elusive huemule deer. Suddenly the way ahead was jammed by dense stalks of bamboo rising like an impenetrable wall on all sides. Alejandro suggested climbing above it, but almost immediately the skies opened and the rain fell in rods. Pitching their tents in a small clearing, the drenched group ate some muesli and tried to dry out their saturated boots and socks.

It was a wretched night, and they rose with some relief at dawn to cut a trail with their machetes by pressing their bodies against some springy stalks whilst slashing at others. The rain fell incessantly and the work exhausted even the fittest. After several days of living on rations everyone looked decidedly gaunt.

Deep in the bamboo Andy came upon an ivy-clad tree and struggled up it to look for a way out of the jungle. Surely there must be an end to the green world which held them captive; but the waving fronds were everywhere – around them a mass of leafy branches, above them the sky. Their trail was taking them in the right direction, but they had no way of telling how many kilometres of bamboo they would have to cut to escape.

The rhythmic sound of their machetes drowned the forest noises. As the small group battled on, the unspoken thought that they might not get out alive was in everyone's mind. Their food was nearly finished and they were growing weaker by the hour; soon they would be at the point of no return and they wouldn't have the strength to retrace their steps. The weather had been bad, but now it became worse. Cold and wet, and down to only one day's rations, the Venturers knew that hypothermia was a real possibility.

I always tell the Operation Raleigh staff that, having briefed the Venturers thoroughly, they should only interfere if disaster seems imminent – the young people should organize and lead their own projects. Tony Painter decided that this point had been reached. Taking the radio, he called base camp at Puerto Montt to tell expedition leader Tony Walton of their predicament. The speedy reaction of the base camp operator raised morale immediately.

'We'll get a chopper in with some supplies as soon as possible. Don't worry,' said the calm voice.

After a meagre lunch the deerhunters began to slash a clearing in the bamboo so that the helicopter could drop some rations. The jungle was so thick that the problem was where to put the cut stalks. Suddenly Alejandro's machete slipped and he staggered, blood gushing from a deep gash just below his knee. Lara and Tony Bush cleaned and bound the wound, but it was obvious that he wouldn't be able to walk. It seemed that the deerhunters were fast becoming prisoners of this green and yellow place.

The rain continued to fall and hunger pangs gnawed at empty stomachs. On instructions from base the Venturers put out orange markers and piled up the driest stalks to light when they heard the chopper. At 0930 hours, on the eleventh day of their ordeal, the bad news came that the only available helicopter did not have a winch or radio compatible with theirs, and that the pilot considered landing in the bamboo too hazardous. The group would have to carry Alejandro out. Disbelief registered on all faces. They could hardly carry themselves out, let alone a casualty. Again the radio crackled to life. The pilot had decided to risk it. The chopper was on the way.

By noon the rain had increased to a deluge and there was still no sign of the helicopter. They huddled in their tents, cold and miserable, close to their radio lifeline. Signaller John Young's eager voice came over the radio from base. 'The chopper's going to lift Alejandro out first. Since there's no winch, you'll have to hook him to a dangling rope. Can you make a harness? It must have chest support and not restrict his breathing.'

Alejandro looked less than delighted at the prospect, but all set to work to fashion a harness from karabiners and slings. Next, they cut strips off Alejandro's wellies - he wouldn't need them in the air - and ignited the rubber with meths. Mercifully the rain stopped and the thin wisp of smoke struggled up through the trees. Not much for the pilot to see. Suddenly, the chopper was flying high and fast right over them. It flew on.

'Oh God, he's missed us,' thought Sally as the noise grew fainter. New directions were given by radio and soon Captain Henriquez, leaning out of the window, saw eleven pale, strained faces looking up at him. A loud crash behind the group made them rush towards the sound. As if by a miracle, staffer Rod Noriega appeared, parting the bamboo. Rod, a Chilean mountaineer who'd been on many Raleigh expeditions, had jumped from the hovering helicopter. Next several boxes of Australian Army rations hit the clearing. At least food would no longer be a problem.

It was day twelve. Still the rain continued, and, apart from feeling a little stronger after a good meal, they were no better off. All day Rod and Paul tried to find a way out of the tangled vegetation. Strong people crawling most of the way without rucksacks might make it, they reported. A helicopter lift was the only solution, but flying in this weather was unthinkable.

Back at HQ, Tony Walton fully realized the acute danger. Helicopters are scarce in Southern Chile and the local Intendente had already given him the use of the only two available in the entire region. If the weather cleared he could get the patrol out, but until then his only resort would be to bring help in. Following Rod Noriega's helicopter jump, Colonel Terry Egan and medic Jim Goodwill, both of the US Airforce, dropped safely to the clearing, bringing with them chain saws and more food. Now the task was to clear a fifteen-metre landing zone for the chopper.

Fate had yet another shock in store. This time it was Andy who, his face streaked with blood and rain, came lurching out of the bamboo. Fixing a rope to a tree his ice axe had rebounded and struck him a cruel blow just beneath his eye. Jim pressed a pad on the wound to stanch the blood. The helicopter was due at any moment and the cut would have to be stitched later. To Alejandro's relief, John Dutton and Tony Bush were delegated to go first. Everyone watched anxiously as the two men were hauled skyward out of the bamboo. Rain and darkness forced the helicopter home, and the deerhunters settled down to another night's captivity.

On the fifteenth day they built a platform in the bamboo sufficiently high to allow them to jump from the structure on to the skids of the hovering chopper. They didn't have time to wonder if this would work. Almost without warning, the great bird was there, its downdraught blasting leaves and twigs against their faces. A rope snaked downward. Seizing it, Sally clipped James Ward on to the line, but as she did so her legs went through the fragile platform. 'Get down,' yelled someone, 'he's coming in!'

The noise was deafening as the Aerospatiale hovered above the disintegrating pile of bamboo, its blades whirling only just clear of the fronds. Working with new-found energy, the deerhunters hurled packs aboard the helicopter and hoisted James, Andy and Lara on to its skids. The machine rose rapidly, transporting its living cargo to safety. Soon the second chopper descended. With their last ounce of strength, the survivors leapt for its bucking skids and fought against the downdraught as they struggled into the cabin.

Sally wrote later: 'I am kneeling on the chopper floor, holding on for dear life: the side door is wide open. The pilot signals that I should grasp the back of his seat. At last we are getting out. My soul lifts as I look down to the land we had tried to cross on foot. Thick, dense bamboo, dark Tolkien-like forest, and the eerie mist. We are escaping nature's grip in a man-made machine. Her force was too strong, her clutch too tight, our attempts to fight her futile. This place was the edge of hell, the forces were evil, the scenery hostile; alone we would never have got out.'

The deerhunters' ordeal made up just one event in Raleigh's 1987 expedition to Chilean Patagonia and, as the year ended, the team changed over and a fresh group of Venturers arrived to test their skills at the ends of the earth. With Gunner Major and explorer Henry Sawrey-Cookson at their head, eighty-eight Venturers and thirty-four staff assembled at Puerto Montt in early January. Henry's grandfather had spent a fortune trying to find the legendary Colonel Fawcett in the Matto Grosso. I hoped he wouldn't have to start searching for any more lost patrols. Henry's deputy was US Army Major Roger Astin, and his staff (as with most Raleigh expeditions) consisted of volunteers from the armed forces of America and Britain plus civilians from many lands who had some expedition experience and youthful spirit.

The new projects would follow our aim of continuing conservation work, scientific research and community aid in an adventurous setting. One group were to explore on horseback, others by boat, some on foot while others would remain relatively static on a giant glacier.

Operation Raleigh's Scientific Director, Dr Robert Muir Wood, describes himself as specializing in hazard. As his subject is earthquakes, the description is pretty accurate. On the barren coastline lies Laguna San Rafael, a tidal lagoon into which tumble vast blocks of ice from the tidewater glacier nearest to the equator. It is sustained by high rainfall and, as Robert reported, 'by the pronounced topographic relief on the tectonically active Western Andean margin'. This area was to be the focus for three research projects investigating and dating subsidence layering associated with past earthquakes; analysing the sedimentation of braided streams emerging from the nearby icefields and studying the tidal and meltwater dynamics of the lagoon.

Laguna San Rafael, 10 February 1987

To reach the site Venturers rowed and sailed 400 kilometres from Melinka in four small fishing boats. Tania Wallis of Exeter was with one group of twenty-five who made the voyage in three weeks, each boat guided by a local fisherman. Progress was often hindered by contrary winds and currents, as they steered through narrow channels and past dangerous whirlpools. In her log Tania wrote: 'The little fishing boats became our homes and the rhythmic rattle of oars in the rowlocks familiar to our ears. We adapted quickly to our new lifestyle of spending the days out on open water and making a camp on an island each evening. We built bivouac shelters with a tarpaulin, cooked on wood fires and drank from streams.

'The islands were similar but each had a character of its own and holds different memories for us. We became familiar with the sights and sounds made by the birds and by the dolphins which swam alongside the boats. We heard the roar of sea lions and the cries of seagulls overhead. An unrepeated glimpse of a distant killer whale did wonders for our rowing speed. One morning we discovered an island covered with penguins and found we could almost walk up to them; they were not used to humans. I was horrified to learn that the locals will kill a whole island full of penguins simply to use as bait for catching crabs.

'To reduce weight we only carried half rations and supplemented the menu with seafood. Our guides taught us their simple fishing technique. They would cast the net in a large semicircle, then row to the middle and beat the water with oars to frighten the fish into the net. We also collected mussels, clams and picorico (a shellfish) which were in abundance along the shores.

'We learned to make bread, baking it in the hot sand by the campfire, and how to make a traditional *curantos* by covering a roaring fire with rocks to heat them up and then removing the wood. On to the rocks we piled potatoes, clams, bread cakes and fish with leaves in between each layer, and completely covered the top with seaweed.

'Travelling further south we felt the icy winds blowing from the glacier and the water became gradually colder. Nearer the lagoon, the sea was noticeably paler, containing the meltwater from the glacier.

'During the last three days we made excellent progress as we began rowing at 5 a.m., under the moon and starlit sky, to catch the early tides and often did not stop to set up camp until after 6 p.m.'

As the little fleet entered the Laguna San Rafael, 23-year-old Mark Hannaford of Tottenham paused at the oars to take in the most fantastic scenery he'd ever seen: 'The rising sun cast a bright orange glow over the lowering mountain range, illuminating the snow and highlighting strands of mist following the currents of the colder meltwater, and spreading over the mirrored surface like finely spun lace. The volcanic atolls standing shrouded by the mist are highlighted against the vermilion background. Entering the lagoon my mind was astounded by the beauty and the unbelievable intricacy of some of the icebergs littering the water, cast about untidily like so many children's playing blocks, all shades of white and blue. In the background was the continual crack and boom of the glacier, itself winding in and out of the hills like a living organism. Insignificant from the distance, up close its spires, arches and blocks crash like distant artillery sending great waves of water out from its base as huge blocks tumble in.'

Our studies showed that the Laguna San Rafael glacier moves up to seventeen metres a day – certainly one of the fastest in the world. Further south was a much larger, unstudied glacier called San Quintin which the Venturers also explored and were probably the first to do so.

In view of plans to develop the area economically the scientists' research has gained renewed relevance. There is interest in restarting an earlier attempt to link the lagoon with the Rio Negro to the south by means of a canal. But as Robert Muir Wood points out, differences in sea levels, future subsidence and the hazard to shipping of icebergs weighing more than 100,000 tonnes, suggest that major construction in this rapidly evolving environment should not be taken lightly.

Inland, Dave Tapply from the Civil Engineering Department of Southampton University was co-ordinating community projects which included repairing schools for remote settlements and installing water supply systems. After five expeditions in this region there are numerous bridges and buildings bearing the Operation Raleigh logo.

Many of our groups used horses to penetrate the wilderness to enjoy the tranquil turquoise lakes and multi-coloured mountains. Relatively few Venturers had ridden before, but aided by the *huasos*, or Chilean cowboys, the youngsters soon learned to stay aboard. When I reached one group they had many funny stories to tell and plenty of bruises to show. Nevertheless they put on a gymkhana and

Sally, my assistant, needed no second bidding to leap into the saddle, but almost instantly was thrown. I decided to take photographs instead!

Whether it was riding the rapids of the Rio Baker in Avon inflatables, or a bucking bronco through the bamboo, working with local people, or nosing a fragile boat through the ice of San Rafael, the Venturers worked hard and will remember the challenges all their lives. Chile gets some pretty bad publicity, often exaggerated. To us the government and people showed nothing but friendliness and enthusiastic co-operation.

The same would prove true in Panama, where Tony Walton was finalizing the details of our next expedition. Embroiled in a conflict with the United States, Panama and her large northern neighbour thrashed out complex questions of sanctions and frozen assets. It was a backdrop that tested our organization of the expedition to the full, but did nothing to curb our adventure on this bridge between two seas

CHAPTER FOUR

Panama

Landbridge to Adventure

(*Expedition Leader*: Major Tony Walton, TD RA)

Cusapin, Bocas del Toro, 8 April 1988

'He's going to die . . . He's going to die . . .' intoned the solemn cluster of Guaymi Indians pointing to Ron Lilley. Stumbling backward in their haste, the people kept their eyes fixed on the tall herpetologist who held a viper firmly behind its spear-shaped head. The angry serpent wrapped its heavy body around Ron's arm, its hourglass markings clearly visible. Ron looked down at his free hand. It was not the snake that worried him: it was the thin trickle of blood that ran down the inside of his palm. He had been bitten by a fer-de-lance, and its bite, as both Ron and the Indians knew, was usually fatal.

Herpetologists tend to be prudent. They wouldn't last long if they weren't. Ron Lilley had been on several expeditions and had done outstanding work with Raleigh in Indonesia. During the fifteen years that he had handled poisonous snakes he had never before been bitten. Now, in the isolated northeast corner of Panama, he had made a mistake which might cost him his life.

An hour earlier, two of the local villagers had come running into the Raleigh camp; there was a dangerous snake near the vegetable plots. From their description, Ron knew that it was what the Indians call the '*culebra bunkong*' – the 'really really' snake, since you really, really don't have a chance if it stabs you with its fangs. When Ron followed them to the river bank, the villagers had jumped and shouted, hacking at the undergrowth with their machetes to frighten the reptile from its lair. Suddenly, it obliged – all two metres of it. Angry and alert, its vertical, diamond-shaped pupils stared at them with the coldness of an alien creature. Ron improvised a snake stick and pinned down the serpent's head. Then he reached into the undergrowth to grasp its head. The thick foliage prevented a good hold, and when he straightened up, there was blood on his hand.

His expression didn't change. Carefully, he forced the creature's deadly fangs into the ground. Venom streamed on to the earth. He placed the animal in a bag, and, holding the writhing sack in one hand and keeping his other hand close to his chest to slow the flow of blood to his heart, he walked back along the forest trail and up the steep trail to base camp. It was the longest walk in his life.

In an instant, Communications Officer Chris Eley was on the radio. While he located a network in Florida, New Zealander Mike Tournier, the assistant QM, and Roger Tillbrook, in charge of community projects, notified Fort Sherman and other US Army bases in Panama. An alert was sent out for a possible helicopter evacuation and anti-venom serum was found. As the minutes ticked by and radio messages flew across the Americas, Ron calmly drank a cup of tea. Everyone was tense, waiting for the dreadful symptoms of poisoning. The venom of some vipers, like cobras, mambas and coral snakes, is neurotoxic, affecting the heart and leading to coma and cardiac arrest. That of the fer-de-lance is haematoxic. If it had entered Ron's system it would break down capillary walls, causing bleeding from every orifice. He would bleed to death - from the inside out.

Fortunately, this grisly scenario never transpired, and, as the expedition progressed, the herpetology teams captured several more vipers - and many other reptiles - during their nightly patrols of the jungle. The scientist had been fortunate. He had stubbed his thumb against the bottom teeth: only the fangs of the upper jaw are venomous.

Isla de Popa, 20 April 1988

Isla de Popa, Sapatilla and Caya de Agua were the islands where Ron Lilley carried out many of his herpetological hunts and Indonesian marine biologist Gayatri Reksodihardjo surveyed the coral reefs. The three tiny Atlantic islands, washed by the Chiriqui Lagoon on the south and the aptly named Gulf of Mosquitoes on the north (actually named after the warlike Miskito tribe of Nicaragua rather than the equally vicious insects), are surrounded by reef and topped with umbrellas of towering trees. Here crocodiles, cayman and sharks lurk in the rich forests of soft and stony coral - gorgonians, sea fans, staghorns and the white-tipped fingers of rusty fire coral. Huge crabs, blue tangs, parrot fish and schools of sergeant majors slalom in between.

Gayatri, a lady as graceful as the corals she charted, had also been with us in Indonesia. She seemed to have the genes of a mermaid for she was never out of the water, and her enthusiasm was infectious. For their part the Venturers were drenched by the almost constant rain and their legs were riddled with white-rimmed bites gone septic, but even so Tony Walton and his deputy, Nick Horne, often had difficulty prising them from the science projects.

Seamus Bennett was one of the youngsters who was hard to budge from the island outposts. A tall triathlon runner and gym instructor sponsored by his local Rotary Club, he had been chosen as leader by the others and had soon learned the scientific language of corals. Another was Michelle Mayers, an unemployed Liverpudlian with an unexpected bent for herpetology, and Singaporean Esther Koh who turned her interest in marine crabs into a full-scale study. Living in such a remote spot did seem to encourage some pretty strange behaviour, however. Blonde zoologist Vanessa Pike once put a collar around a cayman big enough to snap off her foot and walked him down the beach like a poodle on Park Lane; 'Jungle Jim' Dewsbury took to climbing nine-metre trees to rescue baby sloths; and Catherine Lucas was transformed into a jungle nymph, plunging into the bush after helmeted iguanas and other reptiles. Matching their antics with a few of his own, Mike Buckingham, who still suffered from a motorcycle injury, helped to sustain both the community spirit and campfire when both were dampened by the almost constant rain.

Isla de Popa and, indeed, the whole of this northeast coast is astonishingly beautiful, drenched in the colours that only tropical downpours and intense humidity can produce. The colours of the wildlife are also iridescent, almost psychedelic: tiny poison arrow frogs, the size and hue of a ripe strawberry; emerald-green basilisks, or Jesus lizards, which can run long distances across water; brightly banded coral snakes and yellow palm vipers; decorative fish and flocks of parrots. It was enough to make a jaded captain – of industry or ocean – dream of shipwreck in these waters.

Shipwrecks were certainly on the minds of skilled boat handlers Grant McPherson and Jon Goring – their task was to prevent them. The waters between the islands and the mainland sites are dangerous and unpredictable, as quiet as a mill pond one moment and as wild as gale force wind the next. Without warning, storms can spin across the Atlantic and hit the coast of Panama, twisting boats 180 degrees and playing hide and seek with them in swells 6 metres high.

Grant and Jon soon memorized the route through the maze of coral reefs that led to the other far-flung project sites. At Cusapin base camp, Venturer John Cox from Liverpool led a construction team building a new house for Fernando Kays William, a brave and cheerful man who had been struck by muscular dystrophy at age twenty-five. Here too, Venturers met the remarkable Mary Migar. That energetic lady, originally from Monmouthshire, has worked for the welfare of people in Latin America for over twenty years. Her unstinting support, and that of her husband, Guillermo, the village leader, had been a vital factor to our being at Bocas del Toro. With Raleigh doctors Jackie Barson and Alan Anderson and a score of Venturers, Mary Migar, who had started the rural clinic at Cusapin,

Opposite: Glaciological research amongst the ice floes on Laguna San Rafael, Southern Chile.

visited the remote villages of Bocas del Toro, treating the Indians who had not had access to a doctor sometimes for months or even years. Sixty years old, Mary kept up a tremendous pace and slept on the beaches with people a third her age. 'It was fun to go back after all these years,' she told us. 'People still live pretty much the same as they did before, although their health is a bit better and the drinking water is somewhat cleaner.'

Superstitions and dreams - which the Indians believe to be certain oracles of the future - still strongly influence everyday life today, and bush medicine continues to be seen to be far more powerful than any Western remedy. No bad thing, according to Mary, since they did the job extremely well long before Westerners arrived.

The British Ambassador, another remarkable lady, gave the expedition great assistance and even joined me on a stormy voyage to some of the sites. Her Excellency, Mrs Margaret Bryan, had served in Havana and Kinshasa before being appointed to Panama in 1986. Her niece, Rachel Garnier, became an ex-officio Venturer. At Chiriqui and Drago beach they patrolled the moonlit sands where leatherbacks laid their eggs, and near the lily-choked channels of the Cricamola delta kept a round-the-clock vigil of tidal changes and sediment dynamics.

To the layman, this Cricamola 'mud project' might sound about as exciting as an exhibition of old socks in a country museum, but headed by the young Cambridge scientist Jonathan French, it provided a fascinating insight into wider environmental problems such as erosion caused by deforestation and the silting up - and subsequent death - of corals. Like all of the scientific studies undertaken by the expedition, it was co-ordinated by Dr Christine Partridge, a specialist in cancer research who had been a project leader for Operation Raleigh in Chile in 1987. Now she often acted as co-pilot for Grant or Jon as they delivered equipment or food and ferried Venturers from one project site to another.

The flotilla they captained was varied to put it mildly - a colourful assortment of rubber inflatables, a fibreglass launch and two dugout canoes of local design known as *Big Log* and *Little Log* - names which accurately described their somewhat basic construction. Although they leaked through the bows and were broached by the most casual of waves, the 'logs' were stable going into a big sea. They had been an afterthought, for the *agua carga* steaming up from Chile with our container-load of boats, engines and scientific equipment, had changed course without warning, transiting the Canal from the Atlantic to the Pacific and continuing on to the United States. Powerless to stop the vessel, Tony Walton and his assistant, Lisa Cuthill, had watched, stricken, as the ship started up the steps of the Gatun Locks. It would take her only nine hours to make that crossing, but it would later take Tony Walton and his team hundreds of hours to replace (and sometimes reinvent) the lost equipment. The 'logs' were but one example of the expedition leader's happy ability to think on his feet.

Tony's business career and his long experience with Raleigh had left him able to find a port in almost any storm. He had been my adjutant in Panama in 1985, sailed across the Pacific with our flagship, *Sir Walter Raleigh*, and had led expeditions in New Zealand, Japan and Chile. After Panama, he would go on to lead others in the Bahamas and again in Chile, taking on responsibility for a handful of reconnaissance trips in between.

The international politics of Central America proved a different sort of storm; one which might swamp his expedition as surely as any rogue wave. The ongoing tensions between Presidents Noriega and Reagan had led to America issuing a travel notice warning US Venturers not to take part in the Raleigh expedition; the loss of essential scientific equipment forced the cancellation of some of the science programmes; and a strike by customs officials and dockers only thirty-six hours before the main party was due to arrive threatened to leave the expedition not only without boats, equipment and a United States contingent, but even without rations.

'A close-run thing, as Wellington would say,' observed Tony. Some thought the thing was lucky to run at all. Like the boat handlers, however, somehow his team found the passage between the reefs.

Chirqui Beach, Drago Beach, 25 May 1988

Jon Goring steered his twin-engined inflatable boat, *David Gestetner*, into the walls of grey water, his right foot alternately pumping the sea out of the craft and air into her pontoons. Ahead, the breakers crashed on to the beach near Rio Canaveral. He pointed her bow towards shore, knowing that the four-metre swells might swamp her at any minute.

Avoiding a direct challenge to the temperamental sea, Jon throttled back and skirted the shore, trying for another entry: it was no use. He shifted into neutral and let the boat buck the waves. Sometimes it was impossible to take a small craft through the surf, and today was one of those days. At his signal, nineteen-year-old Karen Phillips, a cross-country runner from Devon, threw her rucksack into the sea and dived in after it. Expedition artist Dave Chisholm, and Alfredo Kays Migar, a Panamanian Venturer, followed in her wake. Kicking hard against the current, they swam towards shore with one hand on their kits, which had been made buoyant by natural airpockets and the plastic bags knotted around them. The sea played rough, forcing them down, making them fight their way to the surface and a lungful of air. Jon watched until the swimmers reached the shore, then he swung the bow to starboard and headed back to Cusapin.

Christopher Columbus would never have believed that air-filled inflatables could survive the waters of Central America, although the Indians had long known how to make rubber balls, shoes and clothing from the milky secretions of various plants. Then, too, the great admiral would have doubted that the vast numbers of marine turtles which fed his crews could ever be depleted. Today, only the leatherbacks survive in this region in any numbers. The green sea turtle, its flesh coloured by the grass it feeds on, is a favourite dish in South and Central America, and the hawksbill has an unfortunate combination of assets that almost assures its destruction: the male reproductive organs are thought to have aphrodisiacal properties; the glossy shells are used for combs, jewellery and spurs for fighting cocks; and its flesh is both tender and succulent. In the last ten years an estimated 100,000 hawksbills have been butchered and prices for their amber shells have soared to over $100 per kilogram (an average shell weighs between 1.5 and 2.5 kilograms). If such destruction continues, marine turtles will vanish from the seas they have inhabited for 200 million years.

Poaching, however, is not the only threat to these huge reptiles. Many drown in fishing nets for prawn and squid, others die from the effects of pollution or as a result of coastal developments which have supplanted their nesting sites with striped parasols and yachting marinas. Oil spills and deballasting by tankers are other death traps, as are the sharp propellers of boats and the floating plastic rubbish which can resemble tasty jellyfish. As hotels mushroom on the shores, turtles instinctively head for the shafts of bright light, mistaking them for the moonbeams which would guide them back to sea. Knowing that the turtles will follow lights, poachers lead them into the jungle with a torch, wait for them to lay their eggs, then slit the neck and bleed the carcase, chop off the base plate and cut up the meat. If the female manages to elude them, the poachers search for her eggs by thrusting machetes in the sand. When the blades come up covered with egg yolk, they start digging.

The turtles have natural predators too. Ghost crabs feast on the freshly laid eggs, and high tides, heavy seas and rain can wash the leathery balls from their nests. After the two-month incubation period there is still more danger ahead. The tiny hatchlings must run the gauntlet of armies of seabirds lining the beaches, while the open jaws of grouper, jack and barracuda await the survivors.

As the greens and hawksbills get harder to find, the hunters - some of them commercial poachers from neighbouring Costa Rica - have begun to raid the beaches of Bocas del Toro, one of the most important nesting areas for leatherbacks. The young people who had swum ashore that stormy morning were part of a Raleigh task force whose aim was to protect these ocean wanderers. Building on the work of zoologist Anne Meylan of the University of Florida, they patrolled the lagoon-backed beaches by night, discouraging poachers and monitoring the density of nesting in the area. In the process, they made friends with local villagers and shared with them their ideas of conservation.

No matter how often Ian Puttock saw one of the huge creatures crawl from the sea to the shore, the sight never failed to send a shiver of pleasure down his spine. The young employee of Barclays Bank in Southampton had spent weeks at Chiriqui with project leader and nurse Gail Taylor, a cheerful and competent woman who would join us again in the jungles of Cameroon. Ian had taken on the role of quartermaster on this isolated stretch of beach. Each night, in spite of a weak right leg resulting from a mild spastic condition, Ian took his turn walking a six-kilometre stretch between Rio Chiriqui and Rio Canaveral and back between midnight and dawn.

One night, Scott Kirkland woke him. From his hammock slung from the branches of a tree, Ian could see the quarter-moon and the palms silhouetted against the silver sky. Flashes of lightning crackled on the horizon, as if a photographer had balanced his camera on the lip of the world and pushed the shutter. Lowering his good leg on to the ground, Ian eased himself out of his aerial berth and sleepily rubbed the red, itching welts already raised by the sandflies. He slapped some insect repellent on his ankles and neck, pulled on an extra pair of socks and headed for the beach. Scott and Alfredo were already there, their figures outlined against the lacy surf. The sky was black, but fireflies winked in the darkness and the constant thunder of the surf made conversation impossible.

Every three days the entire twenty-two-kilometre beach between Rio Canaveral and Rio Chiquiri was charted for tracks, nests and false nests, and measurements were taken of any leatherbacks they found, since the turtles go into a trance as they lay their eggs. The Venturers walked, kicking up phosphorescent showers as wave after wave arched and broke against the land. Ahead of them a slow, dark shadow slid across the beach. In the sea, the two-metre-long leatherback could shoot through her element, but shackled to the land, her movements were heavy and cumbersome. Paying no attention to the human intruders she climbed the sandbank and began leisurely to dig her nest. Her efforts were in rhythm with the waves. It would take her about an hour to excavate the sandy pit and at least another to lay almost one hundred eggs, cover the nest and return to the sea. In one of nature's remarkable feats of organization, if the sand was above a certain temperature all the hatchlings would be male, if below, they would all be female.

At Drago beach, a remote stretch of sand which disappears over the border to Costa Rica, other Venturers were also engaged in protecting the huge turtles during this crucial time. At the approach of Grant's resupply boat, a pride of pelicans, strung out one behind the other, struggled into the air, their clumsy movements mocked by the effortless flight of the egrets. Here, the high tides and huge swells made body surfing a favourite sport among the Venturers. For Calum Morrison, recollections of swimming with the turtles and surfing under a moon, his body alight with phosphorescence, still vie with less pleasant memories of vicious biting ants and sand so hot it raised blisters on his feet.

'I just about fell over my first turtle last night,' wrote the tall Venturer. 'We found her just as she was making her nest and watched her deftly dig around a stump, making a hole flipper-deep. We sat behind her so as not to disturb her, and I experienced a feeling of awe, trepidation, fear and excitement - all simultaneously. Words are not enough to express what I felt as I watched her lay. Tears streamed in large globules from her big, sad eyes. Her lungs pulsed with huge breaths. Every breath hard-fought; they rocked and shook her whole body. Taffy - Tim Allsopp - and I left her to cover up her eggs and went off in search of more turtles. We found a false nest and a poachers' trail and returned in time to find her heading for the open water and safety. We waded in with her up to our thighs and she swam off, devoid of clumsiness. I could only wonder why people would want to kill such beautiful creatures.'

From the Atlantic to the Pacific, 16 April–12 May 1988

Tim Allsopp and Calum Morrison were also two of the first Venturers to walk from the Atlantic Ocean to the Pacific. The horizontal S-shaped country of Panama bridges the continents of North and South America. During the three-month expedition, Venturers would cross that bridge every which way. Early on, project leader David Taylor-Smith had found a silver ring fashioned into the shape of a horseshoe. It was to become the good luck charm of the patrol that was known simply as 'Number 2'.

Nick Horne's idea of a good time is to 'trek through somewhere on the way to nowhere', climbing as many mountains as possible in between. It was Nick, with his experience and his logistical skill, who worked out the different routes. More at home in the bush than just about anyone, it seemed to the Venturers that he took a fiendish delight in taxing them to their limits. From his 'office' high on a hill in Cusapin, he unfolded the only map available - thirty years old and drawn on a scale of 1:50,000. Taking a red pencil and a ruler he drew a line from the mouth of the Rio Changuinola down the 80th parallel. If they made it to Boquete, he reasoned, they might just manage to reach the Pacific, climbing the steep-flanked Volcán Baru on the way to the town of David and the coast.

The expedition members soon discovered that a few things had changed since the map was drawn. The delta, for example, had altered entirely and they spent the first day of the trek knee-deep in swamp. Punta Blanco, which they took to be a settlement, turned out to be just as the name describes – a large, white rock. From there on they took their bearings on more reliable features than villages and river beds. They also made a crucial decision: if they had not reached their half-way point, Boquete, by the time they had used up half their rations, they would turn back.

They suffered a bit and learned a great deal. One 'Panamanian hour', for example, was worth two or three ordinary sixty-minute time spans; rations designed for twelve days could be stretched – albeit leanly – to sixteen; and one's feet and groin, if not treated with daily doses of anti-fungal powder, could slow one down something awful. In that extreme heat, they shared the weight of the heavy radio and safety ropes and discovered that whilst climbing a steep hill, a five-minute rest every half hour made an equally steep cut in water consumption. Boquete was a welcome sight after two weeks of walking. It also marked the end of the toughest part of the traverse. Dehydrated and on half rations, the trekkers slept for a few hours, then shouldered their packs and headed for Volcán Baru. It was 3.15 a.m. They reached the summit at sunrise. Dawn on the mountain ridge arrived quickly and in technicolor. It was the highest point in Panama. At almost zero degrees fahrenheit, it was certainly the coldest.

'To the south we looked over the town of David and to the Pacific beyond,' recalled David Chisholm, the staff artist whose skilful cartoons captured the hardships while making light of them. 'Further east a storm flashed a warning just as the sun came up, accentuating all the ridges of the volcanic slopes with their contrasting light and shadow.'

They had traversed jungles and mangrove swamps, camped on beaches and banana plantations, crossed high-wire bridges and swum rivers with ropes made fast to the far shore. They had shared their tents with friendly armadillos, climbed trees for coconuts and caught fish and crabs to supplement their meagre rations. Blisters, septic bites and foot rot were the badges of their Isthmus crossing. They had been hungry most of the time, but they had reached the Pacific. With them they had carried a small bottle of water from the Caribbean. When they reached the southern sea that the Spaniard Vasco Nuñez de Balboa first saw on 25 September 1513, they emptied it into the Pacific, symbolically mixing the waters of the two great oceans.

* * *

Balboa's discovery resulted in gold for his king and slavery for the Indians. Treasure was transported across the Isthmus to waiting galleons. Farther out to sea, other ships rocked in the swells, biding their time to snatch the prize. One of the most successful pirates was a Devon sea captain, Francis Drake, who hid his ship in a secret harbour camouflaged by thick mangroves. At dusk he would slip from the inlet he named Port Pheasant, and thread his way through the reef in pursuit of unsuspecting victims. His forays helped to share out the king's ill-gotten gold.

Over three hundred years later, during World War II, the German Navy found a Panama inlet equally useful. From here a deadly U-boat had stolen out to sink the Allied ships entering and leaving the Canal. According to the local Indians, a group of US Naval personnel had spent long months in the jungles of Cusapin watching for the submarine in the lagoons of Bocas del Toro. Like Drake, they patiently awaited their quarry. One evening, as the dying sun lit the peaks of the Great Divide, their long vigil was rewarded. In the gathering dusk they spied the sinister raider edging through the shallows. According to U-boat expert Harry Cooper of the US Shark Hunters Society, it seems likely that she was U 153, a Type 9C long-range submarine. Launched in Germany on 5 April 1941, the seventy-six-metre Seawolf had already made an impressive string of kills when she was sunk west of Colón by USS *Lansdowne* on 13 July 1942. She was also attacked by US Army Squadron No. 59. It must have been quite a fight.

The Indians' story proved too much of a temptation. Nick Horne and a team of Venturers set out to find the secret base that had wreaked so much destruction. A few kilometres west of Cusapin the shore ended abruptly as the cliffs plunged into the sea. Giants of the rainforest cast their branches over the water, forming a natural canopy that would hide almost any craft. Those ancient trees had seen it all, but old bottles and rusty fuel drums were the only evidence of the historic hideaway.

Somewhere in the Jungle, 7 June 1988

With her punk fringe and long blonde hair, nurse Penny Pepper could easily pass for a Venturer. The 27-year-old Leicestershire lass had two other tough expeditions to her credit – Cape York and the Torres Strait of Northern Australia. Never one to blanch at the sight of blood, Penny had, without batting an eye, stitched up machete cuts and treated the pus-filled sores, weeping infections and grotesquely swollen feet of various Venturers. Being both useful and attractive, one of the local men had offered to buy her for a pig, a cow and some coconuts. It was an offer her colleagues had seriously considered.

As one would expect, Penny was fully conversant with malaria and leishmaniasis – a disease caused by blood parasites carried by the little black sandflies which are found all over Central and South America. She could put people right off their supper with her lurid description of the Triatomid – the kissing bug. 'They're about five centimetres long,' she explained brightly, 'with pointy noses. They bite you around the mouth when you're asleep and defecate into the hole which lets the parasites into your bloodstream. Some call it Chagas' disease. It leads to heart failure and there's no cure.'

What nurse Penny Pepper wasn't prepared for was the sight of her own leg swelling to outlandish proportions during the trek across Panama. Halfway up a mountain, in a jungle flooded by rain, her right leg expanded hugely, then subsided to a rather misshapen lump. This was the work of no ordinary mosquito, she knew – a prognosis confirmed by the doctor in Santiago. He hadn't bothered with an anaesthetic, but had simply sliced her leg open with a scalpel. What happened next made even this tough lady feel a little green. As the pressure was suddenly released from her swollen leg, a lump of blood shot across the room, followed by a huge, yellow larva and a good amount of pus. 'It was something straight out of *Alien*,' howled Penny. 'You could see the creature's eyes.'

They found another in her jaw. The jungles of Panama are not for the faint-hearted.

CHAPTER FIVE

Pakistan

Along the River Indus

(*Expedition Director*: Wing Commander Jawaid Iqbal, Pakistan Air Force)

(*Field Leader*: Clive Barrow)

Domel, Northwest Frontier Province, 21 April 1988

The sweat fell like drops of warm blood on Mary Harding's neck. It was only 8.30 in the morning, but already the heat was fierce. The steep track zig-zagged up the mountain, past the tiny clusters of houses made of mud and wood that sheltered families of seven or more. After only one week in this hot, northern corner of Pakistan, Mary was shedding burnt skin by the handful and her mouse-coloured hair had turned to gold. As the sun broached the serrated mountains, the heat struck her like a physical blow. The trousers and long-sleeved shirt she wore in deference to Muslim custom seemed to draw the rays like a magnet. Slowed by dehydration and altitude, she and her companions stopped to catch their breath, gaze at the camp below and have a sip of tepid water tinged with the metallic flavour of purification tablets. To the west were the mountains of Kohistan, raised by the geological collision of the Asian and Indo-Pakistan plates. To the east were corrugated hills of granite and marble, carved into terraces of wheat, maize and onions.

These mountains were the home of a few farmers and cowherds, plus soaring eagles, leopards, black bear and bandits. That April the leopards and bandits seemed to have gained the upper hand in a valley just east of Kashmir. The big cats had slaughtered two horses in the past month and the bandits – specifically, 'Babu' – had retreated to his mountain fastness with a new pair of villagers to hold for ransom.

Babu's talents in the kidnapping business and our wild surroundings – much of it under tribal law – had led Brigadier Jan Nadir Khan, the head of the Adventure Foundation (Pakistan) and the chief co-ordinator of our expeditions in the country, to recruit a few gun-toting guards. Their job was to protect the remote science camp perched high in the Black Mountains of the Northwest Frontier Province.

When I arrived in Pakistan, I heard that Babu, a rather popular renegade, was asking for 30,000 rupees to release his most recent victims. Such a sum would be difficult to raise in this land where barter is the most useful currency and no one has much ready cash.

'If the ransom is paid how can you know that he will keep his word and release his hostages alive?' I asked.

'Babu is a Pathan,' came the very logical reply. 'The Pathans are men of honour.'

Although the Venturers were within Babu's wide-ranging territory, there was little to fear from the bandits as long as one didn't stray far from the tracks that linked the scattered huts. On that hot, spring morning, fragrant with pine and jasmine, danger seemed as remote as the hills of Kohistan.

As they climbed, Mary and her companions – Ian Lever and Joanne Calvert, David Achilles, Belinda Morris and nurse Julie O'Brian – gave toffees to the children they met, who stared at them with wide, brown eyes. Thin puppies raced out to greet them, at once cowering and wagging their tails.

'*Salaam aleikum*. Peace be with you,' the Venturers greeted the shy women.

'*Wa-aleikum salaam*. And on you peace,' came the reply.

By the time Mary and the others had gained the summit and begun their descent, the remaining sweets had melted in the appalling heat to a sticky mess of silver foil and sugar. Suffering from what would soon become an expedition-wide bout of 'tummy trouble', a polite phrase which in no way describes the undignified and time-consuming affliction, Mary raced on ahead, searching for a bit of cover or, if she could make it, the camp loo.

The track she picked skirted one of the houses, and Mary wondered briefly if she should cross the yard. Her decision was the wrong one. As she ran forward she heard a fierce growl, and a huge mastiff charged her. Mary spun round and leapt up the bank but she was just a fraction too slow. The beast bit deeply into the soft underside of her thigh. Her scream brought the others running.

To Mary, the iodine and the penicillin jab administered by Julie seemed almost worse than the bite. Once back at base camp, radio contact was made with Abbottabad for anti-rabies vaccine and expedition doctor Gulzar Ahmed Jamal came up from the village of Dhodial. The massive injection of immunoglobulin was followed by eight more – two above her shoulder blades, and two each in her arms, thighs and stomach.

The dog, one of the Kohistan breed renowned for both its ferocity and skill in herding sheep and cows, was brought down to camp every day for ten days to satisfy the doctor that he was still alive. 'Dabu' was a large, mangy creature whose ears had been severed at the skull to enhance both his hearing and his frightening demeanour. If he didn't die, the doctor assured Mary, she could be certain that he wasn't rabid. The shaggy hound lived and became quite a favourite. As far as I know he is still keeping vigil at that hut in the hills.

The work at the science camp was focused on botany, ichthyology and geology. As in the previous expedition of 1987, the Pakistan Museum of Natural History in Islamabad had sent us some of their most talented scientists: amongst them, Dr S. R. H. Baqri, director of the earth sciences division, who had been with us in the Karakoram Mountains the previous year. In 1987, the task of his Raleigh team had been to chart the rocks of Hunza, the country of the Ismaili mountain people who are followers of the Aga Khan. This year Dr Baqri and his research associate Hamid Daud would focus on the Siran Valley, known locally as Bhogarmang. Other members of the museum staff included zoology research associate Mohammad Rafique and Drs Malik, Afzal and Nazir. With an energetic team of young people, botanist Dr Nazir, nicknamed 'Missy' by the Venturers, managed to collect 1600 specimens of flowers, leaves, lichens, liverworts and fungi in only two and a half weeks.

'One botanical expedition to the Black Mountains was made in 1818,' explained Dr Nazir. 'At that time there were no tracks in at all; they came from India through the mountains. Dr Steward from Britain published the first list of plants in 1972, but the Hazara region has remained almost entirely unexplored. We may well have found a new species or genus here.'

Those studying the animals of the region were even more convinced that they had found life forms as yet unknown to science. There are over 6000 species of freshwater fish and the expedition probably added two more to the number. Using a variety of nets and traps, the Venturers spent long hours wading in the freezing rivers and were rewarded with a collection of 676 fish from ten known species. But amongst the muscular snow trout (*Schizothorax plagiostomus*) which can swim up a column of water, and the tiger-striped hill stream loach (*Shistura alepidotus*) that lurk beneath river stones, the netsmen found two unusual fish whose peculiarities of barbels and adipose dorsal fins indicated a new species of catfish, the genus *Glyptothorex*. If so, Rafique will bestow the rather grand species name *adventurensis* (as a reference to Operation Raleigh) on one of the whiskered fish, and *domelensis* on the other, after the river in which it was found. The discovery of a new species of lizard completed the hat-trick, and the expedition might well have stumbled upon a new mammal as well – a black and white civet with razor-sharp fangs and a remarkably bad temper.

The aims of the Raleigh fisherfolk included more than pure science. By noting the altitude and water temperature where various species were found, their research will help to determine whether brown and rainbow trout and the common carp can be farmed in the Siran River and its tributaries. Since the trout prefer the icy upstream water with its high oxygen content and the carp enjoy the easier life downstream, the two can co-exist quite happily. One day they may provide a cheap and effective source of protein and iodine for these mountain people whose anaemia and goitres indicate a need for both.

Mary Harding was back in action the minute her doctor ceased giving her daily jabs and gave her – and the dog – a clean bill of health. She still limped for a bit, but resilience is a typical attribute of this curly-haired physiotherapist who enjoys some notoriety as Shropshire's only lady basketball referee.

It was six in the morning when she headed up the hills yet again – this time with Dr Baqri and a team of Venturers. Their job was to map the largely pre-Cambrian rock formations – only about 523 million years old. Some of the molten intrusions are even younger: movement that began some sixty-five million years ago, when the continents began to collide, continues to toss up new mountains in a land that is still being formed.

Twenty-year-old Californian Erick Couch chipped off samples and didn't seem to mind their weight in his rucksack as he climbed higher into the mountains. Nadir Imtiaz Khan, a Pakistani Venturer and a credit to the Pathans, carefully numbered each rock and noted its location, while geologist Ian Lever calculated dip and strike values. When completed, their data map would tell the geological story of the Siran Valley, and, like Raleigh's other science projects, will be of practical as well as scientific value in the future. The pockets of tourmalines, garnets and other semi-precious gems could mean extra income for the local people; areas of schist and granite, rich in potassium and aluminium, will indicate where the soil is fertile enough for agriculture and forestry, and the discovery of fine-grained marble beds could also eventually yield jobs and income.

Dhodial, 5 May 1988

Dawn broke at 4 a.m. At the village of Dhodial, only twenty-six kilometres from the Raleigh science camp in the Black Mountains, the call of the Muezzin drifted across the countryside and suddenly fell silent. From that hour until sunset, no food or drink would pass the lips of the expedition director, Wing Commander Jawaid Iqbal. The expedition had coincided with Ramadan, the holiest month in the Muslim calendar; the holiday's strict discipline extended from one new moon to the next. It would last from 18 April to 17 May.

Before beginning his morning prayers, the Wing Commander glanced at the gathering clouds and frowned. The storm was moving north towards the Himalayas and the foothills of Kohistan. On those forested ridges and snow-filled gullies still called the 'Land of the Savages', a group of Venturers was searching for the Western Tragopan, one of the most elusive and rarest birds in the world. They were led by the able scientist Guy Duke, thin as a knife himself, whose strenuous search would soon whittle his companions down to size. Dr Gulzar, who had treated Mary Harding, was with them, but still Jawaid and field leader Clive Barrow were worried since they had been out of radio contact for days. The stream of oaths uttered by Pat Langan when no report was forthcoming from the mini-expedition still rang in his ears. Pat, a tall, sandy-haired logistics officer, was an experienced member of numerous Raleigh expeditions; organized and punctilious, he hated to lose a sack of lentils, let alone an entire team. Happily they turned up safe and sound.

The thunder rolled across the mountains and lightning silhouetted the trees against the grey dawn. Jawaid could smell the rain long before it struck the parched earth of Dhodial. This, he knew, meant the end of the cool season. From now on, the expedition would be caught in spiralling temperatures which would not abate until the outbreak of the monsoons in July. The intense heat and the fasting required by Ramadan would both take their toll on the building project here in Dhodial. Without water and food, the local stonemasons were unable to work through the heat of the day, putting a heavier burden on the young people who laboured with them. Most of the Muslim Venturers had tried to keep the fast, but soon realized that they would have to make the choice between doing a full complement of work or adhering to the dictates of Ramadan. The wisdom of the seventh-century Prophet Mohammed had provided an acceptable option, however. The Prophet had proclaimed the dignity of labour by turning his own hand to sweeping, mending, digging trenches, milking goats and building; his followers are permitted to break the fast to take it up at a later date if continuing would interfere with their work or endanger their health.

The Venturers' ambitious job at Dhodial was to build an eight-room house in the SOS Children's Village, one of many throughout the world dedicated to raising and educating destitute children. Working in the sizzling 100°F heat, the Venturers and masons soon completed the stone base wall and started on the brick interior.

The heat was only a minor inconvenience compared with some of the other material, linguistic and cultural difficulties. Cement was as rare as gold dust, communication on the site was tricky since the Westerners were slow to pick up Urdu and the Pakistani workers were no better at English, and the idea of females working on the project was initially greeted with derision. In a country where women are rarely seen outside the house – and then usually veiled from prying eyes – the children and even the director of the village, Mohammad Ishaq, watched with some amazement as Gill Hughes slapped cement on the exterior walls, Sara Beesley and Helen Gouldsbrough smoothed the mortar and checked plumb lines, and Marie Nash hoisted bricks alongside her male companions. Modestly covered from head to toe even in the intense heat, the girls' energy and diligence soon won them a grudging acceptance.

The thorough briefing on the customs of Pakistan given by Lt-Col. Tony Chadburn had done much to help the multi-national team adapt to their host country. A retired soldier with the Frontier Force Rifles, whose family have lived in Pakistan and India for four generations, Tony had encouraged the Venturers to adopt the country's customs as their own. 'Girls should not automatically offer to shake hands unless the Pakistani man offers his first,' he cautioned as part of a useful list of 'Do's and Don'ts'. 'Eat with the fingers of the right hand only, the left is used for "other purposes" and the more orthodox do not like to be touched with the left hand. If you are in doubt regarding a situation, wait and watch how your hosts do it and then follow suit.'

In the end, the building project was one of the most successful undertaken by Raleigh. Its progress was monitored by many people, amongst them contractor Mohammed Iqbal Qureshi, a founder member of SOS and a committee member of the Adventure Foundation; the highly respected Brigadier Jan Nadir Khan, secretary of the NWFP committee of SOS and the chief co-ordinator of our expeditions in Pakistan; and the remarkable Begum Mahmooda Salim Khan, Pakistan's first woman cabinet minister, a pioneer of planned parenthood and an effective force in raising the status of women.

The substantial sum saved by the Venturers' voluntary labour – 50,000 rupees in a country where the per capita income is about 6500 (£1 = Rs.32) – was donated to the village by the contractor. He, in turn, had received an infusion of labour during the difficult period of Ramadan. The SOS Village gained a new house for eight more children, and the expedition members had formed unique and lasting friendships with the people of Pakistan. It all added up to what students of international relations call a 'win-win' situation.

The expedition in Pakistan had not started out auspiciously, reflected Clive Barrow, set as it was against a tapestry of peace and violence. First, a mini-revolution in the Amazon had forced us to abandon the expedition to Brazil and hastily set up alternatives in Guyana and Pakistan. Jan Khan, Tony Chadburn and Roger Chapman had burnt quantities of midnight oil to ensure the success of this expedition in Pakistan. Then at 10 a.m., 10 April 1988, the day after the main party arrived, a mysterious and devastating explosion at an ammunition dump near the Islamabad airport killed at least 100 people and wounded over 1000. Had their plane landed twenty-four hours later, members of the Raleigh expedition might well have numbered amongst the casualties. The end of the expedition was marked by yet another tragedy: the aircraft in which the President of Pakistan, General Zia ul-Haq, and the American Ambassador, Arnold Raphel, were travelling was blown out of the sky. The President had taken a very personal interest in the two Raleigh expeditions in Pakistan, and had encouraged the Adventure Foundation's help and involvement.

Against this backdrop, the Geneva peace accords strove to end the eight and a half years of bloody war in neighbouring Afghanistan, the Soviet Army began its withdrawal from Kabul, and some of the 5 million refugees who had sought shelter in Pakistan and Iran began to trickle back to their country. The 3.1 million Afghan refugees who had fled to Pakistan were welcomed as brothers despite the undoubted strain their presence placed on the economy. 'We have gladly accepted them,' explained Venturer Nadir Khan; 'they are Muslims and their battle is our own.' In a world where political refugees are regarded too often as an unwanted problem, which it is hoped will simply vanish, the attitude of the Pakistan people was a powerful lesson for our young people. Only fifteen kilometres west of the children's home, 9695 refugees lived in shadowy limbo. Some members of the expedition accompanied the three British doctors on a visit to the refugee camp near Dhodial. The Venturers sat on mats in tiny rooms overflowing with pillows and children and asked about the hopes and fears of those who had fled; the doctors - Ann Hennell, Leslie Godfrey and Sue Cox - asked about tuberculosis.

In the crowded houses and market places of Third World countries, death is in the air. Whenever a TB carrier coughs or sneezes, tiny droplets of moisture carrying the infection are flung for some distance. Inhaled by others, the disease continues on its deadly round, causing at least three million deaths each year. Childhood immunization programmes and the availability of effective, albeit expensive, antibiotics, have succeeded in virtually eradicating TB in industrialized countries. In tropical and developing countries, however, such as Pakistan, India, Sri Lanka and parts of Africa and Southeast Asia, the bacillus is still taking its toll. The three young British doctors had joined forces with Ayub Medical College doctors Safdar Zaman and Jadun Huma to screen remote settlements and refer those suspected of being infected to the local TB clinic. With them they brought a supply of drugs the cost of which had been sponsored, in part, by the Poor People's Welfare Organization, a Pakistan charity, and in part by Raleigh sponsors such as Astra Pharmaceuticals, Merck Sharp & Dohme, Abbott, Roche, and Merrell Dow Pharmaceutical.

The arrival of the Operation Raleigh doctors was usually broadcast from the nearest minaret. Word of mouth is powerful in a Muslim country and inevitably

Above: Herpetology in Panama.

Below left: Lucy Baker of London working with a mobile health team in Panama.

Below right: Jungle patrol exploring Panama's rainforest.

Above: Venturer Marie Nash of North Carolina crosses a swollen river in Pakistan.

Below: Sarah Beesley of Widnes at the SOS Children's Village at Dhodial, Pakistan where she helped build a house for orphans.

brought hundreds of people from miles around to the clinic. In a few days the doctors would examine, diagnose and prescribe for almost a thousand people, an impossibly high workload in the West.

Completely relaxed in the intense heat and noise of the crowded, hilltop clinic, Dr Ann Hennell, a slim, blonde GP, waved away the clouds of flies and got on with the job. The room was so packed with interested relatives and the simply curious that from time to time a 'bouncer' had to push people out of the door. Privacy was impossible. 'How long have you had this lump? Do you vomit every day? Do you cough blood? Sweat at night?' Ann's questions, and those of the other doctors, were translated by medical students from the college and the answers noted by Venturers on their clipboards. Those records would be of vital importance in the continuing attempt to stem what Dr Safdar Zaman termed the 'iceberg phenomenon of TB'. Although Ann, Sue and Leslie found the incidence of TB lower than they had expected – it is possible that many of those with the disease could not walk over the hills to the health centre – they also found that unless they used their stethoscopes on each patient and doled out some tablets, their patients would be dissatisfied with the consultation. Many had come in order to see 'the English doctors', and often checked their prescriptions with Dr Huma, a gracious, widely travelled lady whose mother had been the first woman doctor in the NWFP. Many patients were genuinely ill, however, and Saul Myerson of London, Tracey Pratt of Sussex, Tory McConnell of Northern Ireland and others recorded many cases of goitres, cataracts, urinary infections, malnutrition and joints stiffened by long years of carrying heavy loads. Occasionally there was a victim of TB. One heartbreaking case was that of a two-year-old girl whose mother refused to take her daughter to hospital because her husband had died there of the same disease. By now, that child is almost certainly dead, killed by an illness that can be cured.

Climbing the steep, rocky path from the clinic to the jeep which would take them back to base camp, the doctors and Venturers discussed the day's work and compared cases. Wild roses and pink heathers grew along the verges and the headman of the village was there to wave them off, resplendent in an elaborately pleated turban. All around were fields of ripening wheat. Soon it would be harvested and the maize would be planted – a staple of both the people and animals of Pakistan.

'It isn't high-tech medicine that's needed here,' commented Sue. 'The solution is far harder: education.'

The weary group nodded in agreement, and continued up the hill.

CHAPTER SIX

Alaska

Killer Whales in the Kenai

(*Expedition Leader*: Chris Robinson)

McCarthy, Summer Solstice, 1988

'If the bear is brown, hit the ground; if it's black, it will attack so run like hell.' That is the rule every Alaskan knows from childhood. Other wisdom has it that you should always retreat, backwards if possible and at the speed required, or stand very still and hope the bruin won't see you.

There are flaws in every argument. Colours can be deceptive, moving backwards at speed a recipe for disaster, and it has recently been discovered that bears possess extremely keen eyesight. Needless to say, the theories are subject to much debate. For Alaska is bear country, and bears are never far away: the polar bear haunts the pack ice, the brown, or grizzly, the interior, and the black the most forested parts of the state.

During the early summer months in Alaska, Raleigh's Venturers had many close encounters with the largest of land carnivores, although strangely enough none were sighted on the islands of Shuyak and Kodiak with a dense population of one bear per square mile. As they climbed the peaks of the remote Wrangells bordering the Yukon, studied the archaeological remains of the ancient Eskimos, built remarkable bridges over salmon rivers in the Kenai fiords and skied the vast Alaskan glaciers, members of the expedition soon learned the 'bear necessities': to hang their food from high branches, burn all rubbish, enter thickets upwind and to sing as loudly as possible at every opportunity. No one wants to catch the creature by surprise.

The bears don't have the same qualms. Mexican-American Martha Jimenez, camping alone on the Harding Icefield, has an indelible memory of her meagre rations being stolen by a marauding grizzly: her mess tin will always carry a set of impressive teeth marks. Nor will Ginger Cook, a Venturer from Maine, forget a sunrise cuddle with a baby bear trying to share her sleeping bag. Knowing that its mother could not be far behind, Ginger spent a frantic ten minutes trying to push the sleepy creature out into the snow.

June in Alaska is the time of white nights, salmon runs and bears, for it is then that the huge creatures, hungry from long months of hibernation, feast in rivers thick with fish. In Barrow, the northernmost settlement in the United States, the sun sets in November and doesn't rise again until the end of January after sixty-four days of night. But the sun stands its own ground in this battle for the skies, lighting the horizon non-stop from May until August. During the summer of 1988 it grilled the US: record temperatures produced a drought that killed the crops. However, in the settlement of McCarthy, population eight, the Venturers shivered in the June cold, while pitching their tents near the freezing meltwater of the Kennecott River. Their woollen socks hung limply from the cottonwood trees, soaked from days of endless rain. Wet or not, they would be worn the next morning when the small group set off for the rock glaciers and ghost towns of the Wrangell Mountains.

There are no roads leading to McCarthy, a tiny cluster of wooden buildings – a bunkhouse, a couple of houses and an hotel – at the base of the jagged mountain range. To reach it, the twelve members on this part of the expedition had used pulleys to haul themselves, their kit and climbing gear over two stretches of boiling rapids coloured grey by volcanic ash. Even in summer, few travellers find their way to McCarthy. Nevertheless, 35-year-old bachelor Mike still pins up a hopeful note advertising for a wife. In 1983 he was shot twice in the head and once in the arm by a crazy stranger new in town. People still talk about how Mike hauled himself up and ran a kilometre to warn the others. It's hard to find anyone tougher than an Alaskan.

The Venturers were becoming pretty tough too. Once expedition leader Chris Robinson and his deputy, Mark Ely, arrived with badly needed resupplies they headed into the mountains. There they would live for the next month, climbing the snowy peaks as they made detailed studies of rock glaciers – the scree-covered ice found in polar regions and nearly all high mountain systems in the world. With scientists Brian Whalley of Queen's University of Belfast and his colleague, John Gordon, they would record and film flow rates, chronology and other basic characteristics of the vast, slow-moving mountain topography.

Food was short, the June nights freezing, and one often woke to find new snow. The nearest stream was a steep trek half a kilometre away – collecting water was a daily chore the Venturers soon accomplished in half an hour, racing through the thick undergrowth of alder and willow with forty-five kilos of water on their backs and a fervent hope that they wouldn't collide with a bear.

Yet no one wanted to be elsewhere. The mountains were their laboratory; endless summits, glaciers and icefalls of remarkable beauty and isolated mystery. To make things even better, an advance party made up of American Ron Boling, Canadian Jane Vincent (a 21-year-old veteran of the Canadian cross-country ski team who is aiming for the 1992 Olympics) and Phil Frankland of the UK had discovered an abandoned hut near the once famous Kennecott Copper Mines. The hut was furnished with a blanket of dead flies and decomposing rats, the walls raked by the claws of an angry bear, but, grateful for the shelter, most of the team moved under its sagging roof. They also discovered the log book of the Kennecott Copper Mines, ruled and penned by a careful hand, and open at the last entry.

Its pages told a remarkable story. Only seventy-odd years ago, fur-clad miners rode up these mountains in ore buckets to work in cold, subterranean pits twenty-five metres below ground. Dog sleds carried supplies between Kennecott and McCarthy, then a town with a wild reputation, boasting a bar, a barbershop, a blacksmith, a Chinese restaurant and a schoolhouse. Diluted whiskey sold for the exorbitant price of a dollar a glass, and the dancehall girls of McCarthy gave solace to the lonely miners.

Where the Venturers now camped was probably once the richest grade copper mine in the world. Almost pure chalcocite, with half a kilogram of silver per tonne, the mines, called 'Jumbo', 'Mother Lode' and 'Bonanza', had made men rich throughout the boom years of World War I. Then, suddenly, the boom was over. If it were not for the rusting earthmover tilted on to its side or an abandoned glove or cap left by a careless miner, it might all have been a dream. The young people of Operation Raleigh were the only inhabitants of one of the world's largest ghost towns.

The Saint Elias are the highest coastal mountains in the world. With the Wrangells to the west, they occupy eight million hectares that follow the arc of the Gulf of Alaska from Copper River to British Columbia. Although much lower than the Himalayas, their high latitude provides challenges similar to those of the Asian peaks: long tongues of ice-flows, temperatures that plummet to sixty below zero, violent storms and walls of ice that drop from rock summits in unbroken sheets. They have drawn climbers for a hundred years, and the Venturers exploring the terrain for rock glaciers, gazed at the higher peaks and planned their strategy. One peak in particular drew the most glances. Bonanza, at almost 2200 metres, is one of the highest in the area and, they suspected, one of the most technically difficult to climb.

Scientific tasks came first, and the work was demanding, but after lunch on 21 June, the summer solstice, a day of alternating rain and snow, a group of five headed out with enough rations for three days. They were a fit and experienced team: climbing leader Nigel Gregory, who had been a Venturer on the New Zealand expedition in 1986; Henry Iddon from Lancashire, who raised funds for the expedition by speed-skiing the mountains of Scotland; Stewart 'Tuna' Wellings, a bear of a fellow and British Telecom union official, whose humour could often retrieve a touchy situation; marathon runner Mandy Mudge; and Scotsman John Lewis, who described himself as 'actively unemployed'. With his kind of energy it was doubtful he would remain unemployed for long.

On that summer solstice bid, only two – Nigel and Henry – would make the top, roping together over invisible fracture lines, false summits and double cornices of new snow. It was impossible for them to secure the belays on the crumbly rock. They agreed that if one fell from the icy ridge, which soon narrowed to a third of a metre, the other would jump off the other side as a counterweight – a rather terrifying technique requiring absolute trust, but used many times in the high Andes and Himalayas. Until the early 1920s it was almost standard practice, according to Nigel.

Bonanza proved a technical and exposed climb, and they needed all the kit they had: fifty metres of 11 mm. rope, harnesses, crampons, ice axes, nylon slings and karabiners. Reaching the top at noon in a lashing wind, they managed to plant one buttock each on the summit and survive the soft snow and raging avalanches on the way down.

The others did not give up. One week and three tries later, Stewart Wellings, John Lewis and Ian Meers woke at 2.30 a.m. for a final alpine start to try to reach their goal, the elusive summit of Bonanza. This time they made it.

During the solstice, five other Venturers were fighting hypothermia and exhaustion as they climbed the twin peaks of Donoho. Staff member Doug Harvey, who had been with us in Australia, Liz McCoy, Lem Kirby, Phil Frankland and Steve Brady had been out for three nights and four days, roping up to cross the glaciers and bushwhacking through thick, wet willow and alder. Leading the way, Lem tightened his fingerhold on the crumbly, disintegrating rock. Behind him Doug accidentally released a rock which plummeted towards the mountain base 1524 metres below. As the boulder crashed towards them Liz, the ponytailed girl from New Jersey, renowned for laughing in any situation, showed another side to her character. Instinctively she threw herself over the two big men to protect them from danger. All was well; the group finally made it to the summit and slid gleefully down the ice face to their ghost-town camp.

Harding Icefield, July 1988

In a land famous for its toughness, 'Black-Ass' Griffith may be the toughest thing to come out of Alaska. This is the land where mosquitoes are known as the state bird, king crabs measure a metre from claw to claw, chinook salmon weigh almost forty-five kilos and halibut are so big and bad they can break a man's leg with a flip of the tail. It is the only place I know where fishermen carry a .44 Magnum. A place where gold nuggets reach seventeen centimetres in diameter and, as the locals say, 'where men are men and women win the Iditarod' – the gruelling 625-kilometre dog sled race from Anchorage northwest to Nome.

Even with this sort of competition Griffith may still come out ahead. Certainly those who crossed the Eklutna Glacier with him, on the trek they dubbed 'The Death March', would give him their vote. Stopping to repair Pitchler's Perch hut, or skiing closely roped to keep from dropping into blue crevasses in white-out conditions, he was still fresh when others were exhausted – people like expedition leader Chris Robinson, still in the running for a NASA position as mission specialist on the space shuttle; Mark Halstead, who runs the London Marathon for relaxation; Brad Barefoot, a business student and windsurfer, who sails up and down the east coast of the United States; and Margaret MacDonald, a TSB-sponsored Glaswegian whose courage and charm made everything seem easy.

At sixty-one, Griffith had no fear of bears, nor time for rest or illness. Flouting all the so-called 'rules', he slept on his food and drank whatever came his way. Naturally, Griffith didn't feel much of anything after supping his nightly brew: a measure of 151 rum, a pinch of nutmeg, a tablespoon of butter and another of brown sugar. He'd top that up with hot water and sit there on the ice with a huge grin on his face. He reckoned that was what you needed to get off the glacier.

Griffith's nickname refers to a casual stroll he once took downwind from Anaktuvuk Pass to Bettles. For the first thirty kilometres the temperature was thirty-five below with a wind-chill factor of minus 100. As usual, his equipment was rather limited – a spoon, water and a box of matches. Past the point of no return and badly frost bitten, he just kept going . . . The man is part of the legend of Alaska.

Raleigh Venturer Christopher 'Streaky' Redding, a lanky fellow who has studied glaciers since he was twelve but had never known the challenge of crossing one, finally figured out why Griffith could keep so far ahead of people one-third his age. 'The man just doesn't stop. He doesn't eat. He just keeps going.' That's his secret.

Like all good leaders, however, Griffith thinks of the needs of others. 'We thought he would be a "go for it bloke at all costs",' said Streaky Redding. 'But he was constantly aware of who was at the back. He was first to the Perch, of course, then dumped his gear – very light it was – and went back to the stragglers, took their load, and skied to the hut with them.'

Caine's Head, Resurrection Bay, 25 June 1989

Not far from Eklutna's eternal ice, another group of Venturers were constructing a string of remarkable bridges over the famous salmon rivers of the Kenai Peninsula, a thick finger of land jutting south from Anchorage into the Gulf. Luckily we had the benefit of John Chesher's advice for the many building jobs we had been asked to do, including ranger cabins at Wood-Tikchik and twenty-two portage boardwalks between the glaciated kettles of the Nancy Lake system. A staff sergeant in my regiment, the Royal Engineers, John knew how to build structures and how to demolish them with explosives. Unless we made a mess of the job the first time round, he wouldn't need both skills.

Working with Senior Ranger Jack Sinclair, who is in charge of the 2428-hectare Caine's Head State Recreation Area, and with others of the Parks and Recreation Division such as Al Meiners, the South-Central Regional Manager, Bill Garry and Chris Titus, the Venturers were to provide access to the park interior, intruding as little as possible on the environment. Only natural materials were used on the bridges: rough-cut timber felled on site; boulders for anti-scour devices around the triangular anchor cribs, and no preservatives which might pollute the river. Yet, the structures had to be strong enough to withstand the force of rivers in spate, heavy snow and the weight of bears fishing the fast waters.

Sophisticated engineering techniques don't always work well in the bush. Equipped with little more than pulleys, 'come-alongs' (a sort of 'endless chain'), one four-wheel-drive vehicle and several axes, it was imagination and stamina that proved the most important tools; most of the other kind broke. One huge tree whose weight had destroyed three 'come-alongs', each with a pulling strength of 2000 kilograms, was finally dragged into place when project leader John Hilhorst, a two-metre-tall New Zealander, hit on a new idea. John, an Outward Bound instructor whose expertise includes kayaking and sailing, fashioned ropes and turning blocks into a rig that's called a 'bully tack' in the boat world. Attached to a pulley system – and an eight-strong team of Venturers – the rig gave a sixteen-to-one purchase (for every unit of strength you get sixteen units for free), and the log gave up the struggle.

The Venturers at Caine's Head in Resurrection Bay worked in one of the most beautiful and hidden corners of the world. Before them stretched the green waters framed by shale beaches and sitka spruce marching up to massive glaciers. Behind them rose the Kenai Mountains and the Harding Icefield – an uncharted sea of ice

1500 metres deep broken by hundreds of lakes, rivers and streams. The bay itself is alive with creatures: black and brown bear, moose, wolves, lynx and coyotes. Sea otters play in the gentle surf, and seals and sea lions in search of salmon are pursued right into the bay by humpback and killer whales.

Here are all five species of Pacific salmon - the red (sockeye), the silver (coho), king (chinook), pink (humpies) and chum (dog) - swimming up the tributaries to the rivers where they were spawned, drawn by the scent of the stream where they were hatched as fry. Their run up the rivers is one of nature's celebrations. Each year there is an early run of kings, while the chums and the pinks start in July and the silvers begin in August and September.

That July the pinks were out in force. The fingerlings had eaten well at sea, and the waters of the bay boiled as the rosy torpedoes headed upstream. Huge gulls stalked the black beaches for offal, while bald eagles screamed down to hook live fish in their gleaming talons.

Mt Marathon, Seward, 4 July 1988

When the Venturers, led by John Hilhorst and his American deputy Lisa Marshall, were not felling trees and building bridges, they kayaked through icebergs calved by advancing glaciers, climbed the surrounding peaks and even ran up a few. But the Fourth of July party at Seward, the town at the mouth of the bay, was not to be missed. The highlight of Independence Day was a race up Mt Marathon - more of a climb than a run up cliffs and scrub, snow and dirt to the 900-metre summit and a free-fall down again. Those who straggle home are often hard to recognize, smeared with the victory colours of mud and blood.

Many train for a year and rest for a fortnight before attempting Mt Marathon. As a special treat the Venturers could enter if they wished. They would still have to do a full day's work beforehand, then hike a few hours to Seward on the morning of the race.

Dressed in ragged T-shirts and torn trainers - the remnants of their best clothes - they arrived in Seward keen to race. The officials counted the entries and ruled that the women could enter (there were still untaken numbers) but the men's places were full. To extend that limit could be dangerous for all. Disappointed but keen to cheer on the girls, Mark Tredwen, Simon Tait and Will Bethell consoled themselves with lashings of junk food they hadn't tasted for months. A few hamburgers and hot dogs later, followed by huge scoops of ice cream, corn on the cob and a couple of cinnamon rolls, they learned there were three empty places. They could run. In five minutes. In whatever they were wearing.

Despite their unusual training procedure, the three British men turned in very respectable times of just over an hour,while Margaret MacDonald was the best of the Raleigh women. But it was their lanky leader, John Hilhorst - an illegal entry - who came in with the top twenty racers and then ran back to meet Margaret who was still going strong at the home stretch. Racing to Seward, the two made a remarkable sight: the small Scots girl chewed up by the mountain and the towering Kiwi urging her on. The officials let John keep his medal.

Wood-Tikchik State Park, Southwest Alaska, 20 July 1989

The ranger fingered his large-calibre revolver. Ahead, fresh bear scat still steamed on the narrow trail and Dan Hourihan hoped that the weapon wouldn't be needed. Thirteen years as a ranger had honed his instinct and his respect for the grizzly. 'Hey bear! Hello brownie!' he hollered. 'We're real bad, bear, you don't want to know us!' The small group following the ranger through the dense woods of alder, birch and spruce made as much noise as possible, hoping the bruin would hear them and keep his distance. The system of long interconnected lakes and rivers nurtures spawning runs of salmon, rainbow trout and grayling, and the park's waters contribute some twenty per cent of the Bristol run of sockeye, the largest in the world. Wood-Tikchik is a paradise for man and bear.

Far below, the rapids on the north shore of the Nuyakut River seethed over huge boulders. The white water graduated from grade three to five, and the thin ribbon-like path wound perilously close to the dangerous drop. The track was riddled with thick roots and boot-catching brush, ripening cloudberries and the blood-red bunchberries clustered between white petals. Those who tried to portage a canoe or a raft around these rapids could easily be pitched into the river below. The alternative was not any more attractive: big Bill Martin, owner of the Royal Coachman Lodge nearby, had fished out many folk who had tried to ride the rapids.

One of Raleigh's jobs in this wilderness - over 600,000 hectares of mountains, forests, tundra, lakes and rivers and the largest state park in the United States - would be to reroute and clear a trail ending in a natural landing bank at the base of the white water. Wildlife surveys, ranger cabin construction and simply exploring this frontier land would all feature in Raleigh's work at Wood-Tikchik, a name originating from the two rivers which roughly define the park's wide boundaries. But the camouflaged C-130 Hercules, generously lent by the Alaska National Air Guard, and the battered float planes that ferried the Venturers from Anchorage to Dillingham and on to Tikchik Lake, carried picks and shovels, dust pans and polythene sheeting as well as tents and Coleman stoves. Also on board was the tall, congenial Dr Robert Shaw, the state of Alaska's chief archaeologist. One of the most important jobs for the Venturers at Wood-Tikchik would be to dig for clues to a people who had lived there thousands of years ago. Probably of Mongoloid stock, they had crossed the land bridge of the Bering Strait from Asia just as the glaciers retreated.

Skeletal remains of these unknown people – probably the ancestors of today's Yupik Eskimos – have yet to be found; they are known only from their stone tools and environment. They built houses of sod blocks, dressed themselves in hides of walrus and seal, bear and caribou, and sewed bird skins together to keep out the rain. Where a man once sat and made an arrowhead of chert or obsidian, or where a woman once butchered fish or game, Raleigh Venturers would live and work, looking for artefacts that might tell the story of Alaska's first people.

Even closer to the Arctic Circle, another intrepid group paddled the icy rivers and vast, open lakes of Canada. They, too, followed the trail of ancient people – Inuit, Chipewyan and Paleoeskimo. So remote are these wild rivers that the Operation Raleigh expedition in Canada was totally cut off from the rest of the world. They had entered the realm of caribou and wolf cubs, whitewater rapids and the ever-changing rhythm of the great Kazan River. It was a voyage through time and endless space, and one that would change them for ever.

CHAPTER SEVEN

The Canadian Arctic

Canoeing the Wild Kazan

(*Expedition Leader*: Lieutenant Commander David Pelly, RCNR)

Keewatin Barrenlands, Canadian Arctic, July 1988

The Canadian Arctic. The last great wilderness in North America. A huge and hungry land of endless vistas, ice and tundra. A land where one can count caribou by the thousands, catch 13.6-kilogram lake trout with unbaited lines, watch magnificent raptors wheel against the sky, and come face to face with wolves, creatures rarely seen, that are unafraid of man.

In the centre of Northern Canada are the Barrenlands, a treeless territory of a million square kilometres once inhabited by the Caribou Inuit (Eskimo). Today the land is empty. The people used the rivers as highways, for the Barrens are laced with wild rivers. Among them are the Back, the Thelon and the river Operation Raleigh had come to explore, the great Kazan that links a handful of jewel-like lakes running northeast to the hamlet of Baker Lake. In seven weeks, the group of thirty-two would canoe 500 kilometres down the river, conducting a series of scientific projects, including the first systematic archaeological study of the Kazan River valley.

The vanished people of the Barrens aided the expedition, for the tall stone cairns they had built, called Inuksuit, were vertical punctuation marks against the horizon, signposts that helped them read the icy river. In fact, the original inhabitants were never far from the Venturers' thoughts. Led by Canadian archaeologists Chris Hanks and Andrew Stewart, the survey of the river valley revealed more of the past at every bend: soapstone pipes and hunting implements, scrapers and spear points, flakes of quartzite, fire hearths, meat caches and tent rings. A wealth of clues to cultures dating back some 3000 years, of several different peoples including the Inuit, Chipewyan and Paleoeskimo. Raleigh's discovery of surface artefacts used by the Paleoeskimo broke new ground, indicating for the first time that these earliest inhabitants of the Arctic had once lived on the Kazan.

If the earliest European explorers such as Samuel Hearne, Father Alphonse Gasté and J. B. Tyrrell came to this remote land on foot or by canoe, we had the modern-day advantage of rail and air. A three-day train ride to the seaport of Churchill on the western shore of Hudson Bay gave the expedition members some idea of the wilderness ahead. Vast lumps of ice floated in the Churchill River, pushed up from the bay with the tide. Beluga whales cruised to within six metres of the shore, venting through their blow holes. All around, the country was flat, broken only by stunted trees and low buildings of corrugated iron.

From Churchill, a bright yellow De Havilland Otter ferried canoes, packs and people across the water-rich country to Angikuni Lake, the first of the five lakes linked by the Kazan River where the trail would begin. Eight times the twin-engined plane rose over the melting ice-floes of Hudson Bay. From now on there would be no outside communication; the expedition members would have no one but themselves to rely on, and no transport but a fleet of two-man canoes powered by paddles and strong backs.

Kassie Heath, a physiotherapist, was on the last flight out of Churchill. She leaned forward, touching the window of the plane with her forehead, her blue-grey eyes scanning the wilderness below. As the Twin Otter came in for a landing over the lake she thought: 'This is it. The beginning. I've got to love it now.' The Twin Otter, its trip completed, turned towards the centre of the lake and took off in a spray of water as it rose into the blue and white sky. Kassie looked around, absorbing first impressions of the bare landscape and gently curving hills of orange and brown and green. A soft rain began to fall as the evening drew in, a silvery backdrop for the double rainbow that suddenly arched across the Kazan.

Angikuni Lake, 2 July 1988

Other, more startling sights greeted the expedition members that night: their first glimpse of the Kazan River, cold and fast and fringed with ice; the first lake trout snapping eagerly at the lure – one needn't starve even if the rations were lost in a capsized canoe. For Hilary ('Hilli') Woodward, however, it was her introduction to the vanished people of the Kazan that made the deepest impression upon her. Gathering firewood near the campsite, the tall, blonde girl stooped to retrieve a branch lying near a rocky outcrop. The pale light caught the whiteness of bones tucked inside the cairn, just visible through the cracks. She straightened her back and looked around. There were signs of man all around, she realized. This was no isolated archaeological site. The landscape was alive and clues to the past were everywhere. But the people who once lived here formed only one part of the whole. To get an indication of the larger picture, the expedition also undertook studies of the environment, its trees, soil, plants, birds and animals, which had provided this vanished people with shelter, food and clothing.

The expedition's first day on the Kazan also brought them their first set of rapids. The river is swift, and the swelling noise of the water alerted the paddlers to the white spume ahead. Now the intensive month of training they had received prior to meeting the river came into its own. Expedition leader David Pelly, who had mounted several expeditions on these wild Canadian rivers, knew the Kazan and its secrets well.

Once in rapids, the canoeist feels a surge of power as the water gathers speed and spills between the boulders. Quick reflexes are needed, along with common sense, instant communication with one's partner and the ability to read the river, a skill which comes with time. Hilli's heart was beating hard long after her canoe had made it safely through the rapids. 'Draw hard!' she had shouted to herself, for the roar of the water drowned her words. It was over in seconds and her strength had seemingly come from nowhere.

As the days of paddling, portaging and scientific work continued, the Venturers learned to read the river's many facets: raging cataracts, long, lazy sweeps, falls and rapids. The land was equally varied, carved by glaciers into gorges and canyons, hard rocky outcrops and gravelly glacial till. Of course there was potential danger in the beauty of the landscape: rapid weather changes could transform the big lakes from glassy pools into two-metre seas of turbulent water, strong opposing currents and standing waves or 'keepers' that capture a canoe and hold it fast.

Three times a boat went over and its pair of canoeists were flung into waters cold enough to bring on hypothermia in minutes. Three times the rest of the team quickly came to the rescue and no one was much the worse for the dunking. 'The main danger comes from not scouting the river before attempting each rapid,' stressed David Pelly, 'and from not carefully judging your ability to handle the white water.' This is necessary because each year the river changes. The amount of snowfall during the winter and the spring break-up of the ice make it a living thing.

The Three Cascades, 11 July

It was late evening and yet still light. The smooth splashing sound of paddles was a musical counterpoint to the twilight birdsong and the low rumble of a distant rapid. The canoes sped down the river effortlessly and slipped ashore for the night. Trout appeared on the menu as if by magic, cooked over firewood that was much harder to find than fish. Walking downstream, a group of Venturers heard the rumble deepen to a roar. Tomorrow they would portage one of the spectacular cascades of the Kazan.

'There is thunder in my ears,' wrote Kassie in her log. 'Little wonder. At this second cascade of the three on this part of the river, there are stoppers with standing waves three to four metres high. It is a spectacle to see this wide river thrown into so much chaos. The river pours over huge, round boulders forming a wall who knows how deep, and certainly not manageable in any watercraft. The cascade is at least 200 metres long, and here the river is the supreme authority.'

As always, the wildness of the river was matched by that of the creatures of land and sky: muskoxen, peregrine falcons, caribou and wolves. The closest encounter with the caribou happened on the far side of Yathkyed Lake, when, hauling their canoes ashore, the stiff-backed Venturers collapsed on the hot tundra. As they roused themselves to gaze at the ridge above, they became aware of the presence of thousands of caribou. The horizon was dotted with them as far as the eye could see, and, when one turned to look again, there were more. Fearlessly, the creatures came right up to the young people, sniffing and snorting and clicking their hooves as they passed.

The muskoxen seemed just as fearless. Taking no notice of Canadian ornithologist Judith Kennedy, nor of Hilli, American Venturer Ashley Wooten or Betty Betsedea, a Dene Indian from Canada, who were mapping an archaeological site, the massive, curly-horned beasts, three large females trailed by their young, strolled into the river and swam leisurely to the other side.

The wolves, too, were with their young. Choi Siu Ping, nicknamed 'Zoe', lives in Hong Kong and had never seen a wolf. Camera in hand, the fragile-looking Chinese girl had set out to photograph the landscape lit by the evening sun. She stopped suddenly. A few metres away was a large, creamy-grey creature staring at her coldly, eye to eye. 'A dog? A fox?' Zoe asked David Pelly excitedly when she pelted back to camp.

'Let's go see,' he replied.

As the pair climbed the river bank of boulders pushed up by the spring ice they heard the unmistakable bark of cubs beneath their feet. Quickly backing off, Zoe and David saw the wolf bitch leap to the spot where they had stood minutes before. She stood without fear or aggression, but more than ready to defend. For the rest of the night a strip of no-man's-land existed between the wolf and human camps.

All in all, there were eight sightings of wolves during the Arctic expedition, two among the caribou herds and one right in camp. A caribou and calf had raced through the camp in the middle of the night; neither they nor the massive wolf that stalked them noticed the amazed expressions of Richard Wilson, a Brazilian-born Scot, and Almon MacNeil, a Canadian engineer.

'Even so late, there was light enough to read by,' recalled Richard, 'but we could smell the wolf even before we saw him. His teeth sparkled against his dark fur and we could see his enormous red salivating tongue as he slung low to the ground. The caribou and calf were off, darting over the river's rocky bank into the water.' Although the wolf gave up the chase and loped away, the calf was a casualty of the life-or-death chase: the cow made it across the river, but the body of the small brown calf floated ashore the next day.

Yathkyed Lake, 17 July

Although the days in the Canadian Arctic were often hot and thick with mosquitoes and blackflies, temperatures plummeted during the pale-lit nights. The ice had not yet melted on Yathkyed – the largest lake the expedition would cross on its way to Baker Lake. The sixteen two-man canoes had split into four groups of four. So vast was this strange new world that none had seen another group since the start. At Padlerjuaq, the river is deep and narrow and the ancient hunters used to wait, spear in hand, for the caribou to cross. Here the Raleigh groups would gather, and cross the lake when the ice retreated.

Over fifty kilometres wide, Yathkyed was a vast expanse of water and white ice that seemed to spill over the far horizon. It would be at least another week before the lake was navigable, reflected David Pelly, glancing at the clouds bunched against the sky. In this northern wilderness, the heat of the sun would not be the force to free them; strong winds and rain were needed to whittle a route through the lake.

The ice-bound delay was put to good use. Surveying the wetlands and the high ground, the members of the expedition discovered over 300 artefacts, some of which will give new leads to scientists studying the inter-relationships of European and prehistoric technologies. Every day they watched the ice lose its grip on the lake, and, within the week, all sixteen canoes were headed for the far shore.

By now, the ever-changing rhythms of the river had become familiar. Most felt in tune with their isolation and consequent reliance on each other. Simon Cremer, a strong, dependable member of the expedition and a science student from England, wrote: 'A wonderful aspect of this was the feeling of gradually becoming more and more a part of the land. River and weather were the dictators of lifestyle; simple needs took over from the complex pressures of life in a "breakneck-speed" society.

'The various scientific projects were also progressing well – brilliantly in fact. My group was initially doing a treeline study with the help of Canadian scientist Dr Glen MacDonald of McMaster University. The work was exciting, since never before had the treeline and the fossil pollen records relating to it been accurately recorded in this area.'

For Simon and the rest, understanding the threads that bound each project to the others made the finds all the more exciting. During the seven-week expedition, 1000 hours of work were put into creating an atlas of breeding birds of the Northwest Territories, and this research, along with pollen and treeline sampling, archaeology, wildflower and mammal observation, was an integral part of looking at the land and the river as a totality.

'We began to see the land differently,' said Kassie. 'It was not just a geographical feature, not just a wilderness to paddle in, not just gentle curves, dynamic waterways and delicate colours. It was far more than that: a working environment that had once been someone's home. That made the whole place so much more alive.'

Baker Lake, 18 August

In early August the sun sets on the river at about 11.30, but even then, the Arctic world is lit by a pale twilight. The final expanse of water, called Baker Lake, lay between the expedition and the welcome David Pelly knew awaited them at the community of the same name. David had often written of the people of the Kazan and had won many friends during his yearly visits since 1982. Nearly the entire village of Baker Lake turned out to welcome the weary but cheerful visitors. People lined the shore, some in caribou skins and beaded ceremonial clothes, as well as a Canadian Mountie in full scarlet regalia, and the Commissioner of the Northwest Territories. Many hands stretched out to help the Venturers ashore.

'Quanuitpit!' the Venturers tentatively tried out their one Inuit phrase. 'How are you!'

That night lumps of caribou were boiled over the community fires, to be served with bannock, an unleavened bread that recalled Scots traders who had passed this way a century ago. Songs and chants that had never before been heard in the remote Canadian North filled the air. Jordanian Venturer Osama Abdeen recited traditional poems; and the entire expedition gave voice to Pakistan's Independence song, which Venturer Arsalan Hasnie of Lahore, a member of his country's national sailing team, had taught them as they crossed the final stretch of water. Eddy Chong, a 23-year-old student and martial arts master from Singapore, stole the show with a crisp and professional display of his talents. In return, our hosts performed drum dances and displayed their expertise with dog whips, used not to strike their huskies but to guide them as they pulled sleds. Finally, as the evening drew to a close, the Inuit performed their traditional 'throat singing', a unique

Above left: Venturers and US Army helicopter crew beside one of the wind-pumps built for the Sioux Indians on the Pine Ridge Reservation, USA.

Above right: Keiteur Falls, Guyana, second highest in the world.

Below: Rafting on the Essequibo in Guyana.

Above: Twin Otter takes off in foggy conditions to ferry supplies to Canadian Arctic expedition.

Below: Abdul Hasnie of Pakistan and American Ashley Wooten on the Kazan River in the Canadian Arctic.

music performed by two women who use each other's voice-box to produce a resonant chant.

Baker Lake was the end of the river and the end of the Arctic expedition. Some of the Raleigh group felt they had entered a time warp. For seven weeks they had paddled towards this place, settled by the descendants of the Caribou Inuit who had once lived along the Kazan. Now the Venturers were learning about the new ways of life flourishing in this remote region, and, as they worked together to build playgrounds for the Baker Lake village children, they could share with these youngsters something of how their own ancestors had lived. These proud and hospitable Inuit were a part of the continuing story of the Kazan.

Much further to the south in the American state of South Dakota, other Venturers were living and working with members of a very different Indian culture: the famous Oglala Sioux. These were the descendants of some of the bravest warriors and finest military tacticians of any people in the world. As I shook hands with Chief Red Cloud, I remembered well that it was only about a hundred years ago that they had given General Custer a very bad time indeed.

CHAPTER EIGHT

The American Rockies and Appalachians

The Wild Country

(*Expedition Leader*: Chris Robinson)

Pine Ridge Indian Reservation, South Dakota, 14 August 1988

The hot wind carried the rhythm of drums across the dusty hills of South Dakota. With it came the low, insistent sound of chanting and shrill notes made by eagle-bone whistles. For days the braves had prepared for the Sun Dance, one of the most important rituals of the Sioux nation. They had fasted and sweated out physical and spiritual impurities in the sweat lodge for four days; most of their lives had been a preparation for the pain they would now endure.

The 1988 ceremony had begun with a good omen. Two eagles had flown overhead on the first morning of the Sun Dance, circling the hill where the tribe had erected a sacred tree and a shelter of pine boughs to shield them from the heat. In the early light, the slender cottonwood tree was clearly visible to Jenny Bond and the small group of Venturers who walked towards it. They had been invited to attend a ceremony few outsiders have ever witnessed. Rules of attendance were strict. No food or drink could pass their lips that day, and they had to cover their limbs with long clothing. To prevent intrusions, the place of the sacred tree was kept secret. Cameras, of course, were forbidden.

Expedition artist Natalie Ellett was able to capture some of the magic on her sketch pad and in her journal. 'From afar the site looked like an ancient monument,' she recorded; 'the pine-thatched structure provided shade, surrounding an inner circle of sage to protect against evil spirits. The circle had four openings, each marked by a different colour; red, white, black and yellow, representing the four colours of man. Strips of similarly coloured cloth were tied around the tree trunk. We sat, with legs covered by long skirts and trousers, in the 110°F heat and watched as the drumming began.'

The music rose to a crescendo then died out. A young girl, accompanied by elders, entered the circle carrying a huge buffalo skull and a pipe, blessing each gate as they passed. Then came the twenty dancers who had gone without food or water for four days; men who were dressed in eagle feathers, long skirts of leather or cloth, with jewellery and garlands of sage tied around their heads, wrists and ankles. Often they collapsed as they danced, weakened by hunger and thirst.

The rituals of the Sun Dance are many and complex, but what happened next was not meant for the faint-hearted. The Sun Dance is the ancient custom the Sioux use to contact the spirit world, strengthen the tribe, bring joy to marriage, heal the sick and settle old quarrels. In the old days, it kept buffalo plentiful and brought victory in battle. The Dance is, therefore, a celebration of life.

For some, like Warwick Cairns, of Berkshire, England, the ceremony struck a chord so deep that years later he will still feel its power. 'One of the dancers lay face down beneath the tree,' remembers Warwick. A razor-sharp knife flashed in the sun, slicing short, vertical lines down his shoulder blades. Slivers of bone were pushed through the cuts and tied to long cords attached to buffalo hide. As the blood flowed from his cuts the Indian stood, then boldly walked forward, dragging the heavy pelt behind him. He circled the hilltop, oblivious to the pulsating throb of the drums that grew louder as he walked. Finally, children jumped on to the buffalo skin to hasten the end of his agony. The thongs of his own skin snapped and he staggered forward. His back would bear the circular scars of his courage forever. The first brave was followed by others. Like him, some dragged the weighty buffalo skin from their backs until the cords tore free of their flesh. Others had skewers stuck through the skin of their chests and the ropes were tied to the sacred tree.

'Pierced through the chest, two of the youngest boys danced together towards the tree,' recalls Warwick Cairns. 'One had staggered a little as he got up, but showed no other sign of weakness. Reaching the tree, they placed their hands and forehead against the trunk, then danced backward until the cords tightened and strained. This they did several times, leaning out harder each time, until, at a pre-determined moment, they both ran back as fast as they could.'

As the young men flung themselves backward, the skewers of bone ripped through their skin. The dancers raised their hands, the medicine man rubbed a grey powder into the wounds and the ceremonial pipe was passed around once again.

Crazy Horse and Red Cloud were two of the most famous masters of guerrilla warfare in history. They, and other great Sioux chieftains such as Sitting Bull, Conquering Bear and American Horse, were the ancestors of the people with whom the Venturers now lived and worked, one hundred years later. Stubbornly resisting white expansion, theirs was the tribe which in June of 1876, wiped out the 7th Cavalry commanded by General George Armstrong Custer. An ambitious young officer, Custer is most famous for badly underestimating the skill of his opponents. Refusing to wait for reinforcements, hc divided his men into four troops. It was the last order he ever gave. The Sioux picked off the soldiers and slaughtered Custer and his entire detachment on the banks of the Little Bighorn.

The battle of Little Bighorn marked the last great victory for the Sioux. Fourteen years later the events surrounding the massacre at Wounded Knee claimed the life of the great Sitting Bull and marked the end of the 'Indian Wars'.

Once the Sioux had been masters of an ocean of grassland stretching thousands of miles. The hills of the Badlands and the plains of the Midwest were grazed by thousands of buffalo which provided them with shelter, food, clothing and tools. Nothing went to waste. Buffalo dung was used for fuel, the flesh of the highly-flavoured hump was a delicacy, as were the tongue, marrow, intestines and liver, and there were at least eighty-six uses of the shaggy-maned bison that did not involve eating. Skilled and resourceful, the Sioux were a people of the open range, a people who even now evoke romantic images of warriors in eagle feathers and fringed leather riding across the endless plains.

Today's reality is shockingly different. Pine Ridge Reservation is a welfare society. There are few buffalo now, but neither are there businesses or industry. To the north are the Badlands, Wounded Knee (now a national historical site) and Mt Rushmore with its gigantic heads of United States Presidents carved into the stone by Gutzon Borglum. To the west, Crazy Horse Mountain and Custer State Park are ironic neighbours, and within one kilometre of the reservation are twenty-four liquor stores grossing one million dollars each year in retail sales. Alcoholism and unemployment, affecting 80 to 90 per cent of the population, are the modern threats to the survival of the Indian people.

Operation Raleigh came to Pine Ridge largely thanks to the efforts of one person – Jenny Bond. Earlier Jenny had herself been an outstanding Venturer in Papua New Guinea; now she had become an outstanding project leader at Pine Ridge in Shannon County, the poorest area per capita in the United States. Jenny saw a need, sought an ally in the Christian Relief Services in Washington, DC, and with Operation Raleigh's skill and manpower found a solution to one of the Indians' many problems, the lack of water.

Once a river had run through the reservation, but it had dried up long ago. Today the nearest source of water was several kilometres away, and the water had to be collected in jerry cans and carted home on foot or in a rusty pickup. Most of it was needed for the vegetable plots. What was left over served for washing and drinking. The acute shortage inevitably led to poor hygiene and illness.

Later in the year and an ocean away, I spoke of the reservation with Gerry Titus, a project leader on one of Raleigh's Kenyan expeditions. An Apache, Gerry had grown up in Pine Ridge in the early 1960s. 'There was never any water,' recalled the Vietnam veteran who is now a SeaBee in the US Navy. 'We had to go all the way to White Horse, on horseback, and bring it back in barrels.'

To Jenny, the solution didn't entail hi-tech engineering, but wind. At speeds of over 70 kph the same wind whipped up dust-devils, uprooted trees, and, on the very first night the Venturers arrived, ripped through the tepee where they slept. This, she believed, was the resource that could be used to pump water from streams forty-five to eighty metres below ground. Christian Relief Services provided a drilling rig and materials and Operation Raleigh provided the manpower. Together they constructed the wind-powered wells that brought water to Pine Ridge.

'This time Raleigh did not have to travel to the Third World to find genuine need,' wrote eighteen-year-old law student Alan Gotto of Suffolk. 'Much of the water under the reservation was alkaline, and unfit to drink, so great care had to be taken in positioning the wells. With temperatures of 110°F in the sun, it was hard work.'

While Alan was at Pine Ridge his group completed a number of wells and water pumps for the local people, including the elderly medicine man, Peter Catches, cave dweller Roberta Kills Enemy and Wilbur Black Feather. Left mute by a childhood accident, Wilbur clapped with joy as they struck water. Then he rolled up his sleeves and set to work planting sunflowers and vegetables in the moist earth.

At night, sitting by the smoky campfire, Venturers heard first-hand accounts of the history of a proud people. Chief Oliver Red Cloud, leader of the Oglala Sioux and bearer of the name of his famous ancestor, sat with the Venturers and brought the past to life. Wearing cowboy boots, jeans and a stetson hat, the chief recounted stories about the wars between the red and white Americans.

'He joked about inviting us back to his tepee, teasing our preconceived ideas of Indians,' recalled Alan Gotto. 'One story he was particularly fond of recounts the meeting between the first Chief Red Cloud and President Grant. Together the two leaders had made a treaty. Negotiations concluded, the great Red Cloud lit a pipe to seal their pact and handed it to Grant. Before lifting the pipe to his lips, the American President wiped the mouthpiece on his shirt. Without a word, Red

Cloud accepted the pipe again and, with a slow, deliberate movement, broke off the end.'

On other nights, Reginald Cedar Face took over the storytelling. Cedar Face was his English name. His Lakota name is Ta Shunke Wakian – 'Thunder and Lightning Horse'. Reggie, an extremely well-educated government health officer, told of the Sioux migrations north to the Great Lakes, the arrival of the horse in the mid-eighteenth century, the Lewis and Clark expedition which led to the first treaty with the American government, the Pawnees (arch-rivals of the Sioux), Fort Laramie and the Ghost Dance fever which swept the Plains. The Ghost Dancers believed in a new religion that forbade contact with whites and the drinking of alcohol, and which promised a new earth for the Indians, rich in buffalo. It was a religion of dreams.

Along with those dreams the Indians found renewed energy which alarmed the white settlers. Tension grew, fears magnified and eventually erupted in the massacre at Wounded Knee. Like many atrocities, the 1890 massacre began with a tragic mistake. Soldiers had tried to disarm a deaf Indian, Black Coyote; his rifle discharged and the fighting began.

Amongst those listening to the tales were Basit Khan of Pakistan and Lorna Burton of England – both engineering students; Hiroko Matsuura of Kobe, Japan; full-blood Lakota Sioux Vine Flood; and blonde, blue-eyed Dawn Paulhamus, another Lakota Sioux descended from a family who combined most of the influences of early America, from Indians, Germans and French to the Pennsylvania Dutch. John Maidens, a zoology/oceanography student, could understand something of what Black Coyote felt when the soldiers shouted at him to throw down his rifle. He too was deaf, as was his fellow Venturer Matthew James, a zoology student from Wales.

Mt Evans, Colorado, 30 July 1988

As the Venturers at Pine Ridge sweltered in one of the hottest summers on record, others shivered in the Rocky Mountain heights. Living on the peak of Mt Evans, at an altitude of 4346 metres, they endured severe cold and tight water rations while they studied the impact of mountain goats on the habitat of the Big Horn sheep indigenous to the alpine region – an area six times the size of Switzerland. They had gone to Colorado, the eighth largest state just west of centre in the United States, and midway between Canada and Mexico. Here trappers and traders once sold white beaver pelts for toppers in Paris, New York and London;

mountain men like Kit Carson and 'Broken Hand' Fitzpatrick sought their fortunes and miners washed the pay dirt in the mountain streams.

Taking a census of the goats and sheep often meant spending days at a time away from camp. 'On the second day of an overnight hike, Chris Wawn and I were cut off from our party on the return journey by thick, freezing fog and lightning storms,' recalls Welsh Venturer Dylan Winder, who plays the trumpet in jazz and brass bands in his quieter moments. 'We had only survival rations, but a packet of hot chocolate tasted exquisite under those conditions.' Despite frozen socks and sleeping bags, the two made it back, climbing along the scree-covered ridges to their mountain base camp. 'Had we been any later, the rescue helicopters would have been looking for us,' said Dylan. 'While we were away, several people were ill with hypothermia and altitude sickness and had to be taken off the mountain.'

As the waxing moon signalled the end of July, the night temperatures fell sharply and many Venturers had their first taste of climbing in the midsummer snow. The Omanis, in particular, had some adjusting to do as the mercury dipped below minus 10°C and the wind chill made even a quick foray to the rocky loo a memorable experience. One night Al-Ghaithy, a marine engineering student from Oman, woke with fever and chills at 3 a.m., the symptoms of exposure and altitude sickness. Without a word, Hiromi Kuroku, a shy Japanese who had hardly exchanged a 'good morning', slipped into his sleeping bag to keep him warm, while Britisher Melanie Davidson boiled up some soup. They were a team. To those at home in Oman and Japan it might have been a bit shocking. Here it was survival.

Resupplying Mt Evans and the other project sites was the hard lot that fell to Bart Greer, the US Army captain who ran the Rocky Mountain programme. An expedition can fail or succeed on the strength of supply runs, and Bart and his team drove endless miles across the United States with rations and equipment. Finding the Venturers was itself a bit of a task since the projects were based in the most inaccessible places: at Mesa Verde – the ancient cliff dwellings of the vanished Pueblo Indians; on the banks of the Yampa River, a remote haven for rattlesnakes and sea snakes, framed by sheer cliffs dropping 700 metres; near the fierce rapids of the Green River and the Y-shaped icefields of the aptly named Mt Ypsilon.

Mammoth Cave, Kentucky, 4 August 1988

In the closing years of the 1920s, a hunter aimed at a bear smashing its way through the low branches of hickory and oak. Wounded, the creature staggered and suddenly vanished. The hunter stood, his rifle raised, watching out for his quarry. A covey of quail rose through the wisps of fog that drifted from an underground sink hole. But the animal had disappeared. Following its tracks, the man stumbled into a cavern that seemed to slope into the centre of the earth. He found himself in a landscape of sparkling white crystals, underground rivers, labyrinths of limestone and absolute blackness. The hunter had discovered Mammoth, one of the great cave regions of the world.

When Operation Raleigh came to Mammoth Cave many years later, 480 kilometres of the underground passages had been charted, but there were many more still to be discovered in this dark frontier. Each month a kilometre of new caverns is found and recorded. Three to five levels make up the cave system and sixty metres down unseen rivers continue to carve their way through the limestone beds.

Deep within the tunnels of Ganter Cave, the Venturers measured their progress in centimetres. Ganter is one of the wild caves of Mammoth; almost three kilometres in length, its carboniferous limestone formations range from pencil-thin tubes to lofty caverns. A textbook example of what cavers call Kentucky karst, it contains pools of water five metres deep, brittle flowers of white gypsum, and frosty pillars of stone that glisten in torchlight. Beyond the reach of the beam all remains dark, and a cold and constant 54°F. The eerie chill in the caves is unchanged by seasonal fluctuations in temperature, and preserves the remains of mummified Indians while supporting blindfish, crickets, bats and salamanders in a habitat of utter blackness.

Joanne Smith lay wedged against the cave walls and realized she couldn't move. Squeezed between tons of rock the girl hunched her shoulders and tried to force herself forward. It was horrible. Behind her face mask, sweat dripped into her eyes and she could hear her breath - sharp intakes that did little to diminish her mounting claustrophobia. For two hours she had crawled down the winding cave into a totally strange environment. Unable to move either her body or her head in the tight passage, she forced herself to relax and to remember that friends were near - Nicola Simpson, Steve Priest, Eric O'Connor, Conor Heaney and leader Tony Hayward. Tony had been an Australian Venturer on the tough Cape York expedition and later worked with Raleigh as a caving instructor in Malaysia, mapping the vast chambers of Sarawak. Along with Mike Godfrey, a Devon man who combined a love of caving with a useful affinity for physics, he headed the Mammoth Cave project.

For safety's sake, they had entered 'The Crawl' feet first. An ungainly position, but a wise decision. The carbide light bounced off the rock, casting an unearthly shadow. As she slowly exhaled Jo found she could slide a bit further. Ahead she could see the huge boots of big Eric O'Connor, a top-notch skier from Denver. 'Surely if he can get through, I can,' thought the girl.

Eric was busy calming his own fears. Not for the first time he wondered what he was doing in this alien place, crawling on his side as he eased his muscular frame through a twenty-five-centimetre gap. After the stifling heat above ground, he had, at first, found the coolness of the cave a relief. Gradually, however, Eric's delight had faded. For the last sixty metres he hadn't been able to turn his head, let alone scratch the innumerable strange insect bites on his shoulder.

Exploring wild caves requires enormous stamina and uncommon courage. 'There was mud and water to slide through and the cold to contend with,' remembers leader Tony Hayward. 'The squeeze in the middle of the tunnel made matters worse. To get through it, you had to remove your safety helmet, stretch your arms before you and tilt your head to one side. Centimetre by centimetre you moved forward, breathing out to reduce your chest size. If you panicked your body would have expanded. And then you'd have been stuck.'

It wasn't fear, but his size thirteen feet that foiled Eric in the end. 'My body was doing all right,' said the big American; 'it was my feet that got stuck.' He had been in the cave for almost two hours when he felt his boots jam against the ancient river bed. No amount of twisting could make them clear the low ceiling. 'That's it for me,' said Eric finally. Ahead of him he could see the soles of Conor's comparatively small size nines; their owner gave a chuckle and swore softly in Gaelic. It was a long way back, but at least it was head first.

To survey the caves, the Venturers stayed underground for days at a time. Charting the wild caves was only one part of the job. Dave Mihalic, superintendent of Mammoth, geologist George Gregory, a resource management specialist, and the Cave Research Foundation presented Raleigh with a number of tasks. Hameed Dhaif, a Bahraini engineering student, Jimmy Bankhead, a 17-year-old Choctaw Indian from Denver, Whitney Warren, Gareth Thompson and others including Orlin Iron Cloud (who next year would take his place in the Sun Dance), researched the caves, destroyed the algae which grew in the light of torches and cleaned the rubbish and graffiti that man somehow seems compelled to leave behind him.

Pamlico Sound, North Carolina, 1 September 1988

Eleven hundred kilometres to the east, on the very edge of the ocean, another part of the US expedition was exploring a very different underwater world: the graveyard of the Atlantic. In the shoaling waters of North Carolina's barrier islands more than 500 ships had run aground on the 'Outer Banks' of the Pamlico Sound.

Raleigh's twentieth-century travellers therefore had their pick of coral-covered wrecks – the SS *Huron*, for example, that ran aground and sank in 1877 taking ninety-eight lives with her. Here on the east coast of the continent Venturers also excavated the newly discovered Pomioac Indian village and made an extraordinary discovery when they found the SS *Curlew*, a Civil War casualty forgotten for 125 years. With Captain John Hilhorst, the New Zealander who had been such an asset to the Alaskan expedition, they sailed through swells and lashing gales, learned to navigate shallow sounds and steer a straight course right through the night. Since Welsh navigator Matthew James was deaf, he shone his torch on to the mouths of the crew to make lip reading easier in the dark.

During the past four years many young people with physical handicaps have taken part in Operation Raleigh. Some, like Matthew, were able to cope easily with the hardships of an expedition. Others found ways to match their abilities with their disabilities – often surprising themselves at how much they could do.

Working with her band of international colleagues, Michelle Redwater of the Lakota Sioux tribe was in Appalachia helping to build a barrier-free trail at Balsam Lake that could be used by both disabled and able-bodied people. First-hand advice was provided by those who would actually have to navigate the forest paths in wheelchairs and by others who were blind or deaf and therefore couldn't spot a twisted root or hear a warning cry of 'Danger!' Janie Robinson, executive director of Patterns, Inc., herself confined to a wheelchair by spina bifida, worked closely with the Raleigh Venturers. They, for their part, would forever be more aware of the frustrations felt by those who cannot always help themselves.

Close to the marshy spit of land where still other Venturers were working on a marine archaeology project, Sir Walter Raleigh had hoped that his settlers of 1584 would build a great city. It was his second attempt at colonizing America. Transatlantic resupply trips in tall ships took a bit of time, however, and when the vessels finally returned to Roanoke Island three years later the settlers had vanished without trace. Their ghosts haunt the Carolinas.

On the eastern shoulder of South America other young people set off to follow a different set of footsteps left by the great explorer – this time in the jungles of Guyana where Raleigh searched for the fabled gold of El Dorado.

Somehow, Sir Walter Raleigh never ran out of dreams. He seemed to have an inexhaustible supply. While neither our expedition nor Sir Walter's own found the lost city, the Venturers did find a little gold, and a few brought home a nugget or two that they had panned in the shallows of the fast-flowing rivers. They also found piranhas and jaguars and rainforests.

Although some may doubt there can be any 'lost cities' when most of the world is known and mapped, the great Inca city of Machu Picchu was found by a history professor from Yale University, Hiram Bingham, only eighty years ago. Perhaps like Machu Picchu, El Dorado may still be there, buried deep in a remote mountain valley, or covered by an impenetrable web of lianas – waiting.

CHAPTER NINE

Guyana

Lost Cities of Gold

(*Expedition Leader*: Major Charles Daniel)

Frenchman's Creek, August 1988

Balancing lightly on fallen logs, the young Parisian wandered deeper into the rainforest, crossing the wine-coloured rivulets that fed into Frenchman's Creek, a tributary of the mighty Essequibo. Before her flew butterflies, motes of white and electric blue lit by sunbeams. Not much sun, however, found its way down to Agnès Boutier and her American companion because the light had to penetrate a leafy canopy of primary forest seventy metres high, supported by buttressed tree trunks and webbed with strangling vines, ferns and fungi.

The deep rumble of a motor echoed suddenly through the wilderness. The two girls stopped, listening to the unfamiliar noises of machinery and man. They and a small group of others on the Guyana expedition were about as far away from civilization as one could be. Under the auspices of Guyanese engineer Terence Fletcher, they were repairing the last of the seven bridges that sixty years ago had allowed the cattle ranchers of the southern savannah to drive their beasts over the hazardous route to Georgetown, the seacoast capital and principal market. The laughter and noise they now heard could only mean one thing: gold miners.

Using one hand to ward off the mosquitoes and blackflies and the other to grasp the vines that fell like sheets from a ship, the girls followed the sounds to a clearing spotlighted by sunshine. The scene before them looked like a stage set: eight men of various hues of black and brown were stripped to the waist. Barefoot and shining with sweat they laboured in their stream looking for gold.

'Hello,' called Agnès, in her lilting French accent. 'We've come to visit you.'

As the girls stepped from the logs on to the creek bank, the men looked up incredulously. They had been in the jungle for weeks; they would stay a bit longer and then sell what nuggets they had found in Georgetown. First to recover from his surprise was Allan Percival Reece, the gang's leader and a true gentleman of the jungle. He gave her a friendly grin and introduced the other 'pork knockers', as the gold miners here are called. Most of the men had the mixed blood and European names (Gerry Hope, John Bennett, Troy Philips and Silvester Domingo) of their adventurous forebears – the great-grandfather of the two Allicock brothers hailed from Scotland. Using nothing more complex than a pump, hose and cylinders of bark, the men worked with an energy bred of fever – gold fever.

Gold is not the only fever known in the humid forests of Guyana. 'It's a fine life,' said Allan as he riddled sand through an oil drum, 'except for the malaria. Everyone has it. That and the kaboura flies.' Allan Percival Reece failed to mention some of the additional hazards that greeted the Venturers in Guyana: piranhas that can strip the flesh from a drowning bullock in seconds; vampire bats that suck blood and can introduce paralytic rabies or Chagas' disease – the horrible illness that killed Darwin which begins like malaria and ends like AIDS; leishmaniasis which first attacks the soft cartilage of the nose and goes on to destroy the other extremities; and onchocerciasis or river blindness, caused by worms transmitted by the bite of the tiny blackfly. The worms find their way into one eye, and, as soon as that habitat becomes crowded, migrate under the skin across the bridge of the nose to the other eye – a disconcerting journey to watch.

Notably, Allan neglected to include real exotica such as furry tarantulas the size of a mop, jaguars, electric eels capable of producing a 640-volt shock, rattlesnakes and aggressive bushmasters whose fangs can penetrate a leather boot. In particular, he made no reference to the dreaded candiru, the 'toothpick fish', which is said to swim up a careless swimmer's urine stream, and enter the urethra. There, I am told, it uses its prickly spines to burrow itself firmly: the pain is said to be spectacular.

Having separated the sand from the larger chunks of quartz, gold miner Leslie Allicock swirled it round and round in a metal batel shaped like a coolie's hat. First the larger pebbles washed over the rim, followed by the coarser sand and finally the finest black grains. Nestled in the hollow of the batel was a coin-sized circle of gold. Agnès looked around her, at the hardworking men out to make their fortunes, the russet waters of Frenchman's Creek and the impenetrable jungle beyond. A student at France's most prestigious business school, the École Supérieure de Commerce de Paris, and sponsored by one of the country's major economic forces, Électricité de France-Gaz de France, Agnès knew that she was watching man's drive for riches at its most powerful level. Here were gold and diamonds for the digging, and somewhere nearby, a lost city of gold. The miners were driven by a dream that had led many to their deaths, among them Sir Walter Raleigh. Theirs was the dream of El Dorado.

El Dorado, Somewhere in South America, Date Unknown

As his father had done and his father before him, the young ruler of the powerful Incas stood silently as his servants coated his body with resin and then powdered it with gold dust. Huge torches lit the night and reflected off his thighs and shoulders as he walked to the edge of the lake. Stepping on to the waiting raft manned by ten attendants, the chief was rowed to the centre where he slipped into the dark, calm waters. Gleaming showers of precious dust washed from his body and streaked the dark lake as they slowly sank to the bottom. With the dust went treasures - helmets, pendants and jewelled serpents of gold and emeralds.

The chief was 'El Dorado', 'The Golden One', master of untold wealth and purveyor of power beyond imagination. Yet his magic was not sufficient to resist the gunpowder of the Spanish. When Columbus landed on the northeast coast of Guyana in 1498, others charted his wake and eventually brought the kingdom of the Incas to its knees. The ruthless *conquistadores* found enough treasure to fill the holds of a hundred galleons but never discovered El Dorado's motherlode. Other famous sixteenth-century explorers turned their ships to the southern continent. They, too, wanted a share of the fabled booty looted from Peru and Mexico by Francisco Pizarro and Hernán Cortés. Many were convinced that somewhere between the Amazon and the Orinoco lay the lost city of El Dorado.

Amongst those who sought for El Dorado was Sir Walter Raleigh. In 1595 he sent an expedition to the mouth of the Orinoco River and penetrated some 640 kilometres inland. The first of his two expeditions brought him hardship and disease; the second, undertaken in 1616 when he was sixty-four years old, sick and partly paralysed from thirteen years in the Tower, brought him death. On his return to England, empty-handed and accused of breaking the peace with Spain, the brightest courtier of Elizabeth I's court was beheaded by King James.

Guyana had taken almost everything dear to Raleigh - his health and his son - but that virgin wilderness never robbed him of his courage or his dreams: 'I never saw a more beautiful country, nor more lively prospects; hills so raised here and there over the valleys, the river winding into divers branches, the plains adjoining without bush or stubble, all fair green grass, the ground hard sand to march on, either for horse or foot, the deer crossing every path, the birds towards the evening singing on every tree with a thousand different tunes, cranes and herons of white, crimson and carnation perching on the river's side, the air fresh with a gentle easterly wind, and every stone that we stopped to take up either gold or silver by its complexion.'

Until his death on 19 October 1618, only two years after his return from Guyana, the old explorer still believed that with just a few more men and a pocketful of gold he would find the kingdom hidden somewhere near the 'Mountains of the Moon'.

Agnès Boutier and the other Venturers rebuilding Bridge 7 – Brian Ross of Ross-shire, Scotland, Marcy Andrew and Julie Halpern of the United States, and a smattering of English including Maurice 'Wicksey' Kell, Mark 'Blue' Millican, Jack Bowyer, George Hadigate and project leader Jeremy Fish, knew that the Elizabethan's dream lived on. 'It's here,' confided Maxwell, one of the youngest of the pork knockers. 'A city of gold, with golden altars and pillars thirty metres high – somewhere in the mountains of Guyana.' Thoughtfully the young miner juggled a three-pennyweight nugget and a tiny diamond in the palm of his hand. 'I'd give a lot to find it.'

'If I had money I'd buy more machinery and I'd find it first,' challenged one of the Allicock brothers. The men turned their backs to the sun and continued to dig . . .

Kurupukari, Essequibo River, 12 August 1988

El Dorado is but one of the fables as big as the Ritz that the gold miners bank on. Another is that 'You can never pollute the jungle.' In this and other beliefs they differ from the indigenous people of Guyana, the Amerindians, who use their land and its resources carefully. Some of the stories of the Amerindians were collected by Dr Sally Anderson, a tall, straight-talking strawberry blonde who had sailed as a Venturer through the notorious Bass Strait on *Zebu* just two years before.

For these imaginative and handsome people, the jungle is as full of danger as it is of useful materials. Here lurks the one-eyed Bush Di-Di who abducts pretty maidens at night, and the masters of the Jambies' arrow, a weapon which shoots tiny pepper seeds into the skin. The elf-like Knoc-o-fo-knoc-o, a creature with straight legs and a large head and belly, will steal your power unless you strike him first in which case he becomes your slave, and the dreaded Kanaime, a person who can turn into a bird or animal and whistles at night to lure you into the forest. If it catches you, the Kanaime will push its iguana tail into your bottom, pull out your intestines, tie them in knots and replace them. You lose the power of speech – among other things – and never, ever recover . . .

The Raleigh camp at Kurupukari was once the resting place for cattle on their arduous journey to Georgetown. Now, as then, the piranhas and caimans have custody of the Essequibo River, the people of the tiny Amerindian settlement of Fairview hunt jaguar, distil medicines from plants and shrubs, pound cassava and collect ripe mangoes as they fall from the trees. Purple orchids still grow in profusion and the legendary river pilots, Captain David Andreis and Captain Roy Bowen, sons of the founders of Fairview, continue to challenge the rapids and chart the ever-changing Essequibo. For three months in the summer of 1988, however, Nick Horne set up his jungle headquarters on the north bank of this wide, brown river. It was a camp of remarkable beauty, populated by kingfishers and toucans, scarlet ibis and laughing falcons. It was also a camp of constant rain and persistent mosquitoes, of chiggers, maggots and blackfly, where piranha and pineapple provided the only fresh food for the expedition. In keeping with local practice, the loo was a ladder slung across the river and daily body checks, by one's 'buddy' for sores and bites in the most intimate of places, were essential for health. It did not take long for the message to spread to other Operation Raleigh sites: Kurupukari was not for the faint-hearted.

It was from Kurupukari that Venturers, in the company of Nick Horne and expedition leader Charlie Daniel, canoed across the river to Fairview to build a school for the village children, from here that they departed to repair the bridges deep in the humid rainforest, and from here they left to cross the swamp and jungle that some called the 'Cattle Trail' but most called hell.

Educated by an Oxford don who had drifted to the faraway town of Bartica, Roy Marshall, an Amerindian of Arawak and French descent, was determined that the children in the remote hamlet of Fairview should have a school. As a youth he had worked as a gold miner and dived for diamonds, plunging twenty metres beneath the Mazaruni equipped with only a hose, face mask and the hope of escaping the bends that tied men up like pretzels. Now, thirty years old, he grew a subsistence crop of bananas, sweet and bitter cassava, sugar cane and pineapples, and fought the armies of brown achioushi ants that attacked his crops each year.

Taking the wave of international young people in his stride, Roy and the other Amerindians of Fairview taught them how to make cassava bread, hunt boar and jaguar, and harvest wood for the school; pump wood bark for the roof and sides, black yari yari for the frames and levelled trunks of palm for the floors. Up at dawn, Venturers such as Catriona Morrison from the Isle of Lewis, Othneil Beckles from Guyana and Lee Ford, Sue Crimlisk and Hugo de Rijke from England, headed off in canoes, going miles upriver to find just the right timber. If their search was successful the real work began, felling the trees and bringing them back to Fairview. Often the tops of the heavily laden canoes barely rose above the water, and the effort of transporting 189 kilos of wood against the current in equatorial heat built muscles that should last for life.

Heading out from Kurupukari, the bridge-building teams slung their hammocks on buttressed trees, built shelters against the constant rain and easily sweated off their high-calorie rations. Their work was illuminated by electric storms that lit the forest for miles. The Venturers cut and dragged massive logs of greenheart (*Ocotea rodiaei*) using chains and ropes and strong, young backs. Like purpleheart, (*Peltogyne pubescens*), named after the crimson sap that gushes like blood and turns a violent purple, greenheart is a remarkably tough and beautiful tree. Both are resistant to termites, marine borers, fire and water, qualities not always essential to their other uses as fishing rods, longbows and the decorative butts of billiard cues.

The interlocked grain of greenheart gives the wood its incredible weight – 1030 kilograms per cubic metre. Dragging their twenty-five-metre logs to the river bed, the ragged Raleigh chain gangs bore a distinct resemblance to the Inca slaves of El Dorado. Occasionally the momentum pitched the huge logs into the river: heavier than water, they sank without any prospect of salvage.

The Cattle Trail, Central Guyana, 17 August 1988

Without breaking stride, John Ayling leant forward, tightening the belt of his rucksack to shift its weight higher on to his shoulders. He had shaved his skull to coax the last bit of coolness from the air, and looked like a Buddhist monk as he slashed his way through the thick undergrowth with a razor-edged machete.

Through the swaying brush, John caught a glimpse of Brigid Averly's flame-red hair. Before her trudged Nicholas Papapfio whose home was Belfast but whose roots were in Guyana, and the universally popular Singaporean leader, Farid Hamid, whose enthusiasm for jungle life was infectious even under the toughest of conditions. Fallen trees and branches vied with creeping vines, mud and swamp. With nothing but jungle in every direction, river crossings provided a welcome distraction, as one tried to keep vertical on slippery logs covered by a metre and a half of dark, fast water.

The Cattle Trail is another of the legends of Guyana: hundreds of kilometres of almost impenetrable track slicing the country from its Atlantic shoulder south to the vast ranches of the Rupununi. The word 'trail' is largely euphemistic. Pioneered in 1922 by courageous ranchers like Sandy McTurk, who hoped to drive his cattle to the markets of Georgetown, it hadn't been used for years, although huge herds of Brahmins once braved the jaguars and piranhas to go from the town of Lethem, on the border of Brazil, north to Kurupukari and the capital. On that tortuous journey, each animal lost an average of forty kilos – if it managed to stay alive.

Now, sixty-six years later, Sandy's great-granddaughter, Diane McTurk, ranched the land at Rupununi; Operation Raleigh had been asked to assess the possibility of building an all-weather trail from these remote areas to the markets of the north. Everyone, and certainly Roderick, the Amerindian guide from Fairview, knew that the trek would not be easy, but no one could foresee the injuries, illness and danger that lay ahead.

Only two days out of Kurupukari an accident happened which forced three people to return to base camp. The track had deteriorated to the point where only Roderick could read the route, following old machete marks scarring the trees. The pace slowed noticeably as expedition members stopped to help companions who had fallen in the thick, slippery mud. It had taken the Venturers three hours, wading through knee-high swamp, to cover about as many kilometres. Neil Hendry, Barry 'Baz' Cochran and Nigel Symonds wielded their machetes skilfully as they carved a route for the others to follow. As Neil slashed his way forward, his bush hat was knocked off by a low hanging branch. When he reached to retrieve it Baz's machete sliced through his hand, cutting the muscles in a long, deep gash.

'Blood poured from my hand as I tried to pull the open wound together,' recalled Neil. Quickly Lorraine Strudwick and Brigid bound the cut and laid Neil on his back. The others built a platform of rucksacks to hoist him above the swamp. That night the mosquitoes came in like Stinger missiles and with no dry wood for a fire, the group spent an uncomfortable night, awakened by the scream of howler monkeys – far louder than any lion or elephant – and by the soft, low growl of a jaguar scenting blood. Fearing infection, Farid sent Neil back to base camp with Baz and Carol Blackburn; both had volunteered without hesitation. Jean Lumb, our energetic GP whose hobby is rally driving and whose nickname is 'Mum', met the trio halfway. Quickly she stripped to wash in the brown river as a 'pre-surgery cleanup', then deftly stitched Neil's hand in an operating theatre of razor grass, vines and towering trees.

Only twelve intrepid survivors remained on the Cattle Trail. Dropping to all fours as they climbed under fallen trees and holding packs aloft as they waded through rivers, it was a very dirty dozen that pushed on, some days covering only five or ten miles as they hacked their way through the belly of Guyana. There was worse to come. The mosquitoes, always bad, became a black wall, leaving a pattern of bites that soon became septic. On the third day, the PRC 320 radio died, unable to withstand a constant bath in bogs and rain. Communication with base camp ended.

They continued on, heading southwest to Surama. The fourth and fifth days were spent in the swamps near the Iwokrama Mountains which they couldn't see: jungle closed in all around them. The thick, slimy water was so deep that soon the

Venturers had to swim from tree to tree, hauling themselves along trailing vines and traversing deeper stretches with ropes. At night they split palm logs and built a hearth above the swamp, managing to light a fire with splinters of a special wood known only to Roderick. The meagre cheer of a hot brew of coffee and swamp water was quickly extinguished. Guyana's cattle trail was testing the Venturers to their limits.

Three days short of Surama, Roderick succumbed to malaria. The guide's illness endangered his life and those of the expedition members. Only he could read the message of the hidden trail-blazes; only he had ever made the journey before. Turning pale under his dark skin, Roderick's temperature soared.

Then a new danger struck. On the same day that Roderick fell ill, Allison Hollington was hit by an electric eel. The pain travelled up from her calf to her shoulder, exploding in waves that racked her slim body. 'Get out of the water! Get out of the water!' screamed Ally as the serpent-like fish, as thick as a man's leg, circled and turned to attack again. The long fin cut a wake that charted its path like a knife.

Near hysterics, Ally's instinctive concern was for her companions. They heard her rising notes of panic and struggled out of the evil water to the safety of tree branches. In seconds Farid had shrugged off his pack and was by her side, dragging her on to higher ground. He knew that most creatures die if struck by an electric eel; a charge of 640 volts paralyses and eventually causes its victims to drown.

The eel's fearful attack on Ally had come out of the blue and made the small band even more aware of the dangers which surrounded them. Some they could see, others lurked, invisible, in this dark and sinister land which they were determined to cross. Roderick did recover from his bout of recurring malaria, but long after Allison's spasms of fear subsided, it still took great courage to shoulder her pack, put on a smile and step again into the fetid swamp that led to Surama. She did.

Kaiteur Falls, 15 September 1988

Guyana was in the midst of an economic crisis when my assistant Sally Cox and I arrived. National bankruptcy seemed imminent as we arrived in Georgetown from London via Trinidad. Georgetown has one of my least favourite airports since it takes two and a half hours and a five-dollar bill simply to pass from one airline to another. I was not in the best of moods.

We had moved our Brazilian expedition to Guyana at a few months' notice after a massacre of Indians on the Amazon, in the very area we hoped to work, led to the cancellation of government permission. The local authorities were keeping the decks clear of foreigners while they sorted out the mess. Meanwhile, Charlie and Jasmina Daniel had been pulled out of the Amazon and were about to be despatched to Guyana.

'Same sort of swamps, bugs, disease, snakes, jungle, mud, heat, rain - so go for it Charlie,' I'd said, stabbing the map with an African dagger.

'Who do we know there?' my practical pal enquired.

Sally passed me the battered address book I carry everywhere. I thumbed quickly to the end of the alphabet. 'Temple,' I said. 'Sir Jack.'

Now that this expedition was coming to an end, and sipping a hard-earned Glenfiddich at the Pegasus, a Trust House Forte hotel in Georgetown which had so generously provided our headquarters, I was relieved that it had all turned out well. Medical surveys had been carried out for diabetes, gastroenteritis and malaria at the river villages of Orealla and Sipurata, botanical studies undertaken, and stellings, or wharfs, constructed for local communities which relied on the rivers as lifelines. Wells had been dug, schools and churches repaired and community centres and bridges built for people who had long despaired of any government help. And, in between, the Venturers had proven they had what it took to walk the Cattle Trail to Brazil, build rafts of bamboo and ikana vines, navigate the Burro-Burro rapids and even body raft for days on end down stretches of river few others had ever seen.

Along with Jack Temple's contacts, we were indebted to those who had come to our aid from the start. Among them were Fabian Liverpool, one of my Sandhurst cadets now in the government; David Small, the British High Commissioner; Clifford Reis, managing director of Banks D'Aguair Industrial Holdings; Bernard Crawford of BIDCO; Colonel Carl Morgan and Brigadier Joe Singh. Joe is a true adventurer who had helped the 1971 SES-backed expedition to Roraima, the mountain of Conan Doyle's *Lost World* which links Venezuela, Guyana and Brazil. Joe cuts a dashing figure in his bright blue combat fatigues, peaked cap, jungle boots and pistol. He loves the wild places and is the inspirational commander of the National Service Corps of young Guyanese who are giving something back to their country.

As September heralded the end of the expedition in this remarkable country, Joe Singh arranged for the only available helicopter - a Russian M18 Hind - to take me to Kaiteur Falls, the second highest waterfall in the world and nearly five times the height of Niagara. It was to prove a fortunate arrangement.

Deep in the virgin forest of the Potaro River, a tributary of the Essequibo which the expedition had come to know so well, the eternal column of water thunders over a cliff 249 metres high and drops into a gorge of rainbows. The Venturers had beaten me to the falls, and they had taken the hard way. Only days before, on 10 September, Grant McPherson, Penny Pepper and their jungle-toughened team had reached this beautiful but inhospitable place. Theirs had been a remarkable achievement: negotiating countless rapids, two-metre 'stoppers' and 1100 kilometres of river in two Avon inflatables equipped with Mariner engines. No one had ever done it before, and I seriously doubt if anyone will ever attempt it again.

Along the way they had panned for the gold and diamonds that had lured Sir Walter Raleigh to Guyana, danced in a pork knockers' brothel, discovered copper and brass helmets abandoned by treasure divers and climbed daily to the top of the falls. Kaiteur's veil of beauty hid a wealth of danger. Two days after they arrived, Mark Millican, an inner city Venturer from Newcastle, awoke with clammy skin, the shakes and a terrible headache. When nurse Penny Pepper took his temperature, it was 105°F. Suspecting malaria, she put him on a drip and made him swallow Fansidar tablets.

Penny Pepper was absolutely right. When Charlie, Jasmina and I flew out again from Kaiteur, we had another passenger with us. We left behind an exuberant team – some of whom also came down with malaria – some words of encouragement and, most important, thread and patches to repair the Avons.

They had made it to Kaiteur but they still had a long way back to Georgetown.

CHAPTER TEN

United Kingdom and Portugal

Closer to Home

(*United Kingdom Leader*: Lieutenant-Colonel Mike Reynolds, KOSB)

(*Portugal Leader*: Commandante Luis Bilreiro, Portuguese Navy)

London, 4 July 1988

The two Inuit boys stood rooted to the spot as the great red monster lumbered remorselessly towards them. Polar bears don't scare these intrepid Arctic hunters but, without even a harpoon to hand, here was something quite different.

'What on earth is it?' gasped Ron Petooloosie who was a long way from his home on Canada's Baffin Island.

'Why it's a double decker bus,' replied one of his new English friends as the vehicle rumbled past. Ron and his fellow Inuit, David Arreak, stared after it in astonishment. Indeed, most of the international Venturers who took part in our British expedition experienced one sort of cultural shock or another. It may seem strange that we should invite young people to explore the United Kingdom, but the request had come from a number of our friends whose countries we had visited and who felt that some sort of exchange would be useful. John Townend, who had led our team in Hawaii in 1985, took on the initial planning whilst Peter Leicester put the idea to our international committees. In early July 1988, twenty-four Venturers from Australia, Bahrain, Canada, Hong Kong, Japan, Kenya, Malaysia, Oman, Pakistan, Singapore and the United States arrived in London. Their style of dress was as varied as their English.

Working closely with our UK division, Mike Reynolds, an adventurous colonel, had set up projects in England, Scotland, Wales and Northern Ireland and Roger Chapman, our plans director at CHQ, had chartered a 30-metre schooner, *Jean de la Lune*. I met the international group as they prepared to leave for the 'British outback' and was immediately impressed by their enthusiasm for this country. The fact that it had rained from the moment they set foot on British soil did nothing to dampen their spirits.

To acclimatize the group Jim Shand, a Birmingham youth officer, had arranged five days travelling in a narrow-boat through the canals of central England. Navigating the confined waterways and the numerous locks, several of the Venturers took a ducking, but they were in fine form when they started their community aid projects.

Around Birmingham they stayed with families and helped at schools, camps and institutions, working mainly with handicapped or deprived children. David Arreak, one of the Inuit, used his patience and charm to defuse the frustrations of some of the deaf youngsters, whilst quadruple amputee Tracy Schmitt of Ontario proved to those less handicapped than herself that physical disability can be overcome by dedication to other people's difficulties.

One of the most unusual tasks fell to Esa Salmam Daif from Bahrain who found himself teaching Arab calligraphy to a class of inner city schoolchildren. Most of them were of Pakistani origin and Esa was able to communicate with them in Urdu, their first language and his second.

In the beautiful Margam County Park in South Wales, the rain was torrential; the team building a log cabin for the disabled were rarely dry. With the help of the Porthcawl Golf Club, Wilkie Burden, our energetic local co-ordinator, had raised £3000 towards the cost of materials and the project had created quite a lot of interest in the community. Ian Grist, Assistant Secretary of State for Wales, came with me to see the job, led that day by Venturer Allan Muna of Kenya. Our conversation highlighted one of the major strengths Operation Raleigh possesses.

'It's strange how Operation Raleigh has managed to link up so many nationalities from different parts of the world,' I told the minister. 'At this moment, in Alaska, there are Welsh building log cabins, in Kenya there are Scots building rhino sanctuaries, and here in Wales we have Africans, Inuit, Japanese, Omanis and Malaysians all working together.'

Meanwhile, on Flatholm Island in the Bristol Channel an ecology study was in progress. Venturer Saffad Syed of Pakistan and his team became used to getting up in the middle of the night to monitor the movements of numbered limpets by moonlight. The Channel waters are rarely calm. Sudden storms toss up walls of green water and effectively cut off the island; this made life uncomfortable for all of the Venturers, but for Tracy Schmitt it caused a serious problem. She had broken one of her artificial legs on arrival, and although the Rookwood Ex-service Hospital in Cardiff had repaired the limb, it looked as if the Canadian girl would have to continue her expedition in a wheelchair unless someone could reach her on the remote island.

To the rescue came the South Wales constabulary who contacted the RAF. Tracy's repaired leg was flown in by a rescue helicopter. When the group arrived in Scotland, Tracy left her colleagues to tackle the hills and once again put her pronounced leadership qualities to good use, working at the Fort William Centre for the Handicapped.

Off the Scottish west coast, *Jean de la Lune* battled through other summer gales, giving Venturers a real taste of Britain's best adventure training area. Seasickness was a new experience for many of the crew on their way to Belfast where Stan Baird, our co-ordinator, had arranged a testing programme.

Reports from Northern Ireland were not good. The newspaper headlines were of IRA murders, ambushes and bombs. Mike Douglis of Los Angeles wondered if he could buy a bullet-proof vest with his American credit card, but the warm civic welcome laid on by the Belfast City Council quickly dispelled most fears. Using bicycles and boats, the Venturers deployed to their camp at Shanes Castle on the shores of Lough Neagh.

The final test, the ascent of Blaven on Skye, stretched everyone's reserves. Alex Wong of California found he'd lost 7 kilograms and Zabrina Hamid from Singapore put in a remarkable performance, carrying a pack equal to half her own weight up the mountain.

In spite of the misgivings I'd had in planning a UK expedition there was no doubt it had been a success; the young people from eleven countries had seen more of Britain than many who live in our islands. Our good friends Robert and Snuffy Mills gave a splendid farewell party for the expedition at the London club, Les Ambassadeurs, and Lord Glenarthur, Minister of State at the Foreign and Commonwealth Office and a great supporter of Operation Raleigh, summed up the general feeling. 'It really has been a case of people from each of the five continents carrying their energy and enthusiasm to the four corners of the United Kingdom,' he said. 'And for some of the very best causes: help for the handicapped and underprivileged, and the essential task of getting to know one another better.'

The Algarve, Portugal, 24 July 1988

The cultural and social ties between Britain and her oldest ally, Portugal, have been greatly encouraged by the Gulbenkian Foundation, which has also done much to support us. Portuguese naval officers have been involved in a number of our expeditions and I was very interested in Engenheiro Luis de Guimaraes Lobato's suggestion that we organize one in Portugal. Luis, apart from being president of the sail training organization, Aporvela, is the Gulbenkian Foundation's administrator. With his backing, a small expedition was planned. Fourteen Venturers from Australia, Britain, Japan and Portugal were joined by sixteen others from the brigantine *Zebu*; their berths aboard were taken by young Portuguese.

The projects were mainly situated in the extreme north and south of the country. Those in the south were based around Monchique, a medieval town situated at the highest point of the Algarve. Here the principal task was to restore a seventeenth-century monastery which had been left a ruin by the same earthquake that destroyed Lisbon in 1755, and the local council gave us *carte blanche* to buy the equipment and materials required. Directed by Jim Bury of London, the team cleared the vast building of thick weeds and shrubs, repaired and protected the walls and helped produce a plan to guide the council in future work, including categorizing the urgency and level of skill required for each task.

Over ten tonnes of materials had to be manhandled to the top of the twenty-metre walls where Venturers perched, mixing cement to repair and cap the walls. The work began before dawn – just as soon as it was light enough to see – and continued until the intense heat of the mid-morning sun threatened to crack the cement. The group were almost arrested when they built a bonfire within the walls to burn some of the scrub. They hadn't known that the danger of conflagration was great and fires were prohibited. Only the intervention of the mayor prevented them spending a night in a Portuguese jail. Quick to make the most of the situation, however, the Venturers persuaded the fire brigade to hose down the freshly laid cement to prevent it from cracking.

Concerned by the effects of tourism on the traditional culture, the local council commissioned us to record the architecture, communications and facilities of three traditional and undisturbed Algarve villages, and the occupations and aspirations of their inhabitants, as the first step in a long-term historical study of the area. The population of one tiny village, where no one was under thirty and most were overdue for retirement, desperately wanted a school. Their hope was that a school would bring children and the much needed rejuvenation of the village. Another village harboured less lofty aims. They merely wanted an extra goat. All were sheltered from the impact of the tourist industry by just a few kilometres of narrow lanes, and the unadventurousness of visitors who failed to find the 'real Portugal'.

In this Portuguese-speaking Shangri-la the expedition was befriended by a Buddhist monk who had fled Tibet, and entertained by a local lady botanist named Zelia Sakai. Previously married to a Japanese and strongly influenced by his culture, she encouraged the young to study herbal medicine, botany and environmentally friendly lifestyles at her beautiful oriental-style home. She had developed effective organic crop protection techniques and was undoubtedly a brilliant amateur scientist. With the aid of Australian Tania Pontel, she revealed the secrets of various massage techniques, which held the interest of all of the Venturers.

The northern projects were in an isolated and mountainous region thirty kilometres from the nearest town, Braganca. Their base was a large house, with a rather grand appearance but with no water, electricity, fixtures, furniture, communications or transport of any kind. Water had to be collected from the River Tuella in the steep valley below – a fifteen-minute walk down and an eternity climbing back.

The tasks included surveys of trekking routes. The Venturers' reports, complete with illustrations by our artists Matthew Cook and Matthew Lawrence, and maps expertly drawn by former Venturer Paddy Clark, gave the embryonic visitor information service a tremendous boost. As in the south, a comprehensive sociological survey of villages was undertaken.

Exploring the Tagus River on the Aporvela, the ketch *Buzio* gave the Venturers a chance to flex a different set of muscles: the boat had an uncanny knack of finding uncharted sandbanks and only brute strength could budge her. Others sailed a racing yacht to an archaeological dive off the coast on an eighteenth-century wreck. With them was Japanese Venturer Yukari Suzuki. She feared becoming seasick and longed to try out the new anti-seasickness remedy: self-adhesive medicated patches worn behind the ear. None could be found, but her friends produced some corn plasters and, with the aid of straight faces and a few white lies, convinced her that these would have the desired effect. Bearing in mind that *Buzio* encountered many a gale on the way home, Yukari's rude good health on arrival spoke volumes about the power of the mind.

When I visited Portugal to thank Luis Lobato and his supporters for their kind help I was very interested to hear of a growing interest by the Portuguese in the development of youth leadership schemes, and of a protocol that had recently been agreed with Britain on implementing others. Hopefully Raleigh has done something to strengthen a new link with an old ally.

London, 30 June 1988

By mid-1987 it was clear that Operation Raleigh had been a success, and many thought it should continue. The management of such a large organization was outgrowing the expertise of the Scientific Exploration Society however, and its council had grown rather weary of the long fund-raising campaign and of the inevitable personality clashes. In 1986, in an effort to sort things out, I had returned to CHQ, now based in a former electricity generating station in Chelsea. The council brought in 'new blood' – some of it in the form of chartered accountant Tony Nowell, formerly Managing Director of Guinness in Malaysia, who became the chairman of the executive and directed our commercial affairs. He found that the 'black holes' in our projected cash-flow were nothing like as deep as some had forecast. Under his careful handling of our resources, we completed the first phase of Raleigh's projected plans with a modest credit.

Another newcomer, barrister Caroline Peel-Yates, was appointed Tony's deputy. She did a superb job in marketing the series of Operation Raleigh TV programmes made by young filmmakers. These were backed by many organizations including the BBC, the Post Office and British Rail. The idea, originally organized by Maurice Taylor, then chairman of our US operation, resulted in a series of six half-hour programmes screened all over the world.

Expeditions thrive on good logistics and I was most fortunate to be able to persuade an old friend, Royal Engineer Major Dick Festorazzi, to take over our vital Support Division and give a boost to the field administration. After long and excellent service, our PR Director, Captain Harry Cook, retired and was succeeded by Stuart Arnold, formerly of the Midland Bank. His many overseas contacts were to prove especially useful. Ably assisted by press officer Alison Blyth Brook, he kept us in the public eye. Otherwise our senior people remained as before with the sad exception of Sally Cox, my highly efficient and charming assistant. But before departing for a job in the Persian Gulf she managed to recruit a hardworking Zimbabwean lady, Barbara Carlisle, to keep me in order.

Luckily we had a most capable team of field directors to lead the expeditions and I was able to leave much of the organizing to them. It was marvellous to know, when I was abroad, that Headquarters was in good hands, and I relied confidently on our Chief of Staff, Geoff Straw.

From the 'Power House', as CHQ was aptly called, we directed planning, recruited Venturers and staff, raised funds, handled publicity and counted the pennies. Indeed, there was an air of economy and thrift which Territorial Army Major, Gordon Raeburn, oversaw as our Financial Director.

Hundreds of companies generously gave stores and equipment. Just to mention a few, IBM's computer – donated back in 1984 – did a magnificent job and was the brain of the organization. Robert Fleming's Bank gave us office furniture, DHL and later TNT helped with a free courier service, and Ernst and Whinney backed up our Finance Division.

Dick Festorazzi's team worked tirelessly with BCB Ltd to perfect palatable, lightweight expedition food and I was delighted when at last Venturers admitted they liked most of the largely dehydrated, high-calorie Raven ration; it had taken over three years to develop. Our Support Division also tested boots, cameras, clothing, survival knives, sleeping bags and tents to get the best value for money; a Raleigh recommendation was also much appreciated by manufacturers.

The British government backed our inner city scheme that provided young people with an opportunity they couldn't get at home. It was going well, with participants from urban areas now taking part in most expeditions. Jamie Robertson-

Macleod and his team in the Markham group had been with us since the start and were achieving excellent sponsorship results, especially in persuading large numbers of major corporations to send young employees on Operation Raleigh. By April 1989, almost 200 of these 'commercial' Venturers were joining us from over seventy firms each year. They came from widely different working backgrounds and, once having mixed with the youth of other nations, returned with a broader, more tolerant outlook, increased self-confidence and a greater ability to realize their potential. Clearly their companies saw this experience as a worthwhile way to develop character and enhance leadership skills in potential young managers.

A worldwide network of national and regional co-ordinators provided vital support; and Venturers returning from expeditions formed support groups to assist others who wished to join Raleigh, provide help within their communities and even run their own overseas projects.

Throughout, we received invaluable help from a wide range of supporters. Prince Charles had been an enormously energetic Patron, raising funds and the morale of all concerned; Princess Alexandra, whose daughter Marina had been a Venturer in 1985, was also an enthusiastic supporter. The Duke of Gloucester, a longstanding member of SES, encouraged the expeditions and attended many gatherings, and stars of screen, stage and radio were most generous with their assistance, as were leading businessmen and senior officers of the armed forces.

One general who visited our headquarters commented, 'Here you see a small number of bright, enthusiastic young people handling the same workload that would probably require the attention of a colonel, two lieutenant-colonels, four majors and a dozen civil servants in the Ministry of Defence.' Keeping the enthusiasm going was not difficult, but efficiency was sometimes hampered by the high turnover of staff, simply due to the fact that many were young men and women who needed to start a proper career. Most agreed, however, that working for Raleigh was fun.

It wasn't always easy for the Venturers who had to raise money by their own efforts. Some did sponsored parachute jumps, others swam the equivalent of a small ocean; Paddy Clark had persuaded a friend to do a sponsored crawl – on land. He managed almost fifty kilometres, enough for an entry in the *Guinness Book of Records*, and raised £800, but when I met him his knees and hands were bandaged and he could hardly walk. 'Greater love hath no man . . .' I thought.

Other fund-raising events included odd jobs, milk rounds, raffles and organizing balls. Angus Forbes found it difficult to excite his colleagues at Gordonstoun until he hit on the absolutely original idea of asking for sponsorship to eat three buckets of school slops! An enterprising chap called Eagle lived in a tree for rather a long time and a fearless girl spent a week in a pit full of snakes.

The ongoing selection tests were also fun to organize. 'It's always nice to watch others suffer as I did,' said a lass from Scotland, grinning maliciously. But those tests were a vital part of the process: we had to be certain that the Venturers could face the challenges in the bush, deserts, jungles, mountains, swamps and sea.

To organize the tests we had the 'Selection Weekend Administration Team' or SWATs, as its members were known, whose job was to think up new challenges. We still asked candidates to find a live python in a dark room, catch it and weigh it: sometimes we varied the test and substituted a gorilla. The minimum rate for hiring live apes was high, however, so the team hired gorilla suits and caused a major traffic jam when they tested them in a run around Trafalgar Square.

On one selection test candidates climbed down into a World War II air-raid shelter. The descent was via a concrete-lined shaft on a windy hillside overlooking Birmingham. The candidates had been given a flashlight and a measuring tape and told that at the bottom of the shaft they would find a wild animal which was quite harmless if they were calm and sensible: all they had to do was to measure its vital statistics. A young female biologist was the first to confront the angry 180-kilo gorilla that shambled out of the darkness emitting awful grunts and smelling pretty vile. Having a great love of animals, she overcame her fear and edged closer to the monster. It wore a muzzle, a necessary precaution to prevent it from biting, she was told. With some difficulty she obtained the required measurements and returned to the surface.

The sight of this pathetic underground prisoner bore heavily on her conscience, however, and she wrote a scorching letter to the press. Almost immediately the cause was taken up by animal rights groups and our phone lines at HQ buzzed with angry enquirers. For several days, our press officer did nothing to refute the reports by which time the story was assuming national proportions. Finally, when it appeared that the whole thing was getting totally out of hand, she let the truth be known: the poor mistreated animal in the air-raid shelter was in fact a Royal Marine officer in a gorilla suit. Everyone had a good laugh but alas our deception had been discovered, and we had to think of another method of testing courage: we borrowed a pet tarantula called Fifi.

Fifi proved to be one of the most effective deterrents of the faint-hearted and wriggled across many a sweaty palm. Eventually candidates discovered that the best way to calm the enraged tarantula was to gently stroke her hairy abdomen, and after a year-long massage, Fifi developed a bald patch. Her replacement cost fifty pounds.

Like large spiders, snakes hold a peculiar fascination for humans. Blissfully ignorant of the continuous rush and bustle on the fourth floor of the Chelsea Power House, a small python can usually be found asleep near the reception desk. Jemima, as she is fondly known, is another favourite at selection tests. One afternoon she was curled up in my in-tray, when a visitor remarked that he had never seen such a lifelike paperweight. I prodded her. Jemima slid gently across the desk. The visitor gasped and quickly staggered out into the safety of the King's Road.

Once I visited a selection weekend at a farmhouse deep in the English countryside. An army sergeant was in charge of the 'test of courage' and informed me that it consisted of a cow in a darkened stable. 'That doesn't sound too difficult,' I remarked. 'Just wait and see,' he grinned. Two bright-eyed young men from one of Britain's better-known private schools arrived, brimming with confidence. 'Right my lads,' growled the soldier. 'In here we have an animal and I want you to locate it in the dark and identify it – no flashlights allowed.' The youngsters entered the stable and a few moments later we heard a loud 'moo'. Then the door opened and one of the young men said, "Well sergeant, we reckon you've a cow in there.'

'Very good, very observant. Now here's a bucket and a stool, get back in there and milk it.'

A few minutes later there was a crash and a muffled yell from within.

'S-s-s-sergeant,' stammered the ashen-faced boy. 'Are you totally certain it's a cow?'

When the light was switched on it revealed a very perplexed bullock. All of the female candidates passed the test with flying colours.

CHAPTER ELEVEN

Kenya

Under African Skies

(*Expedition Leaders*: Lieutenant-Colonel Mark Watts, MBE LI
Lieutenant-Colonel Mike Reynolds, KOSB)

Tum, Northeast Province, Kenya, 6 October 1988

Crouching low to the ground, the *moran*, or warrior, drew his blunt-tipped arrow and aimed it at the steer's jugular vein. Three other *morans*, their ochre-daubed bodies glistening in the sun, held the animal still and filled leather vessels with the blood that flowed from the shallow wound. As the steer raced to rejoin the herd, the marksman lifted a gourd to his lips and drank the thick, warm liquid. The *moran* singled out a second donor; once tapped and released, it would not be caught again for several months.

The harvest of blood is a part of everyday life amongst these warrior-farmers. For centuries, the staple diet of the agile Samburu has been the blood and milk of their herds. Harriet Robinson, a long-limbed American from North Carolina, watched as a warrior stirred the liquid until it congealed into a crimson pillow on the stick. 'Like candy floss,' thought Harriet as she watched with fascination. Heated over the fire, the rich, red clot of blood was a treat for the Samburu children, who devoured it with gusto. Then, with the care of a painter mixing his oils, the *moran* poured the remaining blood into a pitcher of milk, blending his palette to a warm pink.

The famous, much-photographed Masai range mostly in the south of Kenya, grazing their vast herds of cattle and goats, but here in the dry northeast fringe of the country the camel is king, and among the patchwork of African tribes that tend them are the Samburu, an offshoot of the Masai, the Turkana and the Rendille. It is said that when a Rendille dies his brother mourns him with one eye and counts his camels with the other.

Like the frugal Rendille, Harriet Robinson and the other members of her expedition seemed to be always counting camels. Their objective was to cross the vast arid spaces of the Chalbi Desert, heading east to Lake Turkana, known as the

Jade Sea, and then southeast to the settlement of Rumuruti. Following local practice, the Venturers walked while their fleet of camels did the heavy work, each animal carrying up to 100 kilograms of food, kit and water lashed to their wishbone-shaped saddles. Intimidated at first by the arrogant creatures, the Venturers were quick to discover that both prow and stern of these desert ships could be dangerous: their sharp, yellow teeth could inflict a painful bite, and their loosely jointed legs could kick out in any direction.

In this autumn 1988 expedition two people took a special interest in the welfare of the animals: Welshman Mark Ford, ex-army and the table tennis champion for West Glamorgan, and Karron Milner, an eighteen-year-old management trainee. Every evening after the camels were fed and hobbled, the two would make their rounds, flushing the pools of pus and dirt from the saddle sores which refilled daily and swabbing the wounds with hydrogen peroxide, bright purple gentian violet or pale blue copper sulphate. The evening air reeked of the medicines whose sharp fragrance mixed strangely with fermented honey - the potent brew of the Samburu - and with dust, dung and the camels' thick green cud.

As the last birdsong gave way to the sounds of the desert night, the Venturers kept one eye on the angular creatures silhouetted against the sunset and one on the meal in progress. Then, when the last bit of Raven rations had been scraped from the pot and carefully portioned out, the Venturers hooked their mosquito nets and sleeping bags over the saddles and slept on the ground. A few hovered near the fire, talking and writing diaries, but well before the moon made an appearance, only the whine of mosquitoes, the rustle of the night-time creatures and the occasional roar of a lion broke the stillness of the sleeping camp.

Although temperatures in the desert dropped low and fast at night, the heat of the autumn sun was intense and waterholes were scarce. As in all remote regions, local knowledge is essential. To make the most of the cool of the morning, the Venturers travelling these northern regions were up at 4 a.m. Breakfast was made and kit packed hastily in the starry darkness. As dawn approached, the light thrown off by the crackling fires highlighted the dark shapes of the sleeping camels. Then the strange dawn chorus would begin, at first a low purr as the creatures swung their serpentine necks to and fro. Slowly the noise would deepen into a loud morning gargle that sounded like water rushing down an old bathtub drain. Reaching a crescendo, the chorus would conclude with a sleep-shattering roar that woke the late risers and birds alike. The noise reminded Area Co-ordinator Paul Bowen of the fighter bombers he flew. After a meticulous campsite cleanup, the group would be off, following the dusty ribbon that stretched as far as the eye could see.

As the summer ripened, the pools of water drew tight as a bosun's knot. Herding the camels before them, it seemed to Harriet and the others that the camels

Above: In the Alaskan mountains.

Below: Khalil Hamad of Bahrain working on the log cabin in Margam Park, South Wales.

Above: Wildlife conservation projects include helping to save the African White Rhino.

Below: Samburu ladies at a wedding in Kenya's Northern Frontier District.

could smell the water; they would break into a trot several kilometres away. Often the waterhole was dry, but occasionally the Venturers arrived a fraction too late to stop the creatures from having a good roll, drenching saddles, kit and supplies.

The expedition pushed on towards the Kowap Mountains and Sosian. Since it was rare to find water during the day, everyone carried two full water bottles and a few had a supply of strong condoms tucked into their kit. Strange as it sounds, condoms are pretty useful in the desert, although for qualities that their manufacturers have yet to advertise. Not only are they light and strong; they can also carry several litres of drinking water in an emergency.

Camels have evolved a similar solution to the dangers of drought. The secret of their ability to go without water (up to a month if there is good, green browse) lies in their elastic, expandable blood vessels. When water is available, camels can absorb as much as a hundred litres directly into their blood to provide a reservoir for emergencies. They would need that reservoir on this desert route.

Along with Venturers and the Rendille tribesmen, Mark Woodgate, the project leader of the trek, also watched the camels. As long as they get a daily quota of about six hours of browsing, camels can keep a steady pace of 4 kph every day, but they have a habit of slipping off quickly if a succulent acacia catches their eye. Given a sudden fright caused by the scent of elephants or by the noise of a slipping saddle, however, they can bolt at up to 35.5 kph. The dangers are very real: during another expedition held in late January 1989, a terrified camel panicked as its heavy saddle snagged a branch and swung beneath its belly. Tearing across the stony ground, it broke its leg and had to be put down.

Mark is a versatile fellow, as much at home in the Karakoram Mountains of Pakistan as he is in the arid lands of Northeast Kenya or programming computers in London. He was well aware that one animal from our previous expedition was missing. Poisoned by a desert shrub, it had been left behind with a local tribe to recover. Mark and the owner of the camels, Jasper Evans, had to find it since camels can die from the poison. Jasper breeds and trains camels – more than 500 at the last count – on his 12,000-hectare farm between Maralal and Nyahururu. Together with the handlers that accompanied all three Kenyan expeditions, he and his knowledgeable assistant, Debbie Atkins, taught the Venturers about their charges: how to extract the needle-sharp acacia thorns from their spongy feet; how to repair the burlap girths and wooden saddles, and utter the magic commands '*Tou!*' and '*Hub!*' with enough conviction to make the camels sink to their knees and rise again once saddled.

Searching for the abandoned beast, Mark, Jasper and Debbie set off in a Land Rover en route for Lake Turkana, the lime-green crescent of water which slices through Kenya's Chalbi Desert and touches the borders of Sudan and Ethiopia. The lake is known as the 'cradle of mankind', its waters once fished by the first men, *Homo erectus*, discovered by the Leakey family of Kenya.

The long, dusty track, alternately whipped by spiralling dust devils and draped with a shimmering curtain of heat, wound past vase-shaped acacias, Samburu warriors who appeared from nowhere, and the occasional pair of ostrich strutting through the scrub. Their search would be a long one, since the tribe had moved, taking the camels to greener browse.

The camel was eventually found, but not on that safari, not on that lake and not alive. Weakened by the poison, hyenas had brought it down near Lake Logipe, and the Samburu, being a practical people, held a feast. The searchers did, however, find an alternative use for one component of their desert kit. Arriving late in the day at Lake Turkana, hungry after several days of limited rations, Mark baited a line and threw it into the clear, green waters, hoping to catch a lake perch for the pot. Jasper watched gloomily as time and time again the cast fell short of the deep water. Mark waded out as far as he dared; the lake harbours a breeding population of about 12,000 savage Nile crocodiles waiting for a change of diet.

'It would work a lot better if you tied a balloon to the line,' observed Jasper. 'The wind would blow the bait far enough.'

Jasper's companions laughed with him. They were out of food, out of one camel and certainly out of party balloons.

Suddenly, Mark had an inspiration. Rummaging through his rucksack, he grinned with satisfaction. Minutes later the fishing line, baited with goat's liver and tied to an inflated condom, was swiftly drifting out to the middle of the Jade Sea.

Matthews Range, Northern Province, 25 October 1988

All of the Raleigh expeditions in Kenya crossed the wide open spaces of the Samburu. Theirs is a dry land that a rain shower can transform overnight. Slight depressions in the ground can become shimmering pools and tiny, bright-coloured flowers chequer the earth. Herding the camels before them, the Venturers kept up a quick march, which nevertheless gave them plenty of time to watch the changing patterns of the land. Often they would see a shadow in the middle distance, a smudge against the ground that slowly grew bigger and became a red-cloaked warrior.

Kenya's northeast corner is not all desert. Sometimes the dusty Venturers would leave their camels in the protection of spear-carrying warriors and climb up into the mountains. The highest peaks of Matthews Range soar 2375 metres above the surrounding plain. It is a steep climb, but once above the flatlands another world appears.

Scrambling over the first ridge at the base of the peak, cadet pilot Pauline Sugden of Air BP caught her breath. No stranger to loops, spins and barrel rolls herself, the 21-year-old RAF Volunteer Reservist watched in amazement as thousands of butterflies rose like a squadron. Clouds of the colourful insects took to the air, performing aerobatics no human pilot would attempt. Large and small, orange and blood-red, black with spots of Wedgwood blue or wings of bottle green, the butterflies turned the woodland into a wilderness parody of a ticker tape parade.

The extraordinary display was even more vivid to eyes that had grown used to the brown and beige landscape of the plains below. Sophie Walbeoffe-Wilson, one of the expedition artists, climbed up beside Pauline, puffing a little from the steep rocks. Sophie is a free spirit who decided to stay on in Kenya after the Raleigh expedition. Having met Wilfred Thesiger, she persuaded the tall, craggy-faced explorer to let her paint his portrait at his home in Maralal. A legendary explorer, skilled photographer and writer, Thesiger was invariably hospitable to the inexperienced people who suddenly arrived on his doorstep. Described by David Attenborough as 'one of the few people who, in our time, could be put on the pedestal of the great explorers of the eighteenth and nineteenth centuries', Thesiger undertook his first expedition – to the unexplored Danakil country of what is now Ethiopia – when he was twenty, about the age of the Raleigh Venturers.

We have many people to thank for helping us in this northern corner of Kenya, amongst them Wilfred Thesiger, the Somali family Hakim of Maralal and Chief Henry Leshornai. Their world is changing at remarkable speed, but they found the time to welcome strangers.

As Sophie's paintbrush recorded the people and animals of the north, there was one creature – the black rhino – living in the Matthews Range which the Venturers knew they would probably never see. Through the work that Operation Raleigh was doing with the Rhino Rescue Trust in other parts of the country, they were aware of the shocking reason why: there had been 20,000 black rhino in Kenya in 1970. Now there were fewer than 500. The huge horned creature, which had wandered the earth for millions of years, was hurtling towards extinction. The elephant, too, was fighting a losing battle against the poachers.

Nairobi, and Tsavo National Park, 14 September 1988

It was early morning when the senior ranger of the Rhino Sanctuary in Tsavo National Park slipped into the Raleigh campsite. The tents and hammocks were scattered around a still glowing fire and ringed with a thick circle of thorns to keep away the big cats. Glancing up, Oliver Mnyambo smiled as he noticed the dead chickens - tonight's dinner - dangling from the branches of a tree; another precaution that was effective against all but the leopards, which revelled in raiding our aerial pantries. Oliver found the young people already up and waiting. Together they climbed the escarpment to patrol the highland for signs of poachers. They didn't have far to go.

Oliver has been a ranger for fourteen years; he had joined the Rhino Sanctuary at Tsavo when it opened in March 1986. This twenty-square-kilometre patch - soon to be expanded to fifty - is home to seven black rhinos, six females and one male. There is also one baby rhino, the first to have been born in a government sanctuary. For a while, the group followed the clover-leaf tracks of the rhino. The baby's tracks were now about the size of a melon, Oliver noted with satisfaction. It was growing. But so was the tiny horn above its prehensile lip, a horn which would grow slowly, at about eight centimetres a year, until it reached its maximum length of about a metre. Even now, the slim comma could be its death sentence.

As they walked, the ranger explained to the Venturers the courtship rituals of the rhino. Betty Muia of Kenya's Standard Chartered Bank; Scottish deer stalker John Pattinson; Andy Johnston of W. H. Smith; Claire Range, a student nurse and Kathryn Crosbie, a primary teacher from Edinburgh, listened fascinated. Just behind them followed Keith Raynor, a tall, calm London lawyer, Bob Spruce, a Royal Engineers surveyor and Parker Payson, an American journalist built like Paul Bunyan.

'Fighting is an essential part of the courtship,' said the ranger. 'This is a time of great danger for the young - especially if the cow has a yearling by her side. The bull, often almost 1.8 metres at the shoulder, has one to six cows, and he'll single out one and chase her until she gets mad and turns and they crash together. Together they weigh about four tonnes - a pretty big collision. During the chase, the baby can be abandoned, easy prey for lions, or it can get lost and die.

'When the female surrenders, she surrenders completely,' continued Oliver, 'but the fight is essential to that surrender. The only other real dangers to the rhino are sickness and man.'

By eight o'clock the sun was already hot and the heat thickened the air. Oliver left the track and set off through the bush. Claire Range touched his shoulder. 'I could smell the scent of death before I saw it,' Claire remembers. 'I'm a nurse, and all death smells the same.'

Ahead, in the bush, the hyenas slunk away, while the braver vultures hopped about the huge russet-coloured mass that looked like a crumpled chamois. Then the Venturers saw the feet and recognized the carcase of an elephant whose ivory tusks had been hacked out. The elephant had been killed by poisoned arrows: it had taken days to die.

It is mostly the local tribesmen who tip their spears and arrows with poison; as yet they do not possess the high-powered rifles used by poachers from across the border. The deadly poison comes from the Acocanthera shrub which grows in Tsavo, and the Kambas have used it for generations. Hunting for food is in their blood. There is some farming, but their land is arid and food is scarce. In the hard dry times it is difficult for the villagers to understand why they can no longer stalk the buffalo and giraffe to obtain bush meat for empty stomachs. With his team of six rangers – 'Breakdown' (named because he has the power of a tow truck and never does break down), Auli, West, Senei, Tumen and Mkaru – equipped with radios, .303 rifles and Range Rovers, Oliver mounts a two-pronged attack on the poachers. Anyone found within the park is relentlessly ambushed, pursued and arrested; outside the park, Oliver goes into the thatched *manyattas* and talks about the urgent need to save the animals. By far the greater danger comes not from the local people, however, but from the marauding bands of well-armed poachers and the wealthy dealers who employ them.

On the same day that Oliver showed the grisly carcase to the Venturers in Tsavo, newspapers around the world reported tht Kenya's President Daniel arap Moi, Patron of Operation Raleigh in Kenya, had ordered park wardens to shoot poachers on sight. The wardens took him at his word. Within a week, war was declared between local and international poachers on one side and the allied forces of park rangers, police and General Service Unit (GSU) detachments on the other. The action was swift, decisive and bloody – like poaching itself.

Only nine days after President Moi's announcement, Kenyan police closed in on fifty bandits armed with AK-47 automatic rifles and Bren guns who had killed two people and seriously wounded nine others in Tsavo National Park West. In other parts of the country, there were shoot-outs between security forces and poachers – the latter fleeing into the hills, leaving behind a bloody haul of rhino horn and elephant ivory worth hundreds of thousands of dollars.

Poachers are driven to such desperate lengths by the huge prices commanded by precious elephant ivory and rhino horn. The poachers themselves get enough money from the sale of a single elephant tusk, for example, to keep their family for a year, but the real money goes to their employers, who make fortunes in foreign markets such as Singapore, China, Japan and North Yemen. Although the Western world cannot wear a halo either, the Middle and Far East are the biggest markets. Many countries are now considering a total ban on such trade. Like human fingernails, the horn of the rhinoceros is made of compacted hair – keratin – but it can grow to over a metre in length. Cherished for its lustrous beauty, the horn is sought after for its symbolic power and alleged medicinal properties. In North Yemen, a Djamblia dagger handle made of rhino horn, heavily carved and polished to an amber opalescence, is a double-page advertisement of its owner's wealth and power. These huge and highly decorated daggers can cost over fifteen thousand dollars. Much better publicized is the Eastern trade in powdered rhino horn for use as an aphrodisiac, although this market is not nearly as important as is popularly believed.

The poachers may also become an endangered species. World opinion is gathering force and many products and sculptures once made of ivory are now produced in synthetic materials. Military opposition to poaching is growing too. In Britain, for example, the Minister of State for the Environment, Lord Caithness, has agreed with President Moi and with Dr Richard Leakey, the distinguished anthropologist and director of the Wildlife Department in Kenya, to bring in the crack anti-terrorist SAS regiment should it be required.

The destruction of the world's rhino population – there are two African and three Asian species – has accelerated to nightmarish proportions. According to the World Wide Fund for Nature (WWF), the total world rhino population has declined by 85 per cent since 1970 and the black rhino of Africa (*Diceros bicornis*) is hurtling to extinction even faster: only some 3800 remain on the continent, and fewer than 500 in Kenya. The leviathan that roamed the earth for more than five million years is one of the twelve most critically endangered species in the world.

One of the aims of Operation Raleigh all over the world is to support those who are already mounting an effective campaign against the wanton destruction of the world's creatures and environment. In Kenya, members of the three expeditions worked with the Rhino Rescue Trust, an organization which was set up in 1985 to build sanctuaries in Kenya's National Parks, among them Nakuru, Tsavo and the Aberdares.

Rhino Rescue is an extraordinary organization, for many of its most ardent supporters are former big game hunters. It was launched at the annual dinner of the Shikar Club at the Savoy Hotel, the night that Kenyan conservationist Peter Jenkins talked of the appalling massacre of the great animals. The Trust is passionately committed to protecting Kenya's wild creatures, and, more importantly, it is doing something about it.

'Getting things done around here is like elephants mating,' jokes my old friend Jock Dawson, a professional hunter who came to Kenya in 1922 and who is now the administrator for Rhino Rescue at Nakuru National Park. 'It's done at a high level, it's accomplished with a great deal of roaring and screaming, and it takes years to produce results.'

Nevertheless, Rhino Rescue is achieving a great deal, fuelled by the active support of patrons like writer Elspeth Huxley; explorer and originator of the Kenyan park system Colonel Mervyn Cowie; and singer Roger Whittaker. Other patrons of Rhino Rescue working alongside Dr Richard Leakey include animal conservationist Daphne Sheldrick; Peter Jenkins, co-ordinator of the entire Kenya Rhino Rescue project; and two founder members, Sir Christopher Lever and Count Maurice Coreth, a tall Anglo-Austrian whom the Venturers quickly adopted into their ranks.

Operation Raleigh's energetic members pitched in with enthusiasm. At Nakuru, a park of alternating storms and sunshine, they worked with Warden Alfayo Barasa, Jock and Enid Dawson, Count Coreth and others to repair solar-powered electric fences, move tonnes of sand and gravel, and construct heavy cement culverts to tame the floods. But the most exciting days were those when a plume of dust heralded the arrival of a stout wooden crate being towed into the sanctuary. The fearful crashing and bucking within it gave an indication of the mood of its two-tonne occupant – a wild black rhino – with a much better chance to survive once within this safe haven.

CHAPTER TWELVE

Kenya

The Lion's Share

(*Expedition Leaders*: Lieutenant-Colonel Mark Watts, MBE LI
Lieutenant-Colonel Mike Reynolds, KOSB)

Maneaters' Camp, Tsavo, Kenya, 25 September 1988

'*Simba!*' The Kiswahili word for lion strikes fear into the heart of the bravest *moran*, and certainly into mine when muttered within close range of the King of Beasts. The Venturers working to help save the rhinos in Tsavo and Nakuru National Parks had quickly learned to protect their camps with a ring of thorns and to hang their fresh meat from high trees. Sensible precautions, I thought. Just how sensible I was to find out the night I stayed at the aptly named Maneaters' Camp not far from the Tsavo sanctuary.

Forty-eight hours earlier, I had arrived in Nairobi at dawn and spent the day being briefed by Mark Watts, leader of our second expedition, by Major Marsden Madoka, formerly aide-de-camp to Presidents Kenyatta and Moi and now Chairman of the Operation Raleigh Kenyan Council, and by committee member Major Hugh Collins. Together, Mark Watts, his assistant Gill Dalton and I visited the Raleigh project site at Limuru Boys' Centre – a remarkable school which trains underprivileged boys to become self-sufficient farmers of sugar cane, cabbage, tea, coffee and dairy products. Founded by the energetic Bob Mein, who came to Africa in 1948, the school is run by an ex-student, Principal Richard Otieno, and funded mostly through charitable contributions. We were contributing in kind, building a massive cement cattle court for the school under project leader Jeffory Westerfield of the US Army Corps of Engineers.

Later that evening I took the overnight train to Mombasa on the coast, and awoke to a sunrise of palm trees and pink clouds etched like Arabic script above the ochre-coloured earth. Sandy-haired Major Peter Barnes, area co-ordinator, and 27-year-old expedition doctor Anne Mackenzie Ross met the train. Before going on to Maneaters' Camp and the promise of a square meal, there were three Raleigh projects I wanted to see: Baobab Farm, a coral wasteland transformed into a rich new ecosystem of fish, plants and wildlife; the water tank and pipeline project in the Taita Hills, headed by Phil and Sarah Groman of Plan International, a non-profit community development organization; and the medical dispensary being built in the misty Kidaya Valley, just a stone's throw away from Tanzania's snow-capped Kilimanjaro.

I was impressed by all three. Certainly, the experiment at Baobab Farm, where two expeditions worked, provides vital answers to problems created by pesticides, overpopulation and pollution throughout the world. In a strip-mined limestone desert, agronomist René Haller has developed a balanced, integrated ecosystem – the first of its kind – which could be developed on an international scale to make arid lands flourish, help feed refugees, and significantly raise the protein consumption of the populations of Third World countries. In just seventeen years the quarry wasteland near Mombasa has been transformed. Now the land is cloaked in a burgeoning jungle. Fish and crocodile laze in freshwater pools, and emus, hippo and Cape buffalo wander through lush pastures. Over 140 species of birds have been sighted and butterflies drift through sun-dappled glades. Honoured by the United Nations for his work, René Haller has wrested life from dead land.

At Baobab, the Venturers merely wrestled crocodiles, carrying the larger males to breeding pools. But first the crocs had to be sexed and measured. For some, like Grant Hogg, a lofty Canadian who made everything look easy, manhandling the crocodiles was, as the Kenyans say, *hakuna matata* (no problem). Nor were rock-climbing solicitor Caroline Easter or 21-year-old zoo worker Rob Edwards worried at the prospect of carrying a writhing reptile over a narrow log bridge with no rails, spurred on by the sight of rows of teeth below. Balance and strength are essential for the task, however, and Sean Rooney, a computer student stricken with cerebral palsy, would have been in danger had he tried to cross on his own. 'You can mostly do whatever you want to,' Sean told me in his matter-of-fact way. 'You just get up and do it.' It was that attitude which had won him a place on Operation Raleigh.

A little help from one's friends is always a good thing, too. Knowing that Sean wanted to cross the bridge he had helped to build, Paul Sullivan, a stocky quantity surveyor sponsored by Wimpy Construction, simply scooped up his tall friend and started over. Stopping in the middle of the bucking bridge, the two men looked down. 'Heng', the largest of the male crocodiles, slithered beneath and smiled his toothy smile. From his precarious position high overhead, Sean gave a salute, Paul found his balance, and the two crossed safely.

There were no crocodiles at the two other project sites in the south, one in the Swiss-looking Taita Hills, and the other high in the Kidaya Valley. There was, however, a great deal of water. For the villagers, getting to it was the problem. Here, Operation Raleigh was helping the villagers build a gravity-flow water supply system consisting of five storage and distribution tanks. The Venturers were also helping to lay fourteen kilometres of pipe. It was a big project. According to project leader Barry Davis of the US Marine Corps, running water will be close at hand for the first time, a great help to local agriculture and, in an area with a high rate of dysentery and guardia, a big improvement in the health of the villagers.

My last stop before heading on to Maneaters' was the medical dispensary at Kidaya. Here in the valley the mist was so dense that one could only see a few kilometres ahead. It was cold and damp, and hard to imagine Raleigh's camel trekkers further north sweltering in tropical heat. For shelter from wind, snakes and scorpions the Venturers had slung their hammocks in the open-sided skeleton of a timber building. On one side soared a vertical grey cliff; on the other, terraced fields stepped gracefully down the mountainside.

Thirteen years is a long time for people to wait for medical help, thought Joshua Otieno, the *fundi* or head craftsman constructing the dispensary. With him was project leader Anne-Marie Gilbert, a green-eyed nurse with an easy style of leadership, who was enjoying her second Kenyan expedition in a row with Raleigh. Joshua picked up a worn lump of cement, automatically checking for scorpions as he did so. The date 1975 had been carved on its surface, the numerals now obscured by a layer of velvet moss. Once upon a time, a government official had decided that the people of these remote and misty hills should have some medical attention, and had ordered the foundations built and the building blocks needed for the rest brought in. Orders are easy; it is seeing them through to completion that counts. The blocks had lain in a mass of rubble until Joshua showed the Venturers how to build the three-room structure.

The following year, 1989, Joshua helped another group of Venturers build a medical dispensary at Opiroi in the north, near the final destination of the camel caravans. That handsome stone building is now called the Taina Flutti Dispensary, a tragic tribute to a wonderful young Italian Venturer who, having completed the rigorous camel trek to Opiroi, had swum with the others above a cold mountain waterfall and slipped over the rocks to her death below.

Taina died on 15 February 1989, only days before the expedition ended. Her death was a heart-breaking accident, and one that occurred when danger was least expected. Swimming with her were a doctor and a climbing expert; aided by the Venturers, they battled in vain to save the unconscious girl's life.

Leaving the cold Taita Hills, we headed for Maneaters' Camp, situated within the vast Tsavo Park. At 200,000 square kilometres, the park is the size of Wales or

Texas, and the largest in Kenya. As evening fell, long lines of women streamed up from the valley to the hilltops, carrying heavy loads of firewood on their heads. The colourful yellows, reds and browns of their *kangas*, the national dress worn in this part of Kenya, seemed equally a part of the landscape and of the vibrant sunset.

At last Peter Barnes turned the Toyota into the gate at Tsavo. Before us fled dik-diks, tiny antelopes hardly larger than hares, spiral-horned lesser kudus, and Grant's gazelle. Four massive black buffalo lowered their horns in challenge at our approach. Intelligent and cunning, these huge-horned animals are among the most dangerous of African big game, and their only natural enemy is the lion.

Prudently, Peter slowed to a halt, retreated and drove in a wide arc around the bulls. We made it to the camp, near the seasonal Tsavo River, as darkness drew in, and found that Anne Mackenzie Ross and Mukhtar Mohammed Yarrow, Peter's deputy area co-ordinator, had already put the steaks on the fire and poured the Glenfiddich. At twenty-six, Mukhtar, a Kenyan Somali, was a man of many parts and a great addition to the expedition. A graduate of the famous Starehe Boys' Centre in Nairobi, he had swapped his nomadic life in Kenya's arid northeast for a job as a clerk with Standard Chartered Bank. It was impressive that the bank agreed to sponsor him for two expeditions in a row – later in the year he would assist leader Clive Barrow in the big empty lands he had known as a boy.

We talked until the fire sank into embers, with only the occasional growl of a lion punctuating the soft African night. But those muted sounds of simba were enough to recall how Maneaters' Camp got its name. It was near here that the shadowy lions of Tsavo took their toll of coolies working on the railway. In his book, *The Man-Eaters of Tsavo*, the celebrated English engineer and game hunter Colonel J. H. Patterson recounted the gruesome deaths of twenty-eight Indians and a hundred Africans.

Pondering these cheerful thoughts, I carried a thimble of Scotch to my thatched *banda*, pulled my mosquito net over the camp bed and was soon snoring soundly.

I woke at first light, and, not knowing the location of the camp loo, stumbled off a hundred metres into the bush. On my return I glanced at my watch. 'Strange,' I thought. It was 6.30 a.m. but in the camp no one stirred. Two cups of coffee later an African head poked out of a tent. 'Have the lions gone?' its owner enquired.

'What lions?' I replied, handing him a mug of steaming coffee.

'You know, those big lions here all night.'

'Very amusing,' I thought, 'but you won't find my leg that easy to pull.' I lifted the pot of bubbling porridge from the fire and together we filled the mess tins.

Like all good breakfasts, it was eaten in silence while Mark Watts and I read the previous week's *Sunday Telegraph*. At 8 a.m. we were off. Only 200 metres further on, and not far from my morning ramble, the land cruiser rounded a bend and there beside the track sat three magnificent lionesses. Their tails twitched rhythmically in anticipation of their own breakfast - us. It was abundantly clear why they still call this place Maneaters' Camp.

Mt Kenya, the White Mountain, October 1988

Sacred to the Kikuyu people, Africa's second highest mountain (after Kilimanjaro) straddles the equator, yet its gothic peaks are forever capped with ice. Here, too, the big cats have a well-earned reputation for ferocity and local mythology tells of one spotted lion, a powerful, heavy-maned creature, which haunts the highlands and is never seen by sceptics.

In 1849 the sceptics, sipping pink gins in the clubs of London, refused to credit the idea that eternal snow could exist on the equator. When Johan Krapf, a missionary-explorer, described the white mountain, his account was ridiculed. But thirty-six years later Joseph Thomson confirmed its existence: '. . . a gleaming snow-white peak with sparkling facets which scintillated with the superb beauty of a colossal diamond.'

Although no one on Operation Raleigh sighted the spotted lion, many climbed the saddle-shaped pass named after it - the Simba Col, which leads to Minto's Hut - and a few of the fittest even dared to climb the classic ice route, Diamond Couloir. Living high on the mountain for days, where they rebuilt huts and latrines, almost everyone made it up the third highest peak, Lenana: a 4986-metre finger of stone whose rarefied air sucks the breath from one's lungs. Amongst them were Sean Rooney and Andy Kelly, who never let their physical limitations interfere with their fun; American Katie Cannon, who was struck by a particularly virulent form of dysentery and lived only on water for days; and tiny Singaporean Shirin Hamid, who weighed about as much as her ice axe and was not much taller.

Often the snow, whipped up by high winds, hit the Venturers horizontally, and caused severe white-outs on the various routes to the Kami, Minto and Austrian shelters. On the lower slopes where visibility was better, giant lobelia and groundsel, weirdly shaped heathers and red-hot pokers rose from the mist like an alien army in the ultraviolet glare of the world's high places.

In spite of the rigorous training given by international climbing experts like Chris Kinsey, Dave Marriott, ex-Chile Venturer Tracey Bryden, John Widman, Ian Macallister and Barry Roberts, there were the inevitable number of falls on ice so hard that an axe couldn't hold. But it was not the scree slopes and false summits, vertical bogs, ice caves and cliffs that caused one pair of leaders, Bob

Churcher and Iona Leishman, to call a group back to base camp. It was a furry, sharp-toothed rock hyrax, an unlikely relation of the elephant, which resembles a guinea pig and feeds on lobelia. In this case, one of the creatures also made a meal of a Venturer's thumb. Not many things worried Bob Churcher, but the possibility of rabies was one of them. Almost two metres tall, the man is built like a mountain, and his huge footsteps left safe ledges in the snow for Sue Foxley and Stephanie Payne, roped behind him, to follow. Having brought the unfortunate Venturer down for doctoring, the exhausted group got up at dawn the next day to climb the mountain yet again.

Inevitably Mt Kenya produced its crop of heroes. There was Sara Chaves, an environmental science student from Virginia, who spent a record forty-two days on the mountain; Gerard Lynch of New Jersey who climbed Lenana three times in one expedition; those with physical handicaps who drew on resources their able-bodied friends would never know; and the few who climbed Batian, Kenya's highest peak and greatest challenge. For them it meant spending nights on ice ledges just wide enough to lie lengthwise, ringside views of Mars at night and Orion at dawn, drinking three or four cups of melted ice and tea in the early morning to pre-hydrate their bodies and, roped together, crossing the knife-edged ridge of Shipton's Notch, knowing that if one fell off the other would too.

Both Batian and Nelion, the two highest peaks, are the remains of an extinct volcano, a gigantic eroded mountain once higher than Everest. The Kikuyu call it *Kere Nyaga* or White Mountain. With frozen tarns, living glaciers and innumerable valleys spilling down their flanks, the peaks stab the sky, rising more than 5000 metres and offering some of the most difficult ice climbs in the world.

'You don't get credit for climbing a mountain, only for climbing up and getting down again,' says Canadian Barry Roberts who made the summit of Batian with Jon Mason, a Venturer sponsored by Shell Oil. In their party was mountaineer Dave Moisley and Venturer Ian Palefreyman, a gregarious 21-year-old who works for the Electricity Generating Board and is a good man to be stuck on a ledge with. It was just as well that he was a good companion, since Ian and Dave waited midway while the other two made a bid for the summit, fuelled by the rations that New Zealander Tim Davey had thoughtfully stashed in the rocks. Using spring-loaded camming devices on the metre-wide pitches of Firmin's Tower, one last icy step brought the pair to the summit platform. They didn't stay long. As the conditions worsened, Barry and Jon took nothing for granted and abseiled down on a double rope side by side.

'You do not conquer mountains,' said Barry. 'You move according to your own abilities, using sound judgement, and sometimes the mountain relents and lets you get up. The hazards and challenges you face on the mountain are objective: storms, cold, wind, snow – things independent of you and your presence. You learn to deal with them by exercising judgement, learned judgement, to get yourself from the known to the unknown, and by asking, "How hard is this? Is it within my ability? Can I control my fear and remain objective and not be lured to the summit with false hopes?" '

Lake Baringo, Rift Valley Province, January 1989

It seems strange that people are frightened of a creature that is stone deaf, has poor vision and, given a chance, would much rather run from a human encounter – the snake. Its sense of smell is extremely keen, however, and it tastes the air with its delicate forked tongue. During the mating season, a female leaves a trail of scent for the males to follow. Trouble occurs when one amorous male meets another on the perfumed track; the two do battle for the right of way in a sinuous dance of combat. Man's fear of the snake dates back to Eden, and many are killed on sight, poisonous or not, to the dismay of devoted herpetologists.

One person who would seem to be a natural candidate to write reptiles into stardom is Jonathan Leakey, the eldest son of the world-famous prehistorians, Mary and Louis Leakey. Jonathan has a number of important finds to his name, although it is his brother Richard who has largely inherited his parents' archaeological mantle. Still a teenager in the early 1960s and on a field trip with his parents to Olduvai Gorge, Jonathan discovered cranial fragments of what became known as *Homo habilis*, an upright ancestor of *Homo erectus* and us – *Homo sapiens*.

His wife Janet, a talented woman who has traversed the world on public transport, managed the famous Tiger Tops Lodge in Nepal and worked as Mary Leakey's assistant at Olduvai, was a great help in the early days of Operation Drake and her support has continued through the years. She and Jonathan still run a small snake farm at Lake Baringo in addition to their other enterprises. At one time the round wire enclosures held a full range of highly poisonous snakes such as black and green mambas, gaboon vipers and puff adders, as well as the non-venomous (or perhaps just slightly venomous) file-snakes, common African pythons and the local Lake Baringo snakes.

Kenya, with its high proportion of poisonous snakes and its troops of scorpions, is at once a treat for herpetologists and a trauma for medics. While some hospitals may stock anti-venom serum, most expeditions can't carry it since it must be kept refrigerated. Only on the tourist route does one find ice on a safari. There are, however, a number of ingenious new ideas to combat snake bite. High voltage shock treatment, administered four or five times direct to the bitten area with a ten-second rest in between, is one of the most intriguing. Any motor with a spark plug - an outboard motor, car, a lawn mower, or, as Raleigh doctors discovered, an electric cattle prod - can be used to produce a high voltage, low amperage shock. The patient usually recovers completely and remarkably quickly.

Even before the first camel trek had covered much ground, two Venturers were on the receiving end of this shock treatment. The land was infested with scorpions, and in quick succession, Elizabeth Hightower was stung on the thigh three times and Jean Philippe Joly-El Ahl was caught on the arm. As nurse Anne-Marie Gilbert pressed the two-pronged instrument into their flesh, it emitted a sinister buzzing sound. Her patients endured an uncomfortable few seconds, and then, miraculously, their bites ceased to sting.

If the camel trekkers to the north of Baringo were trying to avoid scorpions, the scientists and Venturers at the island-studded lake sought them eagerly. Eibleis Fanning, assistant director of science at CHQ, had sought Richard Leakey's advice and he had suggested that Lake Baringo might provide a host of important projects for scientists. He was right. To determine the interrelated reasons for the rapid silting up of the lake, studies were made of rainfall, fish and animal life, livestock grazing habits and the lake's chemical, plankton and silt levels. Jeremy Adams of British Drug Houses provided much of the expensive equipment needed for the work - spectrophotometers, microscopes and water sampling machinery. In addition, Dr Kate Monk and scientists from the East African Herbarium, and from universities such as Moi, Kenyatta, Nairobi, York and Reading, supervised the collection of over 5000 insects, including over sixty species of grasshoppers.

Climbing the rock cliffs of the Mukatan Gorge and exploring the lake and its islands, the expeditions were constantly aware of the astonishing beauty of Baringo, one of the string of lakes that punctuates the Rift Valley. Most are basins of sodium carbonate - plain washing soda - where only pink flamingos thrive, feeding on molluscs and blue-green algae.

By contrast, Baringo and Naivasha are the only true freshwater lakes in the valley and harbour a vast array of life. But it is the milky tea colour of Baringo that tells of the danger threatening the lake. Massive erosion caused by drought, overgrazing and wood cutting has made the brown water thick with sediment and Baringo is silting up. Each year it grows smaller and could disappear entirely in only fifteen years. With the water will go the grunting hippo and sly crocodiles, great populations of tilapia and barbus fish, aquatic plants and the habitat of hundreds of species of birds. Nor will *Homo sapiens*, the species largely responsible for the death of the lake, escape. The people of Lake Baringo, Njemps, Tugen and Pokot, who fish the waters and graze their flocks, will lose their livelihood.

Murray Roberts, a Kenyan whose family has long lived by Baringo, is trying to find workable solutions to these daunting problems. For over a decade, Roberts has experimented with developing alternative sources of fuel and fodder, and a number of Raleigh teams have worked with him. His goal is to save the lake, rehabilitate the denuded land and improve local management of it.

The hardworking science teams came up with some remarkable finds. In a country where belief in charms and witchcraft is still widespread, the scientists were sceptical of reports of a special root that cleared the muddy water and left it fit for drinking. 'But the locals showed us where to find the plant,' said Dr Meg Huby from York University, an energetic member of two Kenyan expeditions who is always interested in new ideas. 'The results were astonishing.'

Ten minutes after Meg and others immersed the root in a cylinder of brown lake water, the sediment fell to the bottom, leaving the liquid as clear as gin. Some scientific sleuthing identified the plant as *Maerua subcordata* (family *Capparaceae*), and its power to transform muddy sumps into palatable drinking water may eventually prove to be of great importance for people all over the world.

There is a different sort of magic in the crystal-clear waters lapping the foundations of Fort Jesus, sentinel of Mombasa. Around the island spreads a glassy green waterway, filled with white-sailed dhows which gave *Zebu*, our square-rigged brigantine, an escorted welcome to Africa. 'Ahead is Mombasa, a low shoreline of coconut palms and scattered colonial houses. The sea is calm and our engine vibrates as *Zebu* motors up the harbour,' wrote Welsh actress Ceris Morris in her diary. 'I feel so proud of her; *Zebu* is so tiny and graceful compared to the huge container ships, rusty and forbidding as they idle away the time at anchor.'

Zebu had been met with warm welcomes all over the world. Hers is a remarkable story.

Above: Loading Jasper Evan's camels at Rumiruti, Kenya.

Below: Raid on expedition rations, Tsavo East, Kenya.

Above: Snow on the Equator. Dawn on Mt Kenya.

Below left: Blind Venturer Ian Toney of Northampton helps to build a medical clinic at Opiroi, Northern Kenya.

Below right: Herpetologist Mark O'Shea with a friendly seven-foot forest cobra, Cameroon.

CHAPTER THIRTEEN

Zebu

Life on the Ocean Wave

(*Ship's Master*: Captain Peter Masters)

Off the Brazilian Coast, 2020 hours, 29 March 1988

'Man overboard, man overboard!' The frantic cry roused Peter Stewart, a 23-year-old British Aerospace engineer, sleeping deeply in his bunk. In seconds he was on his feet stumbling up the ladder.

'Is this a drill?' a voice called out of the darkness. On deck the light of the three-quarter moon showed the fear and tension on the faces of the watch. They knew that somewhere in the black, heaving ocean one of their friends was fighting for life. This was for real. Flares went over the side to mark the spot as the ship's bell sounded the alarm. The crew rushed to emergency positions. Frantic hands heaved the tarpaulin off the Avon inflatable boat and hauled it to the gunwales.

The accident had happened only minutes before. Steven Law, a member of an RAF Mountain Rescue Team, had been helping American Bob Procter to stow the bowsprit sails. The job was almost finished and he leant backwards to tension the ropes. With no warning the footrope on which Steve was standing snapped, and he plummeted into the sea. As he sank beneath the waves he felt the relentless pressure of the ship's bow over his back, forcing him down. In desperate need of air he struck out underwater and surfaced amidships. A thought flashed through his mind: 'Thank God she's under sail – the propeller's not turning.' As the brigantine swept past, Steve heard the bell ringing and shouts of 'Man overboard!' He knew they'd search.

The water was warm. Thinking quickly and clearly Steve swam hard for the fishing line that was always astern. His arms were weighted down by his anorak and guernsey but he found the line and seized it, wrapping it around his clenched fist. It stretched and bore his weight, but cut into his fingers like wire. He let go and kicked away from the line, remembering its razor-sharp hook.

The glimmering yellow flares receded astern as the crew sought to stop the ship – no easy job when a brigantine is under full sail. With a muffled thump the huge main staysail fell on to the deck. The Venturers dived at it, pulling the canvas clear of the rescue boat. Peter Stewart tried to hook up the inflatable but the crew had hauled on the winch rope early. He yelled for slack, but it was too late, the hook and its locating ring were ripped clean out of the wooden rail and disappeared into the rigging.

Agile as a monkey, Tony Flaherty, the bosun, leapt up the shrouds for the winch rope. Seconds seemed like hours. Again came the shout 'More slack!' This time Peter got the hook on to the waiting harness. 'Haul away! Haul away!' yelled Tony. Slowly the boat was lifted clear of the deck and manhandled over the side.

Captain Peter Masters, who had skippered *Zebu* for almost four years, brought her into the wind whilst Nick Broughton, the mate and owner, trained a searchlight on the bobbing flares. Overhead, loose canvas flapped as second mate Kev Jordan and Australian sheep farmer Rob Hanekamp donned life jackets and clambered down into the tossing inflatable. A sudden swell almost pitched them into the sea. The Mariner outboard roared to life and the boat headed off into the darkness, skimming over the waves towards the smoking flares.

The hood of Steve's waterproof had filled with air and was forcing his head under every wave. Sucking in a deep breath he dived, pulling off his harness and then struggling with the Velcro cuffs that refused to go past his watch. He was free. As he surfaced he could see the black outline of *Zebu*, about 800 metres away and turning back towards him. He was tiring quickly but swam towards her with strong deliberate strokes.

The search beam passed over Steve's head. 'Oh God, have they seen me?' he wondered. He saw the Avon, but it was going away from him. Filling his lungs and kicking himself high out of the water Steve bellowed, 'Over here, over here, starboard side.' Swiftly Kev swung the craft round and came up beside him bobbing in the dark sea. It had only been twenty-one minutes. To Steve it was a lifetime. The crew cheered as he was helped aboard. Back in his bunk Peter Stewart remembered the Captain's words: 'I suppose there must be successful rescues of people who fall overboard, but I have never heard of one.' 'Thank God he has now,' thought Peter.

Cairns, Australia, 14 November 1986

Zebu was halfway round the world when she left Cairns and headed up the Great Barrier Reef bound for Japan, where, with the generous help of our sponsor Nippon-Denso, we were mounting a large-scale expedition.

Reaching the Solomon Islands the team carried out a task on Gizo. We had built a clinic here in 1986. Now the Venturers erected a strong concrete wall around the local prison. Labouring in the sun they finished the task in one day. Even the inmates were impressed. Then someone noticed that there was no gate. 'Don't worry,' smiled the warden. 'This is an open prison, people come, people go.'

Egholo village on Gizo gave *Zebu* a great reception and gifts of beautiful carvings. The Venturers had little to give in return, but produced a motley collection of relatively clean clothes. Next day the villagers came to say goodbye wearing their new gifts. Young and old appeared in a variety of T-shirts and two tiny boys marched up and down the quayside, stark naked, each proudly wearing a single wellington boot. Her huge square-sails unfurled, *Zebu* continued on to Japan.

Rats are always a worry for any ship's captain and in Cairns Peter Masters had enquired if the port had many. The beefy dock foreman grinned: 'Not many – the snakes get 'em.' The idea of snakes coming aboard alarmed Peter even more. 'No worries,' replied the Aussie, 'the crocs usually get those.' Before they reached Okinawa, however, several rats had been spotted skulking below. Knowing how particular Japanese authorities can be, Peter feared that if they arrived with the rodents they'd certainly be regarded as barbarians from the West. So anchoring a day early behind an island, all hands set to, scrubbing the decks and hunting rats. Strangely, not one could be found and it was with some trepidation that they sailed in to Okinawa the next day.

The health officials came aboard and solemnly presented their questionnaire. On the subject of rodents the form asked, 'Has there been an abnormal death-rate amongst your rats?' Peter wrote, 'No,' and they were welcomed to Japan.

Osaka, 6 April 1987

By the time the Venturers of the next expedition arrived, the little ship had reached the port of Osaka. One of the newcomers, Mary Scott, a nurse from Princes Risborough, remembers trooping down to the dock to be greeted by the smiling, if somewhat grubby, crew. That night she wrote in her diary: 'Being a Venturer on *Zebu* is very special; a cocktail comprising the challenge of sailing "olde style", the cultural experiences of the places that we visit and the diverse and wonderful people on board.'

The waters of coastal Japan were not the most welcoming and although Peter and his crew had briefed the Venturers on some aspects of sailing a brigantine, nothing could prepare them for the misery of seasickness. Mary's first full day on the ocean was spent huddled in oilskins sitting at the stern, staring at the grey horizon and willing her stomach to adjust to the swell.

When they first saw her, the newcomers were amazed at how small *Zebu* looked.

The deck is a compact twenty-four metres, surrounded by the 106 ropes needed to manoeuvre the thirteen sails. Below was a room – the size of Mary's modest bedroom at home – to accommodate fourteen of the sixteen Venturers. The remaining two slept in the tiny saloon. It was cramped, but when all hands were at sea working, eating and sleeping watches, the ship was comfortable enough. In hot weather most slept on deck, accepting the risk of being drenched by a sudden tropical squall which could soak all within seconds.

Everything seemed small, bar the rigging. Mary had never been afraid of heights before, but there is a difference between just being high up and having to rely on your limbs and co-ordination to keep you there. Eventually, of course, they got used to it and grew in confidence, but it took time and practice to feel comfortable going aloft. It also took teamwork. When manoeuvring the sails was necessary, the essential thing was to help each other. '"Teamwork" and "supporting each other" sounds corny, I know,' wrote Mary, 'but it happened almost naturally and we needed it.'

Although the young sailors' stomachs soon settled, the swells that caused the seasickness didn't. Nor did the water get any warmer, and, as waves showered the bow, those on watch often froze. There were three watches: starboard, port and for'ard. Each was responsible for sailing, four hours in every twelve. Most Venturers had never sailed anything before, let alone a vessel like this. *Zebu* was very much a working ship and being immensely strong, could withstand any weather. She went well with the wind but couldn't sail to windward, which made it difficult to get out of awkward situations.

Safety procedures were drummed into the Venturers from the start and the hours spent on watch would count towards Royal Yachting Association sailing certificates. Days were spent sailing, working, sleeping, cooking and eating, but there was time to relax too and watch the sunsets.

The 12 p.m. to 4 a.m. watch had the additional responsibility of baking the next day's bread. In the stormy waters off Japan the dough practically kneaded itself as the boat bucked like a bronco and the hopeful bakers skidded about the saloon in a haze of flour. Under Jane Broughton's expert guidance, all *Zebu* Venturers learned to prepare mouthwatering meals, even if they had to sift the flour for weevils and maggots and catch many of the ingredients with a line thrown over the stern. Whilst those on land endured dehydrated and army composite rations, the *Zebu* team grew almost portly.

Finally they reached Tokyo, where five helicopters circled overhead as the vessel gently motored into harbour. A band and Miss Tokyo waited on the quay. The crew explored the city and their week-long stay gave them ample time to meet new friends, delve into the complex culture, and visit the largest fish market in the world. As they watched the people, the people watched them: their wanderings were screened on Japanese television. However, it was the famous hot *sentos* or Japanese baths that were most appreciated by the Venturers for on board *Zebu* they had washed in cold, salty seawater pulled up in buckets, or not at all.

Japan also gave the Venturers the chance to get the ship in tip-top condition before their voyage to Micronesia. Then, sails struck again, they headed south. Their sailing skills improved enormously as they voyaged in the open sea. Although the ship had radio contact, the speed and pressures of Western culture seemed a lifetime away. Dolphins streaked across the bow wave and whales cruised by. Kevin and Tony, the for'ard watchleaders, were keen naturalists and charted a panoply of marine creatures, among them sea snakes and all things finned.

'One morning we caught 68 kg of dorado with one thin fishing line slung out the back of the boat,' wrote Mary in her diary. That's a lot of fish even for a hungry crew of twenty-two. Cries of 'Dorado again?' greeted every meal. 'We all took turns in the galley with varying results.'

There were a few days when the sea turned to glass and the Venturers pulled in sail and leapt off the boat for a swim. Some of the more adventurous even dived off the high rigging. It was strange to swim with the unbroken horizon above and thousands of metres of blue nothing below.

The Nau Islands, 8 May 1987

After eighteen days at sea, land was sighted. The atmosphere on board was euphoric. The ship anchored within sight of white sand and palm trees in clear turquoise water off the remote island of Fananu. The local people, who see a boat about once every three months, were more than amazed to sight a square-rigger, and canoed out to greet the crew, bundling on deck to chat and ask questions. Sign language sufficed where pidgin English didn't.

The villagers soon discovered that Mary was a nurse and asked her to see the sick. Some were very ill: a small boy had a huge leg abscess; an old man, probable meningitis. *Zebu* hadn't the drugs to treat them and even if she had, Mary would have needed to monitor their progress; luckily the local hospital boat was due within a few days. Later our crew contracted their own illnesses and ailments, mainly infected cuts and a few burns from the galley, but there was one case of malaria too. Sensibly, the ship's comprehensive medical kit contained everything from antibiotics and dental fillings to painkillers and diarrhoea remedies.

At Fananu the Venturers found extraordinary beauty. The island was tiny and easy to walk around, its lush green vegetation trimmed with a collar of fine white sand. Villagers gave them garlands of flowers and shinned up trees to cut coconuts. The young sailors swam with the village children in the clear blue waters of the reef, studded with coral and fish of every hue.

The next sail took *Zebu* to Moen, a larger island, to re-provision and on 15 May she crossed the equator, much to the delight of the permanent staff. Foul odours began to bubble from the galley and Peter Masters emerged from his cabin dressed as Neptune, complete with beard and trident. As drums sounded a stately beat, the rest of the old hands followed dressed in a variety of ridiculous costumes. It's all a tradition, and every ship crossing the equator has a similar ceremony. On *Zebu*, lists of 'crimes' were read out before Venturers were immersed and force-fed with an exotic green goo made of dried egg, fish and other delights. Labelled 'octopus vomit', 'porpoise pus' and 'dolphin snot', it was the grimmest mixture imaginable. They had 'crossed the line' and were rewarded with a swig of rum each, before being put into a bosun's chair under the bowsprit to be lowered into the waves. A great way to clean off.

The Arafura Sea, 1 June 1987

The three months aboard raced by too quickly, but by the time they neared Australia, the Venturers found the effects of the swells exhilarating rather than nauseating. Three had managed to get their RYA Watchleader's Certificate. At Darwin, *Zebu* was dry-docked for a thorough overhaul and from there they bade each other farewell. As one group departed, another arrived.

Darwin, Australia 7 July 1987

Janet Wardle, a deaf 20-year-old student from Chester, found that the voyage from Darwin to the Seychelles with the southeast trade winds ever-present gave her just the sort of sailing she wanted. Her diary records a variety of other experiences: hunting cockroaches in the heads, clearing flying fish from the decks, cooking in a heaving, hot galley and watching carefully prepared dishes crash to the floor. But Janet's worst moments took place aloft, when she rolled the sails in the swaying yards with only a footrope to steady her.

Ceris Morris of Cardiff had also experienced fear in the yards. In her log she wrote: 'I've only been aloft once and I'm terrified. I make it as far as the platform which encircles the foremast halfway up, but only just manage to scramble on to it; you have to swing out and up, always keeping three points of contact with the rigging. It demands great faith in one's body strength and co-ordination. Triumphantly I stand up, not realizing that I'm to be stuck there for the next twenty minutes because I can't get back down! Tony Flaherty tries to coax me down but my body freezes. I'm frustrated and frightened and on the verge of tears. Eventually, somehow, I descend and stand on the deck, trying to stop my hands shaking. I know I should see it as a personal challenge, but there are other challenges to win – going down to the galley without being sick for instance!'

On a more practical level, Ceris also described the problems of getting a good wash. 'I'm trying to have a decent wash every day. This involves standing on the foredeck in my bikini, soap and flannel at the ready, with an empty canvas bucket. This is lowered over the side, more difficult than it sounds, because of the danger of losing the bucket as the ship hurtles through the water – the punishment is to make another, a long and fiddly process. Then of course there's always the danger of losing oneself overboard with the bucket. I usually ask someone to tip the water over my head – a request more often than not met with a wicked grin and a faster reaction than hauling a halyard. The most annoying thing is that ordinary soap doesn't lather in seawater. In their highly efficient way the Japanese on board have brought seawater soap.'

Corporal Simon Molyneux, a young British soldier in the Royal Electrical and Mechanical Engineers, found his skills put to good use in the engine room, but will never forget landing a 29 kg tuna that took four pairs of arms to pull aboard.

Then there were the magical ports of call: Christmas Island with its millions of vividly coloured crabs; Cocos Keeling where the graceful Malaysian people sang songs of welcome, and Chagos, inhabited only by fairy terns and brown noddies, forever darting from one tree to another, oblivious to the thunder of a US fighter from a nearby base flying low over the golden atoll.

The next group of Venturers joined at Seychelles and Nick Broughton took some of them night fishing in the dinghy. They caught more than they bargained for. Paul MacIlvenny of Hexham watched the line sink gently, then go suddenly taut, nearly pulling him into the pitch-black sea. 'It's a monster,' the Geordie boy shouted in excitement. 'It's coming up.' Seconds later there was a loud bang right under their feet as a two-metre-long black tip shark, with its mouthful of razors, sliced through the rubber hull. Somehow they got the creature aboard without sinking.

If the Venturers found the shark's reception somewhat hostile, it was positively friendly compared to the one they encountered at Grande Comoroes. Here the people are Islamic fundamentalists, very suspicious of newcomers in general, and of those who visit the French Foreign Legion outpost at Mayotte in particular. To compound the Venturers' difficulties Peter Masters came down with hepatitis, which although fortunately not of the contagious type, also gave us cause for concern at CHQ. Good square-rig skippers are a rare breed nowadays, and not easy to replace.

At three o'clock in the morning on Wednesday 23 December, *Zebu* rounded Cape Agulhas, leaving the Indian Ocean behind and sailing into the Atlantic. The seas off this southernmost tip of the African continent were moderate as she beat into a fifteen-knot, west southwest wind. At dawn she rounded Cape Point and was alongside Cape Town harbour by Christmas Eve.

Cape Town, 24 December 1987

The stopover was not purely one of convenience to indulge in seasonal excesses shoreside. It was most important to slip *Zebu* for her regular six-monthly overhaul. As she slowly came out of the water on the harbour's synchro lift, the crew were happy to see the excellent state of her hull: very little fouling and all seams in good condition.

Christmas is traditionally a time for family reunions and *Zebu*'s stay in Cape Town was no exception. Waiting to take a line on the dockside was one of the early *Zebu* 'family', Karl Strempel. Karl had worked on board during the original refit in England and had been in the crew which crossed the Atlantic to the Turks and Caicos Islands. An old hand, he was under no illusions that it was just his cheery face and bushy beard that Nick and Jane were so pleased to see: he knew they were really after his notable brawn and considerable skills as a shipwright.

Each day Karl would come along and happily work until the sun went down. Sunset was the signal for his invitation to the hardworking crew to come for a drink or a *braai* at his home. This festive spirit enveloped the docks and the two Japanese Venturers on board, Eiji Unakami and Teiko Seki, were quickly adopted by the crew of a Japanese ship when they went in search of genuine soya sauce and miso soup. Others spent a merry night singing sea shanties on board a Polish vessel, where the spirit was as alcoholic as it was seasonal. Many local people arrived every day and took the off-duty crew and Venturers on day trips, and generously provided picnics and mementoes of their visit to the Cape.

Work progressed apace and soon *Zebu* was back in the water and ready to set sail for St Helena. The New Year was welcomed in style with dancing and a *braai* on the top of Lookout Hill, Cape Town's twinkling lights laid out like a fairy carpet below.

After a few very cold days, unseasonal rain and overcast skies, the famous wind known as the 'Cape Doctor' decided to blow. All plans for departure stopped as *Zebu* waited for a lull, but at last they could be off. Whatever the weather outside the harbour mouth, there could be no turning back into the wind. Under course

Above: Great Korup Bridge, Cameroon.

Below: *Zebu* – homeward bound.

Above: Colonel John Blashford-Snell and Martin Venables of Stratford, East London on a marine biological project in the Bahamas.

Below: Timothy Woodburn of Arnside, Cumbria with the drug smuggler's plane discovered in the Bahamas.

Opposite: Lord Nelson entering Southampton water.

Above: An Avon strikes a powerful stopper wave on the Zambezi.

Below: A close call for Peter Enzer and Tony Walton on the Zambezi, but the faithful Mariner started first time.

and lower topsail, the brigantine was making a good five knots in a Force-6 gusting-7 gale. The wind backed to the southwest and abated as they left the land behind and soon they rolled in the westerly swell.

On 10 January the swell eased and more sail was set as the galley watch concocted a twenty-first-birthday cake for Basingstoke Venturer Gordon Davis. It was a long way from home where he would otherwise have been inspecting fuel pumps for Harrier jump jets. This was a day's run of 248 kilometres, with all sail set except for the topgallant. The temperature crept up and touched 21°C, enough to encourage the hardier to endure a seawater shower. The accompanying screams did nothing to disturb the concentration of the girls doing aerobics or those playing in the first round of a Scrabble competition. Not content with the topgallant giving the ship a comfortable five knots, Nick dug deep and produced his 'bonnet', which was set below the course. Now with only the water sail to go, almost every stitch of canvas was set.

St Helena, 22 January 1988

The historic island where Napoleon I died, a prisoner, in 1821, loomed against the horizon. Vertical cliffs rose 550 metres above the pounding surf and volcanic peaks towered above them. St Helena is noted for the dangerous rollers that crash against its rocky shores: here, in 1846, thirteen vessels were wrecked at their moorings. According to the navy hydrographer, sharks 'of great size and voracity' inhabit these waters and *Zebu*'s crew took extra care in going ashore. The governor and people of this lonely island off the west coast of Africa gave the young crew a hearty welcome and a tour around the home of the world's most famous exile.

Salvador, Brazil, 16 February 1988

When the sixteen Venturers forming the next expedition joined *Zebu*, the temperature was 36°C at the town dock. The sweat ran off their backs in rivulets as they toiled in the almost unbearable heat. Once at sea, however, the breeze gave them some respite as they headed for Belem.

They were another excellent crew, varied in ability, but always willing. For example, Brian Primey, from Toronto, was so agile in the rigging that it wasn't until he asked someone to pass him his artificial leg that the others discovered his handicap. Then there was Michael Crane of Cornwall, sponsored by the South West Electricity Board, who was a keen amateur naturalist. 'After refuelling we were off once more towards Amazonia,' he wrote in his diary. 'The bioluminescence around the ship was incredible, like an electric storm, hundreds of tiny flashes lit up the water, particularly in the bow waves. It made night watches pass quickly, as we tried to examine the sources of the light by using special photographic materials. As we neared the Amazon delta, the colour of the sea changed from turquoise to bottle green and murky brown, and had so much debris in it we had a continuous bow watch looking out for large logs that could damage the ship.'

Sailing up the Amazon River, they were lucky to sight a school of rare dolphins and made out a report on them for the use of conservation organizations. Four days later, when Steve Law went overboard, *Zebu*'s luck held again: he was rescued before the crocodiles got him. Good fortune deserted them later, however, when the main engine seized up, but picking up the trade winds, they reached Barbados, 1126 kilometres away, under sail.

Antigua, 4 May 1988

On reaching Antigua, *Zebu* finally completed her circumnavigation. In December 1985 she had called at this tropical island on her way out. But many kilometres of sailing still stretched ahead as the gallant little ship proceeded via the British Virgin Islands, Bermuda, Portugal, Jersey and France to her home port of Southampton. When she tied up on 8 October 1988 she'd been away four years and had travelled 70,000 nautical miles, crossed the equator six times and visited 135 ports in forty-one different countries. Three hundred and fifty Venturers of twenty-three nationalities had helped to crew her and had all returned safe and sound. It was a remarkable achievement for Peter Masters and his staff; all very different people, with diverse backgrounds and cultures, they had shared the challenges, the hardships and the fun. The seasickness and climbing the rigging may have been hellish, but the goodbyes were hardest of all. This was not the end of Operation Raleigh's sail training, however, for yet more Venturers were off to sea on another ship.

CHAPTER FOURTEEN

Across the Atlantic to the Turks and Caicos

Ship to Shore

(*Atlantic Crossing Leader*: Lieutenant-Colonel Frank Esson, AAC)

(*Turks and Caicos Leader*: Leslie Holliday)

Southampton, England, 14 October 1988

Zebu was barely home before the formidable STS *Lord Nelson*, a 43-metre, square-rigged sailing barque, began to plough the Atlantic swells. Her route would take her from Southampton via Plymouth and Madeira south to the Canaries. If the trade winds were favourable she would speed on to Antigua, then head north to the islands of Grand Turk and Providenciales, part of the West Indian Turks and Caicos archipelago. If all went well, hers would be an adventure of 8000 kilometres. On their ocean crossing, the Venturers would make thousands of sail changes and spend hours aloft, working on the yards thirty metres above a sometimes angry ocean.

Packing for this expedition had been difficult. The joining instructions issued by Gerald Oliver from London's CHQ were succinct. Only one kit bag per person would be allowed, and no rigid-frame packs. Crossing the notorious Bay of Biscay in October would mean long and very cold night watches. The second half of the expedition, however, past the coral beaches and mangrove swamps of the Turks and Caicos Islands, would be tropical. In addition, reef surveys and underwater conservation projects were to be the basis of many tasks Operation Raleigh was to undertake in the West Indies. Those with their own equipment arrived laden with flippers, demand valves, masks and wet suits draped across their shoulders.

Les Holliday, a scientist kindly loaned to the expedition by British Rail, who would head the Turks and Caicos half of the expedition, was at the quayside on the morning of departure. The crew would see him next in the very different climate of the West Indies. Lining the docks of Southampton were hundreds of other wellwishers, including members of the Jubilee Sailing Trust, a non-profit organization which had built and designed the three-masted 400-tonne sail-training ship to enable both able-bodied and disabled people to meet the challenges of the sea.

As the band struck up and colourful streamers arched through the air, *Lord Nelson*'s twin, 260-horsepower engines growled impatiently and she left Town Quay in style, escorted by a troop of dinghies, a plume of water launched by a ship's fire tender and the impressive salute of the QE2's foghorns. Once in the Solent, her engines would be silenced and her sails hoisted, 1000 square metres of canvas which could capture the wind and propel her through the open water at speeds of over twelve knots.

In the spring of 1912, to huge fanfare, a very different ship had left from Southampton and set off across the Atlantic. She never made it. The unthinkable happened. The world's largest and most technologically advanced ship was gored by a black iceberg as she steamed past Newfoundland on a moonless night. After inspecting the damage, the man who had designed the ship reported to Captain Edward J. Smith that her condition was fatal. Then he sat down in the lounge, his head in his hands. Both he and the captain went down with their ship. On 15 April, at 2.20 a.m. SS *Titanic* sank, taking 1522 lives with her.

The man largely responsible for finding the wreck of the *Titanic* had quietly boarded *Lord Nelson* at the start of the expedition and sailed with her as far as Portsmouth. He was a tall, trim American who knew more about the sea and salvage than almost anyone. Others had tried to locate the remains of the huge luxury liner, but her grave had remained a mystery, her secrets buried four kilometres beneath the sea. For his search Dr Robert Ballard had organized an experienced team of French and Americans who were on first-name terms with a sophisticated array of technology such as *Alvin*, the three-man submersible; *Argo*, the search vessel; *Knorr*, the Wood's Hole research vessel and *Jason Junior*, a little robot worth half a million dollars. *Jason* was a swimming eyeball that spied on the murky deep, photographing the places nothing else could reach. All together they found the *Titanic* on 1 September 1985.

A leading member of the Explorers Club and an officer in the US Naval Reserve, Bob told me of his plans to use this remarkable deep sea search system on other challenging quests. Indeed, less than a year after he stepped off *Lord Nelson* at Portsmouth, Ballard and his colleagues discovered yet another sunken landmark of the past: *Bismarck*, the pride of Hitler's navy. Crippled in May 1941 by HMS *Prince of Wales*, *Bismarck* had fled south towards France and was finally torpedoed after a six-day chase. Only 115 of the 2200 crew survived. Like the

Titanic, she was a casualty of the Atlantic Ocean, and she, too, was thought to be unsinkable.

Bob Ballard made a deep impression on the young crew of Venturers who were heading for open water. His message was clear. No craft is unsinkable. Eight days and 1769 kilometres from Southampton, they would remember his words as they fought a southerly Force-10 gale in the Bay of Biscay.

Bay of Biscay, Trafalgar Day, 21 October 1988

'As we headed for Madeira the winds were unpredictable and stormy, with lots of Force 7s,' remembers Mike 'Taff' Nilsen. 'The ship handled them well, but the weather was building up and the radar showed squalls. It was going to blow.' After only a week at sea, the whistling Welshman, a pipe-layer for British Gas, had conquered his seasickness. Having sailed on the STA schooner *Winston Churchill*, Taff had the confidence of an old salt. Remarkably, all of the Venturers soon learned their way around the 140 ropes accessible from the deck – 250 all told – called braces, falls, tacks, clews or bruntlines, but never just rope, and the twenty-two sails that could scoop the top and bottom off a trade wind and harvest any breeze in between.

The gale continued for most of the day, and those on watch from 8 p.m. until midnight brought in some of the sails. It was during the second watch that the storm struck. 'Let's get those topsails in,' bellowed Jamie Green, the bosun, as the winds increased and the cold rain whipped the night. As the ship swung through an eighty degree arc and the sea boiled beneath her, the watch handed the main course and four of the men began the precarious climb up the mast to sea stow the huge sail. Taff and Hans Bruning, a student at the University of Arizona, managed to stow the starboard course while the bosun and Ian Patrick stowed the port side. The age-old rule is 'one hand for the ship and one for yourself', but an extra appendage would have been useful. The men clung to the rigging with their knees and elbows while the ship bucked and the wind sought to rip them from their perches.

Even then the job was not complete. The topsails, too, had to be stowed away against the fury of the storm. With the main course lashed tight to the yard, the Welshman and the American continued higher up the ratlines, eyes fixed on the heaving canvas. As they sought for footholds the wind pressed their bodies hard against the salt-encrusted sheets and tore the shouts from their throats. For a moment Hans and Taff lay against the ratlines, conserving the energy they needed to fight the elements.

Far below they could see the tiny figures of the rest of the watch. Amongst them were Carolann Seavers and Dawn Meredith, the only girls who, with Louise Auchterlonie – and in far calmer weather – had leapt from the course yard to the sea far below, emerging from the waters with massive blue bruises already blooming on their thighs. Next to Dawn was Karen Butler, a girl sponsored by the TSB Trust Company, who displayed a different kind of courage; a courage which grew even stronger during the three-month expedition. Karen has spina bifida, a condition which is likened to an unzipped spine which fails to close. She is unable to feel anything in her legs and could injure herself without knowing it. 'I'm one of the lucky ones,' says Karen, her legs thickly padded to protect her if she fell. 'The majority are in wheelchairs.'

For Karen, climbing the rigging felt like trying to climb a ladder of air. On the first try her mind was gripped with an icy fear and her legs wouldn't obey, despite words of encouragement from her friends and the gentle banter of expedition leader Frank Esson just behind her. She had come back down to cries of 'Good try!' with Taff carefully setting her feet on to each slippery rung. Two days before arriving at the Turks and Caicos she tried again, and this time went right to the top without stopping. Very slowly Taff and Frank moved her legs over the futtock shrouds and set them on the yard, then she collapsed on to the safety of the platform with a happy sense of relief.

Karen's eyes still light up with the memory of that moment fifteen metres above the sea. 'It was my first chance to see a sunset aloft,' she says smiling; 'everyone else had seen it for six weeks. The ship looked totally different; I could hardly hear the voices on deck, and, when ship's doctor Jane Dunbar came and sat with me, we looked out at Salt Cay and Cotton Cay and at Grand Turk on the other side. But I knew I was supposed to be on watch, and as I came down everyone cheered. I was handed a *piña colada* to celebrate and had a kiss from Hans.'

Karen Butler's act of bravery was one of many that just being on board seemed to encourage. *Lord Nelson* is a very special ship, designed by naval architect Colin Mudie. All decks are level, with no steps, and there are electric lifts to give access to the disabled. Chart desks, compasses and other navigational aids are at wheelchair height; as the director of the Jubilee Sailing Trust, Major Peter Thompson, points out, the ship's namesake was also handicapped: Viscount Horatio Nelson, who joined the navy at age twelve and became the most famous of Britain's naval heroes, had lost an eye and an arm in battle.

Now, under skipper John Fisher and expedition leader Frank Esson, who had sailed on both *Zebu* and *Eye of the Wind*, life on *Lord Nelson* settled easily into a routine of four-hour watches, 'happy hour', when the ship was scrubbed until it shone, and galley duty, although the ship's cook Kitty Wilkes surrendered her domain with reluctance.

Short of sleep though they were, there was still time to watch the changing moods of the sea. One never grew weary of the magic of whales gliding in slow motion across the bow, of the silver arrows formed by flying fish, of tired birds resting briefly on a shroud, or, most of all, of the dolphins.

Madeira, 1 November 1988

It was during the midnight to 4 a.m. watch, about fifty kilometres off Madeira, that Italian Venturer Andrea Bellardinelli first saw the dolphins. Scanning the port side for a pinprick of red or green – the port and starboard mast lights of a passing ship – the 21-year-old Ph.D. student of marine biology chatted with Emily Catlet of New Jersey. Emily had never liked sailing, but she had worked three years to be on that midnight watch, years when she sold Christmas trees and worked as a lifeguard, barmaid and waitress during hours sandwiched between studies at the University of Wisconsin. Somehow, aboard this ship, she had learned to love the sea.

Conversation soon tailed off. It was 2 a.m. and Venturer Mark Booth took the large hydraulic wheel. With no moonlight to mark the limits of sky and ocean, they merged into a blanket of black velvet shot with stars of silvery plankton. Andrea felt himself nodding off. He roused himself, pulled on a jersey against the chill and started for the galley to make coffee for the rest of the watch.

Suddenly Andrea saw a streak of light flash under the boat, a torpedo launched by a phantom ship no watch would ever see. The Italian stopped and rubbed his eyes. When he opened them again, the sea was alive with light, an underwater fireworks display of slim, arched bodies plunging through the foam, shaking droplets of silver from their backs as they raced beside the ship.

The dolphins played all night with their square-rigged toy. When dawn lit the mauve hills of Madeira and Porto Santo they were still there, a sea-escort leading *Lord Nelson* towards the first land the crew had seen in weeks. As the ship neared Funchal Harbour in the early afternoon, the yards were braced and the skipper gave the order to harbour stow the sails. As if they heard his command, the convoy of dolphins turned like a well-trained squadron, rising smoothly over the waves, and headed back to sea.

A month later, when they arrived in the Turks and Caicos, Andrea and the other Venturers would befriend a wild dolphin, stroke him and swim with him and learn from his antics. 'JoJo' had left his pod to seek the company of humans.

He may still be there, streaking through the bay where the Venturers pitched their tents on the dusty shale, or perhaps like the dolphins of Madeira, he has returned to the deep.

If the coming of three-masted ships in the early fifteenth century made the discovery of the New World possible - single masts couldn't be built any higher without snapping - it was the faithful trade winds that powered their myriad sails. Raised by the cool air from the North Pole blowing into the high pressure areas of the equator, the trade winds carried sailors from Europe across the Atlantic to the Caribbean at a reliable five knots. These were winds which took the tiny *Nina* and *Pinta* - fifty and fifty-four tonnes respectively - and the ninety-tonne flagship *Santa Maria* from Palos, Spain, to the Caribbean in 1492. Their journey changed the world for ever.

Almost five centuries later, Captain John Fisher skippered his tall ship along much the same sea route, heading south to the Canaries and then finding the favourable trades which would drive him west to the Turks and Caicos and on to the Bahamas. Few people agree on where Columbus made his first landfall at 2 a.m. on 12 October 1492; at least nine islands have their champions - Cat, Watling (San Salvador), Conception, Samana Cay, Plana Cays, Mayaguana, East Caicos, Grand Turk and Egg. Local historians and scientists like Si Marvel and Chuck Hesse will long argue the fine points of currents and winds in order to locate the true landfall, since Columbus' log and chart are missing.

Wherever he landed, it proved a bad day for the people he called 'Indians'. The gentle Lucayans, also called Arawaks, were either enslaved or killed by the Spaniards who followed Columbus. Those who survived on land usually died at sea, forced to dive for pearl oysters in up to five fathoms of shark-infested waters, or else perished in the suffocating holds of the Spanish slavers. Even those who managed to stay alive during the crossing usually came to a grim end: the chain gangs digging for treasure in Hispaniola, the island that is now Haiti and the Dominican Republic, succumbed not to gold fever but to syphilis and other European diseases. In less than eleven years an entire people was exterminated.

Columbus made three more expeditions to the Caribbean, searching for a back door to the riches of the East by sailing west. When he returned to Spain in 1504, Queen Isabella had died. Ferdinand let the brilliant admiral die poor and dishonoured, and today his grave, like the site of his first landfall in the New World, is unknown.

Providenciales, Turks and Caicos, 29 November 1988

'Wake up, Sonya!' said Carolann in a loud whisper. 'You wanted to be up before dawn!' Gently, she shook the little figure lying on the deckhouse roof and Sonya Hendrickson from Canada awoke in a flash; she had been on the midnight to 4 a.m. watch and had only had an hour's sleep. She smiled her thanks and looked at the horizon. A thin line of light was just visible, but at 5.30 in the morning the sun had not yet risen. The moon hung in the sky, keeping company with a few bright stars. The water rippled softly in the calm of the dawn.

'Perfect,' thought the pretty, dark-skinned Canadian whose father comes from Nevis, one of the West Indian islands they had passed. Grabbing a single crutch, she went to wake bosun's mate Sian Williams and together the two girls started up the ratlines. After forty-seven days, 5380 nautical miles and 132 hours of night watches, *Lord Nelson* was nearing Providenciales, one of the largest islands of the Turks and Caicos chain. The tiny self-governing British crown colony is made up of thirty small islands – only a few of them inhabited – sprinkled over thousands of square kilometres of ocean off the southeast coast of Florida.

This would be their base for the next seven weeks, and here they would live as close to the sea as they had on board ship. As she carefully placed each leg on the rungs of the rope ladder, Sonya stopped at the fifteen-metre-high narrow wooden platform. The yard had been raised to make the royal taut, and the creamy white sails propelled the ship silently through the water. After a bit, Sian went down, but Sonya stayed, determined to watch the sunrise. She remembered the first time she had reached the royal with Gill Cozens, a blonde civil servant from London. Gill had been terrified of heights, and, halfway up, with her legs trembling and her heart thudding, she thought she would never reach the top. 'I wouldn't have, if it hadn't been for Sonya,' she said later. Too shaky to sit or kneel, Sonya had told her firmly to lie down on the platform until the fear seeped away. 'Reaching the royal was my greatest achievement,' recalled Gill. She went up every day after that.

A fall from any height would have been far more serious for Sonya than for Gill. The nineteen-year-old has a disease called osteogenesis imperfecta, or 'brittle bones', a genetic condition that means her body produces only half the collagen it needs; whereas others' bones can bend, hers will break. Somehow, Sonya never seemed to worry. Although she stopped growing at 1.40 metres – her twin sister is thirty centimetres taller – and inevitably suffers many fractures, she has taught handicapped children to sail, and herself has learned to scuba dive and to downhill ski. She uses two skis and two outriggers when she skis in the Blue Mountains of Ontario. Now, as the trade winds carried *Lord Nelson* to Providenciales, she had climbed to the royal alone. Her timing was perfect. As she hauled herself on to the yard, the last sunrise of the voyage burst from the horizon and turned the sky to gold.

Later that morning the trimaran *Tao*, skippered by David Mathews, cheerfully ferried Venturers and gear up the Leeward Channel, giving them their first good view of the island. Ahead, 'Provo', as the local people call Providenciales, and the Leeward Cays lay scattered east to west, protected by a magnificent fringing reef and tempered by the constant trade wind that had taken the square-rigger across the Atlantic. These coral outcrops support as many as 3000 different species of animals and plants - an invaluable genetic resource. Under the leadership of marine biologist Les Holliday and his able diving officer Katy Burke of Belfast, they would undertake a series of projects monitoring the health of the reefs, assembling data and proposals for national underwater parks, restoring an impounded drug-running boat for use as a marine research vessel, in addition to helping the community generally and learning to live off the sea themselves.

Base camp was basic indeed. The strip of dusty shore came equipped with sandflies, mosquitoes and hundreds of razor-sharp conch shells. Expedition members completed the arrangements, erecting tiny Vango Force-10 tents, a first-aid tent, a ramshackle canvas kitchen, a couple of air-compressor stations and a large marquee that escaped its stony anchorage and tipped over in every gale. It was home.

It didn't take long for Katy Burke and her staff to get people up to sports diver level. After Dr Anne Morgan and nurse Joanna Panton had double-checked medical records, everyone was expected to do at least two dives a day and to brush up on the theoretical aspects of scuba diving he or she had learned aboard *Lord Nelson*. The tests were formal and rigorous; Katy and her team would keep people practising in the water for many extra days rather than give them a pass for an indifferent dive.

The 'Reefwatch' project was the linchpin of the Turks and Caicos expedition. In 1984, Les had organized an Operation Raleigh survey of forty kilometres of reef on the north coast of Provo which stretches from Pine Cay to Northwest Point - the coral graveyard of gold-laden galleons homeward bound from Hispaniola. Since then, he had systematically surveyed South Caicos, Grand Turk and Provo, recording the impact fishermen, divers and sailors have had on the coral and recommending areas for protected marine parks. Already eighteen parks had been approved, and Les, a scientist, writer, scuba training expert and underwater photographer, had played a vital role.

'The concept of Reefwatch is brilliant,' thought Ian Patrick as he finned swiftly through crystal-clear waters twenty metres below the surface. His buddy, Dawn

Meredith, swam close beside him and gave the 'OK' signal. The divers admired the view and recorded the sightings on the waterproof slates they carried. Five key fish families had been singled out for biological sampling. These were the fish which would provide clues to the health of the reef: butterfly fish (*Chaetodontidae*), which feed on coral, and whose numbers indicate the health of the coral beds; angel fish (*Pomacanthidae*), which feed on sponges; trigger fish (*Balistidae*) and puffer fish (*Tetraodontidae*), which feed on sea urchins, the spiny creatures which thrive on algae which in turn live on nitrate pollution. Thus increases in the urchin colonies provide a clue that pollution is also on the rise. The last of the five key species is the grouper (*Serranidae*), perhaps the most important fish to the artisanal fisherman – the man who fishes for the pot.

In addition to the Reefwatch format, Les had organized two other levels of observation; aerial surveys and detailed profiles. When this long-term study is complete, Operation Raleigh will have helped to provide data on biological resources, environmental threats and practical conservation measures.

Some steps could be taken immediately to help prevent the destruction of the reefs. Taff had managed to borrow an underwater hammer drill from his employers and sponsors, British Gas. The idea was to dive to the bottom, drill a few ten-centimetre holes, place steel pins and refill them with cement. Later, buoys would be attached so that boats could tie up rather than drop their anchors into the wonderland below, smashing in a minute the star coral, elkhorn and sea fans that had taken years to grow.

The job was tricky enough for humans; no one had reckoned on the 'help' of a wild dolphin. Attracted by the high-pitched squeal of the drill and the rather attractive vibrations it made in the water, JoJo managed to bring work to a halt more than once. JoJo, an Atlantic bottlenose dolphin (*Tursiops truncatus*), had left his pod in 1983 to live at 'Club Med', a resort he found to his liking near the shallow waters of Provo and Pine Cay. He is about ten years old and may live to be thirty if he is both lucky and smart. The odds are against him: only a few dolphins have ever deserted their fellows for the company of humans, and most of them are dead – killed by a vandal's bullet, caught in a fishing net or struck by a passing boat. Nor is there safety in numbers. On Britain's coast, for example, chemical pollution, pesticides and intensive trawling by fishing vessels may wipe out the remaining dolphins within the next five years.

Ancient civilizations revered these silvery mammals as gods, and they feature in frescoes in Crete's temple at Knossos painted about 1600 BC. The Roman historian Pliny the Elder recounted the famous story of the friendship between a boy and the dolphin who carried him on his back, and pined to death when the child died. Every year the papers carry stories of surfers saved from sharks, and ships guided through stormy seas by these intelligent creatures. Other dolphins have been known to catch fish and offer them to humans, and some fall desperately in love with the bottoms of rubber boats and even make amorous advances to divers in neoprene wet suits.

Dean Bernal is probably JoJo's best friend. Working with Chuck Hesse, president of PRIDE, the acronym of the non-profit organization 'Protect Reefs and Islands from Degradation and Exploitation', Dean has been swimming with dolphins since he was about the age of the child in the Roman story. Every day he spends four to five hours in the water with JoJo playing hide-and-seek behind the pilings, tossing shells or just speeding through the water to burn off energy. 'Most people think that JoJo is Flipper,' Dean cautioned the Venturers. 'He's not. He is a wild animal who shows when he's upset or happy by his eyes and his body movement. He's often moody and can ram, bite or butt a swimmer, especially if you try to touch his blow-hole - his "nose". He can sense your emotions and he responds to them: if you ever feel uneasy, get out of the water immediately.'

Swimming with the silky grey dolphin was an unforgettable experience for all of the Venturers, who devised a 'dolphin watch' to provide PRIDE with additional information on his behaviour. Sonya was especially honoured by his faithful visits when she stayed in the boat as dive marshal, but Dean remained his firm favourite. JoJo would click happily when he saw him, sometimes surfacing between Dean's legs to give him an ocean ride, knowing just when to bring him up for air.

Dolphins can become suddenly aggressive, however, and the muscular power that makes their play so entrancing can threaten human lives by setting crafts adrift, overturning small boats, moving anchors and even pinning divers to the sea bed. Some have been known to butt swimmers in the chest and smash up surfboards. Occasionally JoJo has pushed swimmers out to sea and, like an overly playful puppy, tried to prevent them from returning to shore. Once or twice he has snatched the regulator out of a diver's mouth and swum off with the hapless human in tow - it was a sure way to get their attention.

West Caicos Island, 15 December 1988

As Christmas drew nearer, work on all projects intensified. Reefwatch, of course, continued, but on stormy days Chuck Hesse gave informal talks on the history and wildlife of the islands, and set the Venturers to work clearing out the sea cages of the conch farm. Queen conchs were once a high-protein staple here -the edible foot muscle of one adult yields a hefty 200 gm. of meat. In the last fifteen years, however, overfishing has almost wiped out their breeding sites in the Caribbean. Chuck Hesse is trying to rebuild the population and show people how to maintain these shellfish as a sustainable resource.

Other Venturers worked with local schools, teaching the children to swim and dive, and surveyed Little Water Cay, searching for reasons why the already endangered iguanas decrease each year. A few set off in a rusty landing craft to do Reefwatch studies in the waters off West Caicos, a remote island inhabited only by ghosts of an abandoned settlement and a very lively population of mosquitoes. Quartermaster Chris Payne headed the small team with an ex-Venturer of the Malaysian expedition, Andy Reid. As a surprise - and a kind of insurance - Les Holliday had included someone else in the team, Hawaiian survival expert James 'Kimo' Moore whose bulging brown muscles and triangular shape seemed to frighten fish into his bare hands. 'You catch a squid, bite off its eyeballs and turn it inside out,' explained the Pacific island Tarzan like a chef revealing a secret recipe. 'The meat is so dense that one will feed us all.' Limpets, crabs, lobster and sea urchins were all devoured raw, but Kimo ate shark only in emergencies. 'If you eat a shark, he will eat you next,' he warned - although Les has seen him rip open one snaggle-toothed monster and chew the liver with gusto.

Among the challenges Chuck Hesse had given the Venturers was the restoration of a derelict nine-metre motorboat. Once she had run drugs between South America and Florida, but had been caught, impounded and handed over to PRIDE for use, if she could be repaired, as a research and marine patrol vessel.

'She's a boat with a past who has paid her dues,' said Chuck to project leader Richard Cole, a boat builder and Territorial Army Royal Engineer. Indeed, she was no beauty, lying beached on a coral spit of land, heavy with mud and slime and surrounded by dead conch shells. As if to hide her sorry condition, heart-shaped vines snaked around the gaping hole in her hull and wound through the split engine beds, rotten frames and deck and wrapped themselves around her rudder, rusted solid in the gland. A small blue wooden dinghy leaned against her starboard side like an exhausted companion and, nearby, a single-masted fishing smack lay broken on the rocks. They had gathered here to die, their graveyard just a few metres away from a stone plaque commemorating the opening of the national park by HRH Princess Alexandra a month earlier.

Only the drug-runner would have a second chance. Under Richard Cole's patience and skill, the Venturers restored her to perfection and delivered her to PRIDE just after New Year. Strong, capable Brian Watson, sponsored by Wiggins Teape, had seen the project through from the start, his large hands permanently covered with the sticky, white fur of fibreglass. The tanned Hong Kong Venturer

Malcolm Crawford turned white with resin and Sonya disappeared for hours, her tiny frame fitting neatly into the hold she laminated. With her new stays, reconditioned engines and sparkling blue and white paint, the proud little vessel shrugged off her past; this time around she would help to save lives.

As the Venturers regrouped to spend Christmas together, another seafaring expedition was celebrating the holiday with a pre-dawn dive, delighting in the colourful reefs of the Bahamas and the delicate plume worms that looked, appropriately, like tiny Christmas trees. Columbus had discovered these islands too, and, on a Christmas Eve 496 years before, the *Santa Maria* had been wrecked in these warm West Indian waters.

The great Italian navigator could never have imagined that one day people would swim like dolphins and breathe air beneath the sea. Nor would he have recognized the surprising craft that these young divers found on the ocean floor. Amidst the patch reefs and coral sand lay a small yellow aeroplane. It was in perfect condition, but the pilot had died.

CHAPTER FIFTEEN

The Bahamas

Tropical Paradise

(*Expedition Leaders*: Major Tony Walton, TD RA
John Parsloe)

Hall's Pond Cay, 5 December 1988

Well after dark, the small Cessna aircraft flew north at wave-top height, showing neither navigation nor landing lights. It had been a long flight from Columbia, dodging radar and storms, but ahead the pilot could just make out the shimmering coves of Hall's Pond Cay and Waderick Wells. It wasn't far now to Norman's Cay and the private airstrip where flares would guide him in.

Recklessly, he lowered the nose a fraction, skipping like a swallow across the sea. The starboard wing barely touched the black coralhead, but that touch was enough. The plane reared and crashed tail-first into the sea, taking with it a multimillion-dollar cargo of cocaine.

To those who live on a crowded mainland, the Bahamas conjure up a tropical paradise, but the reality can be very different. The Venturers discovered an archipelago of rare beauty but one where drinking water was scarce, the blister-raising poison wood grew in profusion, and where a stiff breeze was the only antidote to the ferocious sandflies. They also found the furry-bodied groundspiders with a span of fifty centimetres, tarantulas which scurry backwards and sideways like crabs, and the most venomous creatures inhabiting the islands, the black widow: a jet black spider with a red hourglass on her abdomen whose bite can kill a man in a matter of hours.

Whoever named the black widow got the gender right, for like the sandfly and the mosquito, the female is the sex to be reckoned with. In the world of the winged insects, the male feeds meekly on nectar while the female goes for blood. The mate of the black widow, too, seems an afterthought of nature. His is an unhappy lot.

Only a third of the size of his deadly partner, he mates once, loses his fangs, starves to death and is devoured by his spouse.

The waters of the Bahamas have a few fangs of their own. Most sharks, with the exception of the great white, are found in the sunlit, mint-green seas cruising the peaks of the submarine mountains which rise from the ocean floor. Off Little Exuma, to the south of the wrecked Cessna aircraft, Gloria Patience, the 'Shark Lady', has hauled more than a thousand sharks into her 4-metre Boston whaler – the largest was a 5.5-metre tiger shark. The skies can be equally unfriendly, for hurricanes rise quickly in the Atlantic. Just three months before members of the expedition flew into Nassau, Hurricane Gilbert slammed into the Caribbean and raged on to Mexico, destroying everything in its path. In a year which was notable for natural catastrophes – vast floods in Sudan and Bangladesh, fires which reduced North American forests to charcoal, and a drought delivered by the hottest American summer in fifty years – Gilbert was the most powerful storm in the western hemisphere in this century.

With such companions, and the daunting projects outlined by Tony Walton and his deputy Dave Chisholm, the Venturers quickly abandoned any thoughts of a holiday. Over the next three months, they would build huge fire-watch towers on the pine island of Abaco, dive through tunnels off San Salvador to map the fish and corals, help scientists to research sedimentology, dunes and reef erosion, and construct one of the most substantial timber buildings Raleigh had ever attempted.

Both Waderick Wells and Hall's Pond are near to the site where the drug-running Cessna had crashed. Both are a part of the 456 square kilometre Exuma Cays Land and Sea Park created in 1958. Whilst the diving team at Hall's Pond, led by Mike Berry, devised a way to lift the plane off the coral reef, project leader Vicki Pepper and a small group living on Waderick Wells were building an eighteen by nine metre structure able to withstand the hurricanes coming in from the north. When complete, it will be used by Bahamian students learning about the marine park, and other conservation groups and scientists. The projects in the park were overseen and encouraged by warden Peggy Hall and her deputies Bob and Anita Raider. The Raiders live on a 1928 Elco, the *Janice L*, a classic Rolls-Royce of a yacht; Peggy's home is the Victory tug, *Moby* which she shares with her yellow dog. Her radio crackled constantly with traffic from passing yachts, the police, the Defence Force, float planes, friends scattered about the islands and from Operation Raleigh. The communications network was quick to report any suspicious boats in the area. Within minutes of receiving a call, Peggy and Grant McPherson, Raleigh's intrepid boat handler who has charted the rivers of Guyana and the seas of Panama, would head off to help someone in trouble or to nab an offender fishing in this aquatic nursery where all fishing is banned.

Often the call would come well before sunrise. Moving quickly and easily, the warden would climb over the stern of her yacht into the inflatable craft already waiting below. Seconds after she straddled the seat behind Grant's broad back, the twin engines roared and the Avon Sea Rider's bow spun towards the horizon. Whipped by the spray, the two figures, one bulky and one slim, rose like jockeys as the boat rushed watery fences two metres high. 'We either rescue them or arrest them,' laughs the silver-haired lady in her soft Irish accent. She sips her evening rum and water as *Moby* rocks in the gentle swell; a Katharine Hepburn-like figure who has sailed these waters for more than forty years. 'If we don't let the fish breed and replenish their stocks we won't have any fish. It's that simple,' she says. 'If immature conch, groupers and crawfish are killed, if reefs are destroyed by fishermen and yachtsmen dumping their garbage, we won't have anything left to protect.'

Andros Island, December 1988

The ghosts of dead pilots are not the only phantoms to haunt the Bahamian islands. They also held a fatal attraction for galleons, ballasted with solid silver and homeward bound from Hispaniola: the Spaniards aptly named this region '*Baja Mar*' or 'Shallow Sea'. Hundreds of millions of dollars' worth of jewels, precious silver and gold lie buried here amongst the bones of brave sailors. This was once the undisputed territory of ship wreckers and rum runners, smugglers and swashbucklers, pirates like Edward Teach – alias Blackbeard, who drank rum-and-gunpowder and shared his fourteen wives with the crew – and bloodthirsty females like Irish Anne Bonney and English Mary Read. Two centuries later, during Prohibition, fortunes were reaped from smuggling illegal liquor, a career which gave a new meaning to 'gin clear' waters. Legend has romanticized the evils of the past; impossible as it seems today, the shades of dead drug-dealers may eventually receive the same treatment.

Each island has its own peculiar ghosts. The caves of Waderick Wells are haunted by shipwrecked missionaries, for example, whose choirs sing when the moon is full; Andros, the largest of all the Bahamian islands, harbours the spirit of 'Uncle Charlie', still diving his blue hole. Andros is a big jigsaw puzzle of an island, cut by a hundred unexplored creeks, mangrove swamps, pine forests, salt lakes and its famous blue holes. These entrances to the earth's centre drop vertically through hundreds of metres of rock; they are freshwater springs carved by time and nature into ice-blue aquariums for neon-coloured fish and needle-sharp stalactites. A few divers enter, and a few remain: Uncle Charlie was one. Whoever he was, locals swear he is still there. Cave diving is a dangerous game; you can't surface if you lose your way or panic; most dead divers have badly cut hands, torn by the rock as they scrabbled against the underwater ceiling. One of our earlier recce parties had discovered Charlie's skeleton, still in its wet suit and imprisoned in a cleft of the great cavern. You don't rescue blue hole divers; sometimes you can't even recover their bodies.

Charlie is a kindly, if unfortunate presence, an element of the eeriness of Andros which few would challenge in the bone-white light of the moon. Perhaps it has something to do with the dramatic underwater mountains which surround the island. And who knows what lurks nearby, in the Tongue of the Ocean, a submerged Grand Canyon which plunges three kilometres beneath the ocean floor.

It had taken days for the fishing trawler laden with lobster pots and Venturers to reach Andros from Freeport. Days when Welsh-speaking Eli Meazey, Australian Jim Miles, Italian Piero Benedetti and their companions fished for mutton snapper and watched the acrobatics of porpoises, turtles and flying fish as they anchored out at night. They reached Mangrove Cay – the middle cay of Andros – at 2 a.m. and were met by project leader Alastair Anton and diving instructor Christine Brearley, who had braved rain and rough seas to ferry them ashore. When the shear pin of Alastair's outboard snapped in the angry swells, however, it was the Venturers who came to the aid of the staff: Jim Miles, who routinely free-dives to fifteen metres on Australia's Barrier Reef, swam past ribbons of poisonous sea snakes to bring them a forgotten paddle.

En route the Venturers had stopped at Driggs Hill to join a local 'disco', beginning their adventure in a manner they meant to sustain. When Tony Walton and Dave Chisholm at their Nassau HQ received a radio request for a rubber repair kit, they assumed that the Avon had suffered a puncture on the sharp limestone rocks. In fact, the Andros islanders had discovered a derelict house with boa constrictors asleep in the rafters, rampaging rats, a brace of tarantulas – and a waterbed in need of repair.

Few Venturers had a chance to try out the elegant bed or enjoy the comforts of base camp. Their usual camp was a waist-deep swamp or some tangled maze of mangrove. 'Almost the whole of Mangrove Cay is reported to be unexplored,' wrote Raleigh scientist Rob Whittaker of Oxford University. 'Access is clearly difficult and no one knows what lies in the interior.'

Young Tam McCordy of Ayr, Scotland, was one who soon found out. Glaswegian Venturer Robin Rafferty – a part-time racing driver who drives speedboats, sails, and is working on his private pilot's licence – led the group deep into the swamp, surprising spiders, egrets and hummingbirds which had claimed the wasteland for themselves. 'Extreme heat and clouds of mosquitoes in the mangrove and button-tree bush made the going difficult,' admitted Tam. 'But it was when we ran out of water that it got a bit tough.'

San Salvador, 10 December 1988

Most dives have one outstanding feature, according to Phil van Zwanenberg: coral, sponges, fish or wrecks. San Salvador, however, has them all. If one had to name a highlight of this underwater world, it would probably be 'The Tunnel': vertical chimneys of coral where the fish swam up to the divers unafraid, nibbling the masks of the young people who were making coral surveys. It was like sharing an aquarium.

In 1988, when Operation Raleigh visited this island, the world had all but forgotten it. In 1992, however, San Salvador will be the centrepiece of the 500th anniversary of the discovery of the New World, choked with historians championing their various theories concerning the first landfall of Columbus.

When the letter arrived, Paul Hancock was busy chipping off the old paint and plaster from the San Salvador jail. The building hadn't been used since 1965 when the only lodger lifted a grille and sauntered out, and the cheerful pink and green structure was being restored as a landmark at the request of Commissioner Joseph Alexis Ferguson. There is no need for a real jail, for nothing ever goes missing on the nineteen kilometre-long island.

The nineteen-year-old athlete was used to a certain amount of acclaim. Paul was a paraplegic who had cycled around Britain twice (each trip had taken forty days), sailed on *Lord Nelson*'s maiden voyage in 1986 and won a double silver in the 1988 Seoul Paralympics in the 50-metre backstroke and the 100-metre freestyle. Now, as his friends crowded around him, the boy with the smiling, blue-green eyes could hardly believe the tribute his Humberside community had paid him. 'Paul Hancock made history in Cleethorpes last night,' ran the article, 'but he was miles away in the Caribbean.' In his absence, Paul had been voted 'Sports Personality of the Year' and had won the 'Disabled Person of the Year Award' for South Humberside. Expedition leader Tony Walton was there to share his triumph.

There are many different kinds of handicaps. Physical limitations are one kind, growing up in a street gang is another, and Garry St Catherine has a knife scar to prove it. A member of our expedition to Southern Chile in 1987, the handsome, black carpenter had once been a member of the 'Tottenham Firm'. Tony was quick to spot his many talents and had recruited him as a project leader for the

Bahamas expedition. Ironically, the task he assigned the ex-streetfighter was that of restoring the San Salvador jail.

'Anyone you admired was in a gang,' says Garry; 'it was the natural thing, an easy pattern to fall into. Before you knew it, your group got bigger, there were dress codes that other gang members recognized and people put a name to you. It's a very small world.' Aware of the rules of that violent world, he had known he was going to be hit as soon as he stepped from the safety of the clubhouse. He woke up in hospital with five holes in his chest. The blade missed his heart by a fraction.

His three months in Chile as a Venturer gave Garry time to think things through. Now, the lanky 25-year-old is successfully self-employed and has started a series of 'Raleigh Adventure Weekends' (RAWS) to teach local youngsters camping, cooking, climbing and communication skills. Garry and other ex-Raleigh expeditioners like Andy Thomson, Dyan Wood, Emma Clarke and Lesley Smith find the names of problem kids from the local probation services – youngsters without direction, charged with breaking and entering or with car theft. Some are on their third court appearance of the year. They see Garry as a big, hard man. He is. A big, hard man extending a helping hand.

Eleuthera, Hatchet Bay Cave, 10 December 1988

Helen Kilmurray emerged from the cave, blinking as her eyes adjusted to the brilliant sunlight. Her helmet felt heavy and she pulled it off with relief, running her fingers through her sweat-drenched mop of blonde hair. Behind her she could hear the high-pitched chittering of the bats that the Venturers had disturbed as they worked in the high-ceilinged chamber, clearing the rubbish and erasing the graffiti left behind over the years.

The twenty-year-old student of environmental science had never before been down a cave, and she was struck by the beauty of the maze of cold tunnels dripping with water and streaked with white, green and red. Stalactites hung like roots from the ceiling and crude steps had been cut here and there by guano gatherers. Behind Helen came Paul Hebden, an apprentice mechanic sponsored by Vickers Defence Systems; plumber and builder Patrick O'Riordan; and Gregory Kreikemeier, an American student specializing in Caribbean marine organisms who was a walking encyclopedia of information and an expert caver.

Now the small group packed their frugal lunch and climbed a steep hill covered by thorns and poison wood. At the top, cliffs fell ten metres down to the sea and the Venturers leapt into warm water that was so clear they could see the purple fans, moon jellies and barracuda as they launched into space. When Dave

Chisholm and Paul Hebden saw a particularly large, dark shadow swim towards them, Greg quickly allayed their fears by identifying it as a southern stingray, *Dasyatis americana*, whose grey, ruffled wings were a little battered and torn by age. Dave invented a new game: when he tossed his knife into the sand, the old ray would follow, lunge at the glittering blade, then brake suddenly when it realized the metal wasn't edible.

The fish had a few games of their own. One early evening as he snorkelled, Pat O'Riordan glanced down and saw a convoy swimming towards him made up by two sharks flanked on either side by spotted eagle rays. At the approach of these ocean-going 'heavies', the calm sea erupted as thousands of small fish raced for shore; silversides and bar jacks leaped and splashed in terror, making the water boil with their frenzy.

It was just after 5 p.m. – the time when all groups made radio contact with Tony Walton in Nassau – that Greg Kreikemeier, Pat O'Riordan and project leader Pat Shirley entered a cave to search for an outlet to the sea. There had to be a tunnel, they reasoned, since the salty water in the lowest part of the cave rose and fell with the tides and a local fisherman had confirmed their suspicions. Crossing the first large chamber, they climbed down the steps carved in the limestone and then dropped three metres into darkness. Their headlamps cast weird shadows on the rock.

Pat O'Riordan felt uneasy. The enormous chamber floor was strewn with boulders, and clusters of bats hung from the ceiling, shuffling and squeaking at the interruption. Once his eyes became accustomed to the darkness he could see the autumn colours of the flowstone, glistening curtains of amber and white, veined with dark streaks where the soil had leached through. On one side of the cavern was a forest of stalactites, and the sound of dripping water echoed in the distance.

Pat felt a spurt of adrenalin as they set off down a long, dark passage, jumping from rock to rock over the cold, clear water that came up to their ankles. Confused by the lights, bats swooped at their heads; he could feel a cool draught on his neck as they passed and smell their droppings pungent with ammonia. Soon he was bathed in sweat, his hair plastered flat beneath his helmet. Ahead was a pool of impossibly blue water which seemed to drop to the centre of the earth. They skirted the edge and continued on, searching for the tunnel which would lead them to the sea.

The passage narrowed abruptly. The three explorers slithered through corridors of mud which made a sucking sound at every step. Often they had to squeeze through holes so narrow that they couldn't move their heads, or inch forward on their toes. Covered in red mud and bleeding from the thin, sharp soda straws that sprouted from every surface, they found themselves in a passageway of glassy pools and washed in the subterranean cavern.

They had been down in the caves for hours and had explored every route without success. It was getting late. Perhaps they had missed the tunnel; perhaps it had collapsed. The latter was a very real possibility, thought Pat as he wriggled through a narrow channel with one arm stretched forward and the other behind. The rock crumbled at his touch and for the first time he felt a stab of real fear. Perhaps they were in a fragile sand tunnel which could collapse at any moment. He tried to ease himself backward but the rock held him fast. And then his light went out.

'Pat! Watch my feet!' came Greg's reassuring voice in front of him.

'Count to ten and don't panic,' Pat told himself sternly. Following Greg's movements exactly, he squeezed through the chimney, and, as his head struck the wall, his torch jarred against its contacts and splashed its light against the clammy rock.

They never did find the passage to the sea for the next moment they heard the project leader shouting their names. Somehow, after hours in the labyrinth, they had ended up directly below the main chamber. 'We were filthy, exhausted and soaking wet but came out talking at ninety miles an hour,' said Pat. 'We were on a high, bursting with energy. The long walk back to base passed in a minute, and we met up with Dave Chisholm on the way.' Only then did Greg learn that Pat had never before been in a cave.

Abaco, 12 January 1989

I was watching the Venturers struggling to erect a 20-metre fire tower on Abaco, a boomerang-shaped island to the north of Eleuthera. Tall stands of pine grew out of the pure white limestone, like Christmas trees in snow, and the air was heavy with their scent. The trees blocked out the sea: except for the fact that the group hauled their drinking water from a blue hole deep in the forest, it was hard to believe that this parched land was part of the Bahamas.

'Props in?' sang out Perry Donaldson in his Northern Irish accent. Answering shouts of 'Props in!' echoed down the line in a variety of inflexions ranging from Ronald Rakete's Australian to James Murray's Scots, Juli Handscomb's Welsh and Alex Cartwright's Bahamian. I was impressed that their work had been accomplished with such basic tools: rope and a 2-tonne car jack. Last year, over 12,000 hectares of trees on Abaco had burned down, Tony Walton explained, often set alight by wild boar hunters. Once the Raleigh teams completed the series of cross-braced towers, foresters like Shireen Chambers, who encouraged the project from the start, would have a far better chance of putting out the flames.

On site, Ian Lothian, a keen local archaeologist, told me about some carvings of old ships he'd seen in the Hole in the Wall cave system on the southern tip of the island. I remembered tales of such carvings in caves off Queensland, Australia, said to have been done by Aborigines to depict the early European vessels that sailed close to the coast.

'I'd like to see them,' I told Ian, and soon we were bumping along in his pickup. The cave entrance was only a few metres off the rough track, and we managed to clamber down a tree rooted in the limestone cavern. Stepping across the boulders, we edged into the darkness. Tony's torch threw a pool of light across the rock. Before us were the crude outlines of sailing ships etched on the limestone - a galleon, a Bahamian sloop and a schooner. It was the galleon that caught my eye - a two-masted ship with a keel, a bowsprit, an early sail configuration - and a date: 1450.

I caught my breath. If the date was genuine, it would mean that someone had beaten Columbus to the New World by forty-two years.

Sanyo had recently presented us with a new video recorder, and as I filmed the carvings by the light of the torch I wondered if perhaps some Portuguese captain, rather than the Italian admiral, had first stumbled on to these islands. The fifteenth-century Portuguese were talented navigators and intrepid sailors. It could, of course, be a hoax. Yet it is just possible that whoever etched this date had never returned to tell his tale - or to write a very different history of the discovery of the New World.

CHAPTER SIXTEEN

Cameroon

A Walk in the Rainforest

(*Expedition Leader*: Nick Horne)

Summit of Mt Cameroon, 11 February 1989

The Gurkha's curved *kukri* flashed in the evening sun as with one smooth stroke he severed the head from the antelope's body. It was a tidy job; the *kukri*, the knife carried by these fabled warriors, is designed to let blood drip away from the handle. Deftly he scraped the head and held it over the fire to burn off the remaining hairs, then chopped up the skull, brains, teeth and tongue and added them to the boiling soup of cocoyams, ginger and chillies. As he stirred this witches' brew, the Venturers skinned the carcase and hacked the meat into lumps, skewering them on to sharply pointed saplings. That night the mountaineers would have fresh meat for the first time in a month. Like the unusually tall Nepalese soldier, they had a lean and hungry look.

Lt. Argun Kumar Gurung was one of two Gurkhas recruited by expedition leader Nick Horne to sharpen skills in jungle survival. Popular members of the expedition, their strength, patience and knowledge made an outstanding contribution to all aspects of the Cameroon adventure. Although we would not kill on this mountain except in dire emergency, the antelope had been shot by a local hunter who wandered into camp with the animal slung over his back. Everyone had quickly agreed that it was indeed 'fair game'.

As Argun added the final touch to the soup – two packets of powdered peas which, reconstituted without benefit of animal brains, were generally considered inedible – his colleague, Lt. Bal Krishna Gurung, was miles away, waist-deep in swampy coastal rivers with some other Venturers. Both men are platoon commanders with the Gurkha battalion stationed in Church Crookham, England. Another battalion is on loan to the Sultan of Brunei and the rest of the 8000-strong force is stationed at the regiment's home base in Hong Kong. All are part of a select group, renowned for courage, who have served bravely in the British Army for over 170 years: in the nineteenth century the British were so impressed with the ferocity they displayed in battle in northern India that we wisely invited them to stop fighting against us and start fighting with us. We have been friends ever since.

That night, under the stars, three hungry teams feasted on Argun's antelope. On the summit of West Africa's highest mountain - a still-active volcano - the young people studying its geology, forests, soils and insects had walked across the hills to the geology camp, stopping at the only spring en route to top up their water bottles. As everyone knows who has climbed the 4070-metre mountain, or read the vivid accounts of explorers such as Sir Richard Burton and Mary Kingsley, Mt Cameroon is dry, offering only a few thin springs at her crest.

Like the Operation Raleigh teams studying the ecology of the volcano, the subject itself - in geological terms - is very young, formed by basaltic lavas less than 10,000 years old. By comparison, some other tropical mountains have been forming for millions of years. The youthful forests of Mt Cameroon and the ancient lowland forest of the Korup - where the World Wide Fund for Nature and the Cameroon government are co-operating in a massive and original conservation effort - were the main reasons we had come to this wedge-shaped country nestled in the crook of Africa. Our work here was part of a comparative study of rainforests around the world - specifically, the Indonesian rainforests of the mountains of Gunung Binaia and Kobipoto, and the La Selva forests of Costa Rica. This study, like the others, would examine the changes in altitude in rainforests and their effects on genetic diversity.

The study had started in the late 1970s, long before the cry 'Save the rainforest' became a tabloid headline. Operation Drake had just set sail, and the Raleigh sequel was but a glimmer in Prince Charles's eye, when zoologist Andrew Mitchell and ecologist Stephen Sutton conceived the idea. In broad terms, the objective was to study species variation in the forests and to try to correlate this with climatic change and altitude, as well as other environmental variables such as slope and soils. With the help of Royal Engineers Mike Christy and John Rimmer the scientists had constructed a portable 'highway in the trees' that yielded valuable information in Papua New Guinea, Panama, Costa Rica and Indonesia. Cameroon was to be the last link in our study; this time we relied on the agility of the Venturers to scale forest giants and on the energy of scientists such as Robert Payton, ecologist John Proctor and botanist Ian Edwards to survey as much of the country as possible. Much is written about the horrifying loss of rainforests - each year witnesses the permanent destruction of an area the size of Ireland. In exchange for the mass extinction of insects, plants and animals, the world inherits deserts, droughts, silted-up rivers, destructive new weather patterns and pollution of the atmosphere. Nearly every natural habitat is at risk, from marine ecosystems and northern forests to wetlands wrecked by pollution, overfishing and development. The tropical rainforests cover only 7 per cent of the earth's surface yet nurture between 50 and 80 per cent of the species to be found on the planet, still less than 5 per cent of rainforest lands are protected.

'It's important to highlight the genetic diversity of these forests,' emphasized scientist Robert Payton of the University of Newcastle upon Tyne. 'There is very little mountain rainforest left in the tropics; many have been cleared on their lower slopes, and it is vital that we preserve those remaining as resource bases for medicines, plant breeding and botanical uses in the future.'

In just one of the fifty-metre-square plots mapped by the team, they discovered no fewer than forty-six different species of trees: the entire United Kingdom contains only thirty. Such hard work will continue to bear fruit: administrators Mark Bovey and Ndam Mourou of the famous Botanic Gardens at Limbe, where members of Operation Raleigh restored the stone 'Jungle Village' amphitheatre, will continue to monitor the plots on a long-term basis.

From this vast biochemical storehouse come the ingredients that make up one in four of the pharmaceuticals in use today: the rosy periwinkle fights leukaemia, the bark of the cinchona tree combats malaria, the Mexican wild yam prevents unwanted pregnancies and the venom of the Brazilian pit viper reduces high blood pressure. Innumerable medical secrets, plus the wild plants that may help to save lives, lie locked away in the vaults of the rainforest.

The immense trees of Cameroon, rising into wet, swirling mists and draped with mossy dreadlocks, are not the only things of mystery in this extraordinary country. Cameroon is a land of ritual, magic and phantoms where hunters use powerful charms to draw animals into their snares, and it is commonplace knowledge that the hunters can also transform themselves into bush buffalo, monkeys, duikers, crocodiles or any animal they wish in order to get closer to their quarry (a somewhat dangerous practice, since sometimes they are shot by other hunters, or even shoot themselves by mistake). It is a country where *ju-ju* societies still remain very powerful and very secret in spite of the energetic efforts of missionaries to eradicate them.

The companions of Cameroonian Venturer Buma Njinimbot, an automobile electrician, listened with astonishment to his tales of phenomena which they might expect to encounter on Mt Cameroon: a huge female goddess, half rock and half human; a magic farm where sugar cane grows untended, and which, if you take it away, will condemn you to a life of wandering in the mountains; and of spirits which possess 'king stick trees' not found in any other forest. The king sticks are found where nothing else grows, and the closer you come to one the farther away it gets. Needless to say, they never appear when photographed.

Westerners, too, have their stories of strange encounters, including sightings of a fifty-tonne, 23-metre-long brontosaurus-type 'thunder lizard', that bears a resemblance to the Loch Ness monster. As he expanded on this information, the tall, always immaculate 24-year-old cast apprehensive glances at the still-smoking volcanic peak. For Buma, as for the rest of us, it was a first ascent of this magic mountain. Like all of the Cameroonian Venturers and staff, Buma was an invaluable interpreter of customs and traditions to those of us from abroad: I would consider any expedition without local participants incomplete. Buma, Maurice Koffi, Boniface Esong, Doris Awusa, Becky Lyonga, Godlove Nesoah and the other Cameroonian members of the expedition worked overtime as informational double agents, describing us to the villagers and the villagers to us as we explored the hinterlands.

The last great eruption of this powerful mountain we had come to explore began on 16 October 1982, the day after the death of the country's greatest chief, Chief Endeley of Buca. After twenty-three years of quiescence, the mountain brought up ten million tonnes of basalt from a fissure on its southwest flank, spewing a river of lava into the rainforest, shooting fire fountains 400 metres into the air and creating dozens of perfectly cylindrical cinder cones, some of which continue to steam today. Bursting straight through the forest for eight kilometres, it had suddenly swerved to the left, avoiding the inhabited valley below. One evening, as I chatted with a relative of the dead chief, the charming 67-year-old international lawyer, Justice Samuel Endeley, I turned to another chief and asked about the eruption. 'It took us three days to stop the mountain,' the men agreed. But they wouldn't tell me how they did it. In any case, they did a good job because no lives were lost.

Dave Spooner, the widely travelled geologist leading the study on Mt. Cameroon, had briefed all the Venturers so that they could detect the warning signals of a potential eruption of this active volcano in the Cameroon fault line. 'The mountain gives ample warning,' said the slim, fit scientist who, appropriately enough, once engineered thunder effects for theatrical productions. 'Before an eruption, the mountain rumbles and shakes for two or three weeks as the pressure builds and seeks the weakest point. There are fissures all across the summit.' According to Dave, the high risk period for a major eruption is not far off, probably the next will happen between the years 2003 and 2010.

Deep in the Rumpi Hills, near the hamlet of Dikome Balue, the Operation Raleigh medical patrols were greeted enthusiastically, but with great attention paid to ceremony. Children rushed out to fill washing bowls and drinking vessels with water for the thirsty travellers. Not to be left out, the spirits were appeased with offerings of whisky poured over a post of the elder's house. Forewarned of this custom, project leader Steve Oliver produced a second bottle, appropriately called Black & White, to toast the gathering, only to be upstaged by the chief who presented him with a bottle of whisky labelled 'Prince Charles'.

Up at dawn to walk in the cool of the morning, the Venturers made the trek south via villages such as Mofako, Bonji and Bafaka on their way to Mokoko and the wide Meme River. Others had taken a different route south, stopping at Lokado, Small Massaka and Bakumba, and swimming in the warm, clear waters of the perfect circle of Lake Dissoni. On the shores of that volcanic sink hole, they set the Tilley lamps in the centre of their camp. As the glass-chimneyed lamps pulsed, throwing out their hot circles of light, hundreds of moths barged against the glass and danced in the miniature thermals. Villagers living near the lake also came to dance, and everyone joined in from Steve Oliver, Bal Gurung, nurse Sarah Ford to all of the Venturers including Pauline Crawford, Peter Kerridge, John Law and Melanie Philipps. This strange celebration lasted through the night, the drum beats drowning out the noise of the jungle.

With environmentally approved hangovers induced by lashings of *mimbo*, a distilled palm wine, Steve Oliver and his group struck camp at dawn and were on the march soon after. Never had they sweated so much; the vicious yellow sweat bees clung to their shirts and crawled along their necks and around their eyes in search of moisture. Even in the coolest part of the day, their bandannas were sodden with perspiration caused by the intense humidity and the effort of crossing jungle waterfalls that plunged over suicidally steep cliffs. Descending into the valleys, their toes slammed into the front of their boots as the weight of their rucksacks propelled them down the slopes. Along the way, they assisted Sarah Ford to diagnose cases of leprosy, tuberculosis and onchocerciasis (river blindness), a disease which leaves white patches of lizard-like skin covering the body. If not treated, the disease kills the optic nerves and may cause blindness. Onchocerciasis is transmitted by tiny worms 'injected' into the bloodstream by minute, black, hump-backed flies called *Simulium damnosum*, which breed in fast-running water. Practically everyone in the remoter parts of Cameroon has the disease.

In a country where the average life expectancy is only forty-six, where simple childhood illnesses such as diarrhoea and measles are often fatal, and where there is approximately one doctor for 10,820 people, the medical team who accompanied the Raleigh expedition were able to make a real, if limited, contribution to the well-being of the village communities. Experienced nurses like Katie White, Wendy Brown and Gail Taylor told the Venturers of simple remedies that could be made from local ingredients (such as rice water for diarrhoea), which the youngsters, in turn, taught the villagers. David Thew, Douglas Ong, Karin

Rencken and David Cumming, doctors with the expedition, inoculated children under four against measles. But everyone on the expedition did come in contact with these and other diseases, and just about everyone – the doctors in particular, it seemed – came down with an exotic variation of 'Montezuma's Revenge' in this hot and humid country. Most people lost at least a stone in weight. The gruelling nature of their work was offset by its importance to the villagers.

One of the most rewarding medical projects, however, was also one of the easiest to administer: examining people's eyesight and providing second-hand spectacles. Dubbed 'Spec-Trek', the project was run by Andrew Orkney, a 27-year-old Yorkshireman whose array of talents includes riding as a National Hunt jockey and practising as a qualified ophthalmologist. It was Andrew who appealed to the UK organization Vision Aid to donate 'recycled' eye glasses to the expedition. Together with Cameroonian ophthalmologist Victor Effimbe, the teams travelled to remote fishing and agricultural villages to dole out spectacles. Occasionally Venturers Sandra Potter from Tasmania, Anna Gawley, a systems programmer with British Airways, Peter Kerridge from Cambridge and Jo-Anne Morrison from London shook their heads in amazement at their new world, a world that meant pushing an inflatable boat filled with spectacles up the jungle-clad Ndian River and testing the sight of the village chief.

'Now I can see,' exclaimed the grizzled chief of Besingi, Billo Ngibili, with dignified delight. When Andrew handed him the large, brown-rimmed spectacles to keep, he took them with the reverence of a man receiving a priceless gift.

The trials of the Rumpi Hill trekkers were only just beginning when they reached their southern destination of Mokoko. For the next few weeks they would push and paddle their rubber inflatables down the Ndian and up the Meme Rivers. Between them the various groups led by the intrepid Canadian David Briggs covered much of the swampy wilderness. Only twenty-six years old, David had been a Venturer in Indonesia and has since led expeditions in Indonesia, the Yukon, Ontario and Alaska. Equally at home in the jungle and on its rivers, Dave and the rest of the expedition had to contend with the constant shortage of drinking water by filtering 175 litres every day. They had to clean and patch the boats, collect firewood and plan each day's advance in accordance with the tides. Up at 5 a.m. to catch the morning tides, they paddled past crocodile slides scarring the sandy banks, watched kingfishers, pelicans and West African river eagles dive for a breakfast the Venturers would have willingly shared, and sometimes woke troops of monkeys sleeping in the high branches. The trees exploded into life as the angry primates shouted their displeasure at this interruption of their private dawn. In addition, the explorers kept detailed reports of the agricultural practices of the small villages, their populations and traditional medicines, and of the inoculations performed by the Raleigh nurses and doctors against measles.

But it was the nights spent in the mangrove swamps that no one will ever forget: nights when they hung their hammocks at eye level so they wouldn't be woken by wet bottoms as the tide rose; nights when they had to paddle over to the wooden platform they built to save the fire from the sea; nights with crabs nipping their bare feet, mud hoppers skipping over their legs and hairy spiders dropping suddenly into sleeping bags and hot chocolate. Climbing into their hammocks was the trickiest part of the evening; stowing mud-sheathed boots on mangrove branches and wiping thick coats of slime from their legs before lowering them into the swaying cradle took great agility. The raucous calls of parrots were almost drowned out by the whine of mosquitoes, but sometimes both were silenced by the gentle music of John Denver's 'Country Roads' strummed by Dean Reorda on the old guitar he carried everywhere.

Mundemba, 25 February 1989

Chief Ngibili's village of Besingi is in the western part of the country, just south of a huge palm oil plantation and the nearby dusty town of Mundemba. It was here, under the towering palm trees, that the Venturers made their principal base camp, ably administered by Kiwi engineer and ex-Venturer Tim Chiswell. From Mundemba, herpetologist Mark O'Shea continued his hair-raising pursuit of serpents and reptiles by launching climbing ropes over the high canopy with crossbows and bringing snakes down from these heights held gently between his lips. Here at Mundemba, entomologists David Lees and Andrew Rawlins set out to make an inventory of the butterflies of the forest and started up the first butterfly farm. It was from Mundemba, too, that members of the bat- and bird-survey projects led by ex-Venturers Amanda Scholes and John Taylor left for the interior of the jungle, and that those intent on exploring the Ndian and Meme river systems departed.

The palm plantation at Mundemba was also the site of one of the most ambitious construction projects ever undertaken in the previous four years of Operation Raleigh: a 120-metre suspension bridge spanning the River Ndian. Expedition leader Nick Horne and Roger Chapman had entrusted the project to Royal Engineer James Lockyer, to Sapper Ian Grant and to Rory McGowan, an engineer with Ove Arup Partners, London. That massive cable suspension walkway, whose construction was primarily sponsored by the World Wide Fund for Nature, was built from the durable, chocolate-brown Ekki wood (*Lophira alata*), a rainforest tree whose grain is so dense that holes have to be pre-bored for every bolt and nail. During the rainy season the Ndian rises almost 4.5 metres and its raging, 64 kph current makes it impossible to cross. For local people, scientists, environmentalist organizations such as the UK-based Deforestation Awareness Expedition whose filmmakers joined us for a while, and for the occasional intrepid explorer, the bridge would be the back door to the heartland of Africa's oldest and richest remaining rainforest – the Korup.

The teams were lucky to have first-class briefings on the problems and goals of the fledgling park. WWF Park Adviser John Hazam and Conservator Nkemi a Tchaie monitored the bridge project almost daily and were invaluable sources of information. John and his wife Diane turned their house into a Raleigh hospital on a number of occasions when Venturers became gravely ill. The Hazams' cheerful encouragement and easy hospitality made them firm favourites with everyone.

The Korup is the great survivor. This dense coastal rainforest just north of the equator is fortunate not to count amongst its riches the things like mineral reserves, agricultural terrain or easily extracted timber, that man holds dear. Over nine metres of rain falls on the forest every year, carried by storms that sweep in from the Atlantic. The heat and humidity are fierce. Not an easy berth for man, the Korup is the perfect environment for over 250 species of birds, 400 species of trees, many rare and unknown fish, moths and butterflies, and creatures such as the forest leopard, the elephant, the beautiful Preuss' red colobus monkey and the elegant drill baboon. It is also the site of an experiment in conservation never before attempted, the goal of which is to protect and manage the park by helping the small-holding farmers to prosper outside the park area. 'The Korup can pay for its own protection, and the local people and hunters can be its guardians,' says Dr Stephen Gartlan, of Wisconsin University's Regional Primate Research Centre, and the scientific adviser of the Korup project. 'In most other parks the people have been rigorously excluded from their lands, they were not told why and not compensated. They could perceive that the parks were for foreigners, and the area became something alien. If a park is to survive in the long term, those living near it must benefit from better health care, housing and running water, advice on farming, fertilizers, food products and crops, and transportation of produce to market.'

Steve Gartlan, and Basingstoke house painter Phil Agland, who devoted five years to making a powerful film on the plight of the Korup, were almost singlehandedly responsible for the government's designation of the pristine belt of coastal forest as a national park in March 1988. In co-operation with the Cameroon authorities, WWF (United Kingdom) has undertaken to manage and conserve it. Theirs is a great achievement, and a startling example of the impact individuals can have on projects of international importance.

'Too often protection comes too late,' says Gartlan. 'It only begins to happen when people perceive that there is almost nothing left.' Although there may still be time for the Korup, the scientist holds out meagre hope for the future of rainforests in general. 'What is left in Britain?' he asks. 'If that country can't protect her treasures it is unrealistic to think that Africa will do any better. Ninety per cent of the rainforest will be gone in the next twenty to thirty years. My task is to identify the priority areas and get them protected so that when the grass roots call comes for protection, there will be something left to protect.'

In this exotic, hot-house world of almost untouched forest, it is not surprising to come across creatures stranger than fiction. Things that look like leaves or flowers suddenly get up and walk away, scaly reptiles watch one's progress through the rainforest with eyes which swivel like gun turrets, and if the ground begins to move it means the armies of driver ants are preparing for battle and the destruction of everything in their path.

Brent Johnson, a student of environmental law in Virginia, shudders as he recalls the driver ants. 'They think, they send signals, they work as a unit,' he says with the emphasis of a general recalling the front. One night the seething army of ants attacked the science tent, and everyone knew that unless their advance was checked, the specimens of live snakes and lizards, moths and butterflies would be devoured long before morning. The ants bite with the tenacity of bulldogs: even when their bodies are wrenched from their heads, the jaws remain locked in the flesh of their adversary. Only by surrounding the insect army with a ring of flaming kerosene did Brent and the other Venturers win that battle. However, a few soldier ants climbed to the top of the tent, searching for a way out of the fiery trap. They found a solution. Forming a living bridge, they encouraged the rest to escape over their backs. For a long time afterwards, when nineteen-year-old Brent closed his eyes all he could see was a river of ants.

Deadly gaboon vipers also seemed to turn up everywhere. Most disturbing, perhaps, was the one discovered by Scotsman Mike May directly beneath him as he answered a rather different call of nature. Even the moths collected by keen expeditioners such as Omani Juma Subait, botany student Michael Bassett and Stuart Lotherington had a few unpleasant traits, such as sucking eye secretions from animals. Under the auspices of entomologists David Lee, David Jones and Ugo Dall' Asta, Venturers learned the technique of setting a lamp backed by a white sheet by the river and collecting the moths quivering on the cloth before the bats and praying mantises swooped down for an easy feed. Another moth-collecting method called for a bit more imagination. It involved peeing on a lady's fishnet stocking stuffed with chicken feathers. The unsavoury object, which might easily be mistaken for a *ju-ju* of the most powerful sort, was then hung on a tree to encourage moths to lay their eggs amongst its various folds and fragrances. Since many of these activities took place in the night, I was particularly interested to hear of the existence of blood-sucking moths as I watched the beautiful creatures barge against the glass chimney of the Tilley lamp.

In the dark hours that begin around 8 p.m. and continue until five in the morning, I knew that Amanda Scholes, John Nelson and their groups were deep in the Korup, checking their mist nets for bats. So far, they had identified fourteen different species of fruit bats and insect-eating bats, ranging between two and twenty centimetres in body length and decked out in yellow wings, red or brown fur, white spots or with leaf-like appendages on their noses. Some bore the remarkably descriptive name of 'hairy slit-faced bats'.

These shadowy creatures have long been associated with graves and belfries. Eerie, flitting shapes, they are unique among mammals, for three remarkable reasons: they breed and give birth upside down – the female's tail forms a pouch to catch the baby as it drops – and they are capable of true flight. I have been reliably informed that there are no vampire bats in West Africa, but lest one become too cavalier about roaming the jungles of Cameroon at night, I should add that those ancient trees harbour an equally remarkable creature, the hammerhead bat, which glides unerringly through the darkness on wings a metre wide.

The motley band of Venturers that gathered at the base of the mountain at seven in the morning looked fit, hard and muscular from the exertions of three months in Cameroon. Now, that fitness would be put to the test in a gruelling 16-kilometre race up and down West Africa's tallest peak. They had volunteered for the fourteenth edition of the Guinness-sponsored international event that demanded exceptional stamina, speed and strength from the men and women who took part. Starting at 915 metres above sea level, at temperatures of 25°C, they would race up the rocky path that rose steeply through the forest, savannah and scrub to the sub-zero temperatures of the summit. Draped with water bottles, chocolate bars, bandages and dehydration powders, the eleven members of our expedition joined the crowd of runners.

Undoubtedly, Operation Raleigh added to the international flavour of the event, entering Nepalese Dev Rana, American Rob Cole, Canadian Rob Haines and New Zealander Tim Chiswell in addition to a healthy smattering of Britishers such as Colin Largent, Mike Bassett, David Jones and Ben Lovering. Maurice Koffi represented his own country of Cameroon. None of the Raleigh team came terribly close to the winning time – Scotsman Jack Maitland's extraordinary three hours, forty-seven minutes and thirty-four seconds – but river leader Dave Briggs was the fastest of our group, followed by a determined Nick Horne and Mike May, who has promised himself that he will wear his Macbeth tartan kilt on his next ascent.

But we never forgot that a mountain is not a playground: like the sea, it rarely gives one a second chance. Just a few days after the international athletes scrambled up and down her flanks, the mountain showed her more sinister aspect. Searching for a new and easier resupply route to Buea, the Gurkha officer, Argun, who had provided the antelope feast, American Brent Johnson and Glaswegian stuntman Rab Allan nearly came unstuck. Falling from buildings and moving cars, Rab has to 'die a lot' in his job. Here, in the harsh world of life and death, the mountain nearly turned the celluloid illusion into reality. Lost in the impenetrable forest for several days, the trio exhausted their reserves of water and food. Even Argun, who could climb faster and carry more weight than almost anyone on the expedition, began to sweat and breathe a little harder. Said Rab: 'It wasn't fun, and we were looking forward to looking back on the experience, but we knew that if anyone could get us out, it was Argun.'

In the end, it was a combination of skill, stamina, humour and teamwork that helped them find their way back to the geology camp on the crest of the mountain at midnight. 'Life is going to be easy after this,' grinned Rab. Most of his colleagues agreed that his words summed up the entire expedition in Cameroon admirably.

CHAPTER SEVENTEEN

Sailing On

(*Expedition Leader,* Lord Nelson*'s Return*: John Parsloe)

Atlantic Ocean, 25 February 1988

Looking skyward, Paul Hunt grimaced as he watched the royal yard start to rotate to starboard and aim for the stars. There was a resounding 'Crack!' as the heavy beam collided with the roller-furling gear at the end of the topgallant yard. Racing from the bridge, the first officer, his face as red as his unruly mop of hair, growled: 'You're going to tear those sails! That's expensive gear, you know – hard to replace in the middle of the sea.'

It was 23-year-old Paul's first mishap aboard the *Lord Nelson*. He was proud to be aboard, and mortified that he had endangered the valuable sail. Paul's family had long been connected with the Blue Star Line, and his father had been a captain with the company. Now Blue Star had helped sponsor the son of 'Peewee' Hunt to bring to life the boy's inborn love of the sea.

Thirty-three Venturers had joined the ship in Freeport, Grand Bahama, and their voyage bringing her home to Southampton would be the second phase of their three-month expedition. After eight weeks of community tasks and scientific projects under the tropical island sun, they were fit, tanned and ready to try out their sea legs.

The test came sooner than expected. On the first leg of the voyage, the 1408-kilometre stretch to Bermuda, they ran into Force-9 winds and heavy seas. Luckily, the strong winds were with them rather than against them, driving the barque homeward at up to eleven knots – 335 kilometres a day on one occasion, the vessel's best ever run. Not all of the crew rejoiced in the speed and the high swells, however.

Leading the team was John Parsloe, a 43-year-old merchant navy officer from Christchurch, New Zealand, who had previously served with us as the mate of *Sir*

Walter Raleigh. A tall, slim fellow, one might take him for a dry-humoured professor – until a wink of his eye alerted the crew that he was about to unfold one of his larger-than-life sea-going tales. John's wide knowledge of seafaring, survival, law and accounting serves him well in his life as a government trouble-shooter and explorer. In addition, he has a well-earned reputation for expertise in the Antarctic, and had been Sir Ranulph Fiennes' ship's manager during the famous Transglobe Expedition in the polar regions.

Two weeks out of Bermuda, the weather did an about-face: now *Lord Nelson* was totally becalmed. 'A passing "high" stole the very last breath of wind from her sails,' wrote Paul Hunt in his log. 'The Atlantic was a mirror, and the only sound was a gentle lapping against the ship's side. The sky was clear, and a full moon bathed the vessel in an eerie glow, turning the masts and yards to silver. Visibility was excellent, and the ocean stretched ahead: now I understand why men fall in love with the sea.'

CHQ, London, 21 March 1989

'She's going like a bat out of hell,' chuckled Geoff Straw as we studied the situation report on *Lord Nelson*. 'She is almost certain to get here early, and if she does, Vic Rudge will have a seizure. All his plans are made to celebrate her arrival at Southampton on 3 April – and not before.'

Never had the prospect of fair winds seemed so unfortunate. Just then Felicity Bowden ('Flis'), our capable operations officer, came in with a report which confirmed our fears: the forecast was for fine weather 'with strong southwesterly winds for the next week'. At this rate, *Lord Nelson* would certainly beat the band. A quick telephone call to John Wild of the Jubilee Sailing Trust solved that problem: *Lord Nelson* would proceed to Jersey, the largest of the Channel Islands, if she arrived early. There she would be well positioned for a majestic sweep into Southampton on the original ETA.

On that Monday morning on 3 April, the sun was just beginning to penetrate the grey clouds as we climbed aboard the launch to greet the ship. Beneath the towering cranes lining the quayside, a growing crowd of well-wishers, friends and families waited in the chilly breeze. Ahead, silhouetted against the distant horizon, was the tall ship. Her masts stood out like church spires amongst the squat container vessels ploughing furrows up the Channel. Her rigging was alive with Venturers furling the sails; it was a scene that could have happened a hundred years ago.

Captain Hugh Munro fired the engines to bring her alongside, and, 300 metres from the dock, her cannon boomed seven times in a stentorian salute. Flis, in her Territorial Army role, answered with the shore gun as cheers rang out, sirens blared and welcoming banners waved in the wind. Press and TV reporters swarmed over the ship, and Vic had arranged a splendid reception with the generous backing of the Mayor of Southampton. The great ship had come home.

London, 4 April 1989

The National Army Museum was packed with guests and Venturers when The Rt. Hon. Richard Luce, Minister for the Arts, opened the exhibition of the work of our young expedition artists and photographers. There was another special guest in the throng. Wilfred Thesiger, himself back from Kenya, viewed the paintings with interest – including the portrait Sophie Walbeoffe-Wilson had made of him in Kenya. It was a happy coincidence, the kind that leads people to remark on what a 'small world' it is. A remark equally applicable to the fact that the Arts Minister had been a District Commissioner in Kenya when Wilfred Thesiger was exploring the northern corners of that country: Richard Luce had been able to give him a bit of assistance in locating extra camels for his expedition.

Later, when he visited the art exhibition, the Duke of Gloucester commented that he was 'always hearing good things about Raleigh'. His words were directed particularly at Operation Weston Spirit, a programme set up to help inner-city youngsters by ex-Venturer Paul Oginsky and Simon Weston, the Welsh Guardsman who was so terribly burned during the Falklands campaign when his landing ship *Sir Galahad* was hit by an Argentine bomb. Simon and Paul had given much credit to their experience with Operation Raleigh as the incentive to set up this worthwhile enterprise.

The involvement of young artists in Operation Raleigh had been instigated by Ley Kenyon – an artist of distinction himself, who had spent some of the last war in Stalag Luft 3 at Sagan, Silesia, after baling out of his RAF bomber over occupied France. There, Ley had been the official artist of the celebrated 'Great Escape' on 24 March 1944, when seventy-six RAF and other Allied prisoner of war officers had tunnelled out of the German camp. Most were recaptured and shot on Hitler's orders; Ley did not manage to get out, but survived. His drawings, recovered after the war by the fighter ace Douglas Bader, were used in the making of the film of that epic story of courage. Later, Ley became a pioneer of underwater diving and even taught the Duke of Edinburgh in the pool at

Buckingham Palace. With Operation Raleigh, he worked tirelessly to get his protégés into the remotest parts of the world where they painted and sketched in jungles and swamps, often with only a stub of a candle for light.

The successful opening of the art show was just one of the events which celebrated the end of the first stage of Raleigh and the beginning of the next. Four days later, over 3000 Venturers, international representatives and supporters piled into London's Royal Albert Hall for a grand reunion, organized by Geoff Straw and Bill Bellars with the help of Kate Pitman and Kate Beurle. The day was packed with TV and radio broadcasts: Peruvian Venturer Sandra Echegaray Samanez spoke on John Dunn's popular BBC radio programme and our press office excelled itself, fielding interviews across the country.

As evening drew in over Kensington Palace Gardens, people from many lands arrived at the Albert Hall. Some wore black ties, others sported expedition T-shirts and jeans, and a number of two-legged lions were seen being chased by gorillas. Knightsbridge had never seen the like. Tony Walton, just back from Zimbabwe, acted as master-of-ceremonies, our Padre, Olympic canoeist Basil Pratt, said prayers, and, against the din in the cavernous hall, I reviewed the progress of the 'Raven Rations Survivors' Club'. Graham Walker, our new Chairman, spoke of his hopes for the future and read a congratulatory message from Prince Charles. The four-thousandth Venturer selected for an expedition, Tim McCarthy from Belfast, and Sandra Echegaray Samanez, whose energy and courage had inspired everyone she worked with, recalled their adventures. Finally, a multi-projector audio-visual show splashed across the screen; afterwards, the party dissolved into splendid informality.

General Sir John and Lady Mogg were in the thick of the disco dancing. Everyone scoured the circular maze of the hall's corridors looking for companions who had come from as far away as Pakistan, Australia and Singapore. Major Hawk Freeman had flown in from Colorado, and Clive Barrow arrived straight off the plane, still covered in the dust of Kenya.

The Lord Mayor of Hull was there too, as was our staunch friend Jim Johnson, formerly the local MP. In the programme was a glowing tribute from Prime Minister Margaret Thatcher who has given consistent and enthusiastic support. It was a night no one present will ever forget, a night which made us recall the achievements of this extraordinary band.

Of course, we had encountered a host of problems during the previous four years. The Venturers faced their own economic trials as they struggled to raise funds for their expeditions, but few of them knew of the battles fought by CHQ and the international committees to maintain the vital flow of cash. Sending expeditions to 'the ends of the earth' often means long and costly negotiations with governments, as well as expensive reconnaissance trips and the necessary boats, trucks, rations, tents, scientific equipment and radios. If, as sometimes happens, political conflicts force us to cancel arrangements, a great deal of time and money has been spent for naught.

Then there is the cost of insurance, of recruitment and of selection tests to ensure we really do get young people with leadership potential. Additional expenditures on research, communications, rent and wages raise the bills to alarming proportions. With careful economic planning, however, we managed to use a bit more black ink than red, and it was time to look ahead. The Ministry of Defence had agreed that I could remain with Raleigh until the end of my service in 1991: perhaps it was felt that the realm would be safer if I were not quite so actively engaged in military operations.

Several government ministries and the majority of our sponsors urged us to continue, and there were plenty of young people who wished to volunteer. Above all, however, we needed a sound management team – like businessmen Tony Nowell, Derek Chidell and Tony Hepper who helped to keep us solvent. As with many international charities, we had to become more commercial in our outlook. In setting up the Raleigh Trust, Graham Walker did just that.

More and more Venturers were sponsored by their companies, convinced that the challenge of strenuous tasks and demanding projects would prove a good investment. The success of the inner-city Venturers had led the British government to send members of the Youth Training Scheme with us, and this meant increased instruction and guidance by the staff. Furthermore, in Merseyside, leading businessmen like Barry Owen had started a scheme to send youngsters from urban areas on Raleigh expeditions. One group of industrialists told me that they judged a young person's time with us as the equivalent of holding a university degree. 'Many people have paper qualifications, but very few have any practical experience of group management, problem solving, teamwork and tackling projects under difficult circumstances. We know that all the men and women who have been on Raleigh have that experience.'

Without a doubt, throwing together young people of different backgrounds, colours and creeds before they have developed any unshakable prejudice does much to foster international understanding. I recall one Christmas Day when the Rotarians of Grand Bahama invited the Venturers to their homes to a festive lunch. Having lived on tinned army rations for days, the expedition members accepted with eagerness. I was a bit concerned about some of the Muslims from the Gulf; it seemed that they were forever on the receiving end of pork and beans for breakfast. On Boxing Day, I met them at a beach cook-out and asked if they'd had a good Christmas.

'Oh yes. Very good,' they replied with enthusiasm.

'Was the food all right?' I asked.

'*Halal*,' – 'Absolutely fine' – they assured me.

'Thank heavens; who did you spend it with?'

They pointed to a gentleman whom I recognized as the leader of the local Jewish community. If we can bring Jews and Arabs together to celebrate a Christian festival, there can be no insurmountable obstacles.

*

In maintaining our international links, it was necessary to take care that words in one English-speaking country were not misinterpreted in another. I received some very funny looks when, during a TV broadcast in Raleigh, North Carolina, I talked about 'Venturers humping their rucksacks over the hills'. In another instance, I remember the Lord Mayor of Hull missing a step or two as he danced with American Jenny Bond who casually remarked that the North Carolinians 'so enjoy shagging that they hold contests for it'. Apparently 'shagging' is a dance common in the coastal regions of the state.

But everyone understood the broader language of the goals of Operation Raleigh – the development of leadership and character. People from all over the world shared hardships and returned to their own countries to help the disabled, the sick, the elderly and the unemployed. They are all answering the final challenge of Drake and Raleigh: 'What can you give back to your – or the world – community?'

There is Terry Linehan, for example, an American boy from a Wisconsin farm who developed a plan to save a small tribe in Papua New Guinea, and carried it through after his time with Operation Drake. Then, along with so many others, there is Paul Mason, a 'punk rocker' from Birmingham, who returned there to counsel drug addicts, and Alison Farmer, a nursing sister, who led a team of blind people up Mt Kinabaloo in Malaysia.

As our numbers grow, it has become necessary to give more guidance to those returning from the rigours of expedition life. Roberta Howlett has produced a booklet entitled *Been There . . . Done That . . . What Now?* In particular, we have formed a close association with the Duke of Edinburgh Award Scheme which operates all over the world and recognizes various levels of achievement attained by young people.

This kind of follow-up is vital, and it is good to see how many Venturer support groups have been established by the young people themselves. By June of 1989, Britain had forty-seven, and there was one each in Australia (Melbourne), Japan (Tokyo), Singapore and the United States (Raleigh, N.C.). The overwhelming enthusiasm to help others generated by Raleigh expeditions is equally strong in other parts of the world. I have seen it as I tramped through the heather with Rognvald Livingstone to see Venture Scotland's bothy – a remote hut in the Highlands. I saw it again as I watched Venturers launch their hot air balloon, *Spirit of Kitty Hawk*, on a stormy night in North Carolina. The young lions are beginning to lead the pride.

Those lucky enough to have jobs to return to often encountered a sceptical reception, however. 'They think I've been on a good holiday at the firm's expense,' complained one Venturer who had sweated blood building schools and dams in the forests of Patagonia. 'Why can't you get some of the bosses to visit an expedition?'

We decided to do just that, inviting sponsoring companies to send the fittest of their executives. One pioneer was Lorraine Green from British Gas, who joined the Torres Strait expedition. Others came from British Rail and TSB. 'Holiday' was not a word they used to describe their experiences. The idea grew when National Westminster Bank suggested running an expedition for executives to 're-motivate burnt-out people and give them the Raleigh experience'. Jim Harris, marketing director of British Airways, thought it a great idea. So did many others, and we set to work planning a four-week programme for 'wrinklies', as the Venturers call those over twenty-six. This new concept was in effect by 1990. Well before the first executive expedition, one secretary telephoned to ask if we could send her chairman to the North Pole for a few months.

These days, people are fitter, live longer and are better off. I feel absolutely certain that these older folk will set off for adventures that would have seemed impossible in the past.

Chirundu, Zimbabwe, 12 March 1989

Once the Raleigh Trust was firmly established, we began planning our new expeditions. From Zimbabwe came a letter from Val Enzer, who had been with us on the Zaire River expedition, urging us to come there. She had married my adjutant from the Junior Leaders Regiment, Royal Engineers, and Peter, her husband, was serving on the staff of the British Army Training Team in Zimbabwe. My godfather, Lord Forester, who had done much to start me off on a life of exploring, had loved this country and often talked of the excitement of the bush.

I flew to Harare and, with Peter, Tony Walton and wildlife expert Des Bentley, set out on a bright Sunday morning to motor up the Zambezi. Our aim was to see an old game warden's camp that might be rebuilt by Venturers.

Rounding a bend in two motorboats, we passed close to a herd of hippo. Suddenly, the head of a huge old cow appeared about twenty metres from Peter's boat. Her tiny eyes stared unblinking, her ears twitched, froth bubbled around the great lips.

Tony had his video out and I focused my camera on the massive head. In the foreground the second boat bobbed in the current. As I pressed the button the viewfinder filled. The hippo was coming straight at the craft in a full charge. Thankfully, the outboard leapt to life at first pull and the boat veered away from the angry beast. 'One very bad-tempered lady who doesn't like being disturbed in her bath,' muttered Des, as we skimmed over the brown water. 'More Africans die from hippo attacks than from crocodiles,' he added helpfully.

Yet, as we sped away, I felt strangely young at heart.

Hawaii, 20 August 1989

When I visited the site of one of our earlier expeditions, I made a night-time trek across the lava flows of the recent eruption on Hawaii's Big Island. By the light of the moon, our small party threaded its way across the still warm, twisted crust, beneath which molten rock ran in a red-hot river. At the coast we were greeted by an awe-inspiring sight. A stream of liquid fire gushed from a low cliff into the boiling sea. Great rollers washed in from the ocean, temporarily engulfing the incandescent fountain and sending clouds of steam hundreds of metres into the darkened sky.

Receding waves carried glowing boulders of pumice into the depths, creating new land. The air was heavy with the smell of sulphur as spasmodic pulses deep within the earth ejected showers of living debris. 'Reminds one of the beginning of the world,' muttered Ken Kupchak, our Hawaiian chairman, who crouched beside me a mere fifty metres from the inferno.

Somewhere, a very long way overhead, the spacecraft *Voyager* was transmitting the results of its exploration as it plunged past Neptune. Like the scene before us, the pictures of that planet showed volcanoes spewing liquid gas and great storms whirling on an inhospitable globe. Nowhere in our solar system has an atmosphere been discovered that might support life as we know it.

Almost exactly one year earlier the space shuttle *Discovery* had transmitted other, more shocking pictures of a planet destroying itself. Houston had requested an aerial survey of the Amazon and Commander Frederick Hauck had taken photographs from the shuttle's windows with a hand-held Hasselblad camera. Those snapshots showed what one Brazilian conservationist called 'a biological holocaust'.

On that October day in 1988, the smoke cloud covered over 2.5 million square kilometres – an area the size of Europe. It was the rainforest burning, the ancient home of an estimated eighty thousand different species of plants and of thirty million species of animals, many still unknown to science.

Our teams in Pakistan, Indonesia, Cameroon and other countries had discovered several new species, although violence in the remote reaches of the Amazon had forced us to cancel our expedition there. The thick smoke that rises every day in the Amazon – particularly in the 'burning season' of September and October, signals the death of a forest and the loss – for ever – of resources which could save lives and bring prosperity to the very people who destroy them.

The Elizabethan era of Sir Walter Raleigh was one of the greatest periods of discovery the world has ever known. Now we have a choice: to continue in that spirit of discovery by finding new ways to conserve the earth's wonders or to witness catastrophe in our lifetime.

Imagine a world without coffee, corn or contraceptive pills, rice, tropical birds or tigers. A world without rubber, rhinos or a host of other riches from the world's wild places. There are so many yet to be discovered. If we continue in our destruction, perhaps we had better get used to imagining a world without man.

IN REMEMBRANCE

Our sympathy and thoughts are extended to the families and friends of the following who lost their lives during the period covered by this book, either on Operation Raleigh or since their return:

Peter White (25) of Romsey, Hampshire.
A Venturer on Expedition 3B in Peru (July 1985) who died as a result of a leaking gas fire in a caravan, whilst working as an Outdoor Pursuits Instructor at Celni Centre, Llangryn, Tywyn, Wales in March 1988.

Brian Seymour (22) of Lanark, Scotland.
A Venturer on Expedition 10E in Australia (July 1987) who died from a brain tumour in April 1989. Brian was an active member of Venture Scotland.

Taina Flutti (19) of Carnobbio, Como, Italy.
A Venturer who died in an accident whilst in Kenya on Expedition 17C in March 1989.

Sadly, space does not permit the listing of all the dedicated advisers, friends and staff who worked so hard to make the operation such a success. However, a report listing the generous sponsors, helpers and Venturers, plus tables of the achievements of the enterprise, is available from:

Operation Raleigh (Report Dept)
Alpha Place
Flood Street
London SW3 5SZ
England

Copies of all books are also available.

INDEX